Transplanting Human Tissue

TRANSPLANTING HUMAN TISSUE
Ethics, Policy, and Practice

Edited by
STUART J. YOUNGNER, M.D.
Susan E. Watson Professor of Bioethics
Chairman, Department of Bioethics
Case Western Reserve University
Cleveland, Ohio

MARTHA W. ANDERSON
Vice President, Donor Services
Musculoskeletal Transplant Foundation
Edison, New Jersey

RENIE SCHAPIRO, M.P.H.
Consultant/Editor
Madison, Wisconsin

OXFORD
UNIVERSITY PRESS
2004

OXFORD
UNIVERSITY PRESS

Oxford   New York
Auckland   Bangkok   Buenos Aires   Cape Town   Chennai
Dar es Salaam   Delhi   Hong Kong   Istanbul   Karachi   Kolkata
Kuala Lumpur   Madrid   Melbourne   Mexico City   Mumbai   Nairobi
São Paulo   Shanghai   Taipei   Tokyo   Toronto

Copyright © 2004 by Oxford University Press, Inc.

Published by Oxford University Press, Inc.
198 Madison Avenue, New York, New York 10016
http://www.oup-usa.org

Oxford is a registered trademark of Oxford University Press

Library of Congress Cataloging-in-Publication Data
Transplanting human tissue : ethics, policy, and practice/
edited by Stuart J. Youngner [et al.].
p. cm.
Includes bibliographical references and index.
ISBN 0-19-516284-6
1. Transplantation of organs, tissues, etc.
2. Transplantation of organs, tissues, etc.–Moral and ethical aspects.
3. Informed consent (Medical law)
4. Medical ethics.
I. Youngner, Stuart J.
RD120.75.T745 2003   617.9'5–dc21   2003040464

9 8 7 6 5 4 3 2 1

Printed in the United States of America
on acid-free paper

Acknowledgments

The editors wish to thank the following organizations whose generous support made this project possible: The Greenwall Foundation, the Musculoskeletal Transplant Foundation, LifeNet, The Cleveland Foundation, AlloSource, Community Tissue Services, DePuy AcroMed, GenSci Technologies, Life Cell, Osteotech, and Synthes Spine.

In addition to the authors who contributed chapters to the book, we also want to thank the following individuals who served on the planning committee or attended the working meetings and whose ideas and comments helped shape it: Bill Anderson, Lori Andrews, Remy Aronoff, Richard Bauer, Patricia D. Brewster, Tom Byersdorf, Allen Carl, James Childress, Theo DeBey, Campbell Gardett, Susan Gunderson, Richard Hasz, Russell Hereford, Thomas B. Higgins, Louise Jacobbi, Linda Jones, Michael Joyce, Rob Kochik, Helen Leslie, Richard Luskin, Frank Maas, Virginia McBride, Max Mehlman, Brad Moore, Haavi Morreim, Howard Nathan, Paul O'Flynn, Randy Rosier, Jeffrey K. Shapiro, Laura Siminoff, Bruce Stroever, Frank Taft, Gloria Taylor, Paul Treuhaft, David Urbahns, Doug Watson, Doug Wilson, Judith Wolf, and Sheldon Zink.

We also would like to thank Carol Adrine, Jan Liber, Donna Olszewski, and Judy Richardson for their invaluable help in planning and running the two working meetings; an additional thanks to Donna for her tenacity and skill with the book's graphics. Thanks also to Tracey Baker for her work on references, Brian Hamilton for preparing the glossary, and to Joyce Collins for helping us over the finish line.

Contents

Contributors

Martha W. Anderson
Vice President, Donor Services
Musculoskeletal Transplant Foundation
Edison, New Jersey

Scott Bottenfield
Senior Vice President for Tissue Recovery
  and Development
LifeNet
Virginia Beach, Virginia

Courtney S. Campbell, Ph.D.
Professor and Director of the Program
  for Ethics, Science, and the
  Environment
Department of Philosophy
Oregon State University
Corvallis, Oregon

R. Alta Charo, J.D.
Professor of Law and Medical Ethics
University of Wisconsin Law School
Madison, Wisconsin

Norman Fost, M.D., M.P.H.
Professor, Pediatrics and Bioethics
Director, Program in Bioethics
University of Wisconsin Medical School
Madison, Wisconsin

Glenn Greenleaf
Director, Tissue Services
LifeCell
Branchburg, New Jersey

Ellen Gottmann Kulik, J.D.
Donor Family Council
Skaneateles, New York

John T. Makley, M.D.
Professor of Orthopedics
Professor of Clinical Pathology
Case Western Reserve University
Cleveland, Ohio

John P. Moyer, M.D., FAAP
Clinical Professor of Pediatrics
Associate Director, Preceptor Development
Foundations of Doctoring Curriculum
University of Colorado Health Sciences
  Center
School of Medicine/Dean's Office
Denver, Colorado

Richard Nicholas, M.D.
Professor of Orthopedics and Pathology
College of Medicine University of
  Arkansas for Medical Sciences
Little Rock, Arkansas

Jeffrey Prottas, Ph.D.
Professor, Social Policy
Heller Graduate School
Brandeis University
Waltham, Massachusetts

Renie Schapiro, M.P.H.
Consultant/Editor
Madison, Wisconsin

Jill Hartzler Warner, J.D.
*Senior Policy Advisor and Counselor for
　Biologics, Center for Biologics
　Evaluation and Research, Food and
　Drug Administration*
Rockville, Maryland

Stuart J. Youngner, M.D.
*Susan E. Watson Professor of Bioethics
Chairman, Department of Bioethics
Case Western Reserve University
Cleveland, Ohio*

Kathryn C. Zoon, Ph.D.
*Former Director
Center for Biologics Evaluation and
　Research, Food and Drug
　Administration
Principal Deputy
Center for Cancer Research
National Cancer Institute
National Institutes of Health
Rockville, Maryland*

Introduction

As a very public debate raged over organ transplant policy during the last decade, transplantation of non-organ tissues, such as bones, ligaments, heart valves, and skin, grew exponentially with far less notice. In 1994, an estimated 6,000 people became tissue donors upon death. By 1999, that number had grown to 20,000, more than triple the number of cadaveric organ donors. And with tissue from one donor going to as many as 50 to 100 recipients, hundreds of thousands more tissue transplants than organ transplants are now performed each year.

This growth in the donation and clinical use of transplanted tissue has spawned a booming industry of often-interconnected for-profit and not-for-profit organizations. A decade ago, tissue transplantation was about a $20-million-dollar industry; today it is estimated to have revenues of $650–750 million, and some experts expect it to reach $1 billion by the end of 2003.

Tissue transplants have saved or improved millions of lives. In addition to the transplants occurring every day at hospitals across the country, the expanded network of tissue banks provides the foundation for a critical emergency-response system. Within 24 hours of the September 11th attacks, for example, large amounts of skin from tissue banks around the country were being transported to the East Coast in anticipation of large numbers of burn patients. But the growth in tissue transplantation and in the industry that facilitates it also raises ethical concerns. And its relative invisibility to most of the public raises additional issues. For example, do people who are considering signing donor cards know that in addition to solid organs, like the kidney or heart, a donor's skin and bones may also be taken?

In the past several years, tissue transplantation has begun to step out of the shadows of its cousin, organ transplantation. The new visibility has come at a price. With provocative headlines such as "Assembly Line," and "Skin Merchants," a series of articles entitled "The Body Brokers" appeared in April 2000 in the *Orange County Register*. Among the concerns these and other media stories raised were that the tissue industry was "commodifying" the human body, making outrageous profits, and irresponsibly allocating skin for "cosmetic" purposes, leaving burn victims without an adequate supply of skin. According to these allegations, the tissue industry was guilty of several transgressions, not least of which was violating the trust of grieving families who had altruistically donated the tissue of their newly deceased loved ones.

The tissue industry and others criticized these articles as inflammatory and riddled with inaccuracies. Nonetheless, the press coverage for the first time brought problems facing the industry to the attention of the general public and their congressional representatives. Several U.S. senators raised concerns with then–Secretary of the Department of Health and Human Services (HHS) Donna Shalala, who in turn asked HHS's inspector general to investigate. This book grew out of a scholarly project that began before the media fury hit, but was motivated by concern from within the industry and elsewhere in the field about many of the same issues. One of our goals was to gather accurate data where possible and note where good data are simply not available.

Unlike organs, which are transported quickly and changed little from donor to recipient, human tissues are often highly processed, radically transformed in appearance, and packaged and stored in tissue banks, often for years. Thus, the commodification of tissues is more palpable—and the role of commerce much more difficult to deny. On its way from donor to recipient, tissue often passes through several organizations, what law professor Julia Mahoney has termed a "chain of distribution" in which "money changes hands at numerous points" and value is added along the way.

These characteristics of the tissue industry raise important ethical questions about the place of altruism in a raging sea of market commerce, the responsibility of tissue banks and organ procurement organizations to the grieving families whom they approach about donation, the safety and distribution methods of tissue, the growing role of for-profit corporations in the field, and the role of government oversight of an industry that, until fairly recently, has been remarkably free of it.

The transplantation of human tissue donated by families upon the death of a loved one—specifically, musculoskeletal tissue and skin—is the focus of this book. But it is only one piece of the expanding topography of the uses of tissue. Research and commercial uses of other human tissues are also growing. Human tissues may be obtained as "side-products" during routine biopsies and surgeries, removed by coroners following autopsies, taken from the umbilical cords of newborns, donated by volunteers, or even sold in response to advertisements. Human eggs and sperm, individual cells, blood products and even DNA are all examples of human tissues now in the marketplace or being studied. These tissues may be used for data banks in genetic epidemiological studies, to create cell lines for research, as forensic or historic evidence, for medical treatments, to treat infertility, or even to create human clones.

Some of these uses have been the subject of books, papers, and legal cases. For example, the National Bioethics Advisory Commission issued two reports, "Ethical Issues in Human Stem Cell Research" and "Research Involving Human Biological Material: Ethical Issues and Policy Guidance." Ethical issues in the use of reproductive tissues have also received widespread attention.

This book is the first comprehensive treatment of the specific use of tissue that begins (most often) with the generous gift of a grieving family and ends up being therapeutically transplanted into a human recipient. The chain of distribution of the tissue between these two defining acts and the large industry that is growing up around it is unique territory within the larger map of tissue use, and that chain raises some unique organizational, regulatory, legal, and ethical issues. We address primarily musculoskeletal tissue (bones, tendons, ligaments and cartilage) and skin for several reasons. First, they are the most commonly transplanted tissues. Second, unlike other tissues (such as corneas), they sometimes undergo significant transformation between donation and transplantation, becoming "products" that look very different from the donated gift. Finally, musculoskeletal and skin transplantation have been the focus of controversial media articles.

As part of health care, tissue transplantation is inevitably entwined in many important ethical issues in health care delivery, such as distributive justice or access. Our ethical analysis, however, focuses on issues arising from the particularities of this enterprise.

We have also limited our analysis to the United States, where the tissue transplant industry is by far the most developed. Tissue banking and transplantation have been in place in Canada and Western Europe for nearly two decades. In addition, with support from the United Nations International Atomic Energy Agency (IAEA), dozens of other countries, including India, Sri Lanka, Bangladesh, and Argentina, have also begun tissue banking. In none of these countries, however, is the clinical demand for allograft tissues nearly as great or the donation and processing technology as extensive as in the United States. The ethical issues highlighted in this book, while perhaps relevant elsewhere, are therefore considered within an American social, legal, and economic framework.

Stuart Youngner conceived of the project that resulted in this book after serving on the Medical Board of Trustees of the Musculoskeletal Foundation (MTF), where he now heads the Ethics Committee. Many persons involved in tissue transplantation agreed that the newly emerging ethical issues needed to be addressed. A planning committee met twice in 1999. The committee focused the themes of the project and decided that it should include the perspectives of all segments of the tissue industry, including tissue banks, organ procurement organizations, the Association of Organ Procurement Organizations (AOPO), the American Association of Tissue Banks (AATB), the United Network for Organ Sharing (UNOS), government agencies (HHS Inspector General's Office, Health Resources and Services Administration, HRSA's Division of Organ Transplantation), orthopedic surgeons, and donor families, as well as scholars from the fields of bioethics, law, religious studies, philosophy, and the social sciences.

Two working conferences were held, at which participants discussed and debated papers prepared by other participants. The first meeting, in Edison, New Jersey, on June 20, 2000, was devoted to presenting background information to the group. It was striking how few national and trend data were available to address issues such as the supply and distribution of tissue, informed consent for donors, and other important and controversial areas. After the two meetings, the three editors further refined the issues, consolidated available information, and worked with selected scholars to fashion specific chapters to create this book.

The book is divided into four parts. Each part is introduced by a brief commentary by the editors. Part I provides background information about the industry, the expanding clinical uses of donated tissue, and Federal regulation, written primarily by those directly involved. Part II offers the important and poignant perspective of two donor families. Before addressing how ethical and policy concerns might be addressed, the two chapters in Part III look at what lessons can be garnered from the treatment of other tissues and organs. In the final section of the book, ethicists address ethical and policy issues in tissue transplantation. We conclude with a chapter by the editors that draws together the issues raised in the preceding chapters and offers some recommendations about the future of the field.

At the end of the book a brief glossary defines terms used in many of the chapters. One comment on terminology is important here: the word "donor" has been used throughout the book to refer to the recently deceased source of the tissue, although the decision to donate is most often made by a loved one of the deceased.

I

TISSUE BANKING, TRANSPLANTATION, AND REGULATION

While public controversy has drawn attention to musculoskeletal and skin transplantation, the details of its development and operation remain something of a mystery, even to those with a reasonable understanding of health care. This section methodically explores where this field came from and where it stands today.

We begin with a basic introduction to the links in the chain: from identification of a potential donor to transplanting tissue into a recipient. We conclude, in Chapter 5, with senior Food and Drug Administration (FDA) officials describing the agency's developing approach to the regulation of these tissues. In between are three chapters written by tissue bank executives and the surgeons who use their products. Chapter 2, by Martha W. Anderson and Scott Bottenfield, describes how changes in tissues, tissue banking, and clinical demand have transformed a cottage industry of nonprofit eleemosynary organizations into an expansive market in which some U.S. tissue banks import and export tissues internationally and where for-profit companies play a significant and growing role. In Chapter 3, Drs. John T. Makley and Richard Nicholas point to the large and growing range of clinical uses of tissue in fields such as oncology, sports medicine, spinal surgery, and dentistry. In Chapter 4, Glenn Greenleaf goes beyond the headline charges that skin is used to puff actresses' lips at the expense of burn patients, to look at skin-recovery organizations, the expanding applications of donated skin, and some of the issues skin transplantation raises.

These are in one sense technical, background chapters, pulling together information in one place and written to be accessible to those without extensive knowledge of the field. Readers may choose to read some of the chapters more closely than others. But amid the comprehensive chronologies and descriptions, the reader will begin to discern how the field has spawned the ethical issues highlighted in later sections of the book.

Implicit in the practices described are decisions with significant ethical and policy implications. For example:

- Whether a local recovery agency sends donated skin to a processor that prioritizes its use for burn victims.
- Whether a processor maximizes the financial gain from a donated bone or looks to less lucrative but perhaps more medically important uses.
- How any particular tissue processor strikes the critical balance in processing tissue between reducing the chance of transmitting disease and preserving the tissue's usefulness.

These chapters portray an industry that continues to undergo dramatic change. We have tried to be up to date, but new developments will undoubtedly occur after the book goes to press.

1

From Donor to Recipient: The Pathway and Business of Donated Tissues

MARTHA W. ANDERSON AND RENIE SCHAPIRO

The procurement and distribution of skin and musculoskeletal tissues (bone, tendons, ligaments, and cartilage) follows its own pathway, one quite different from that of solid organs or other tissues such as corneas, heart valves, or veins. This chapter introduces the reader to the many steps and parties involved in that process, from the death of a potential donor to the distribution of the donated tissue (allograft) for implantation into a patient. The chapter also offers a primer on some of the business aspects of that process—where money changes hands and why the industry has become so attractive to for-profit companies. Subsequent chapters expand and build on the material presented here; this chapter is intended to introduce the reader to the basic system as a framework for the more expansive discussion that follows.

An organization that recovers, processes, stores, and/or distributes tissues for clinical transplantation is referred to as a tissue bank.[1] Tissue banking encompasses a wide array of tissues (e.g., bone, tendons, ligaments, heart valves, blood vessels, skin, dura mater), and the scope of activities pursued by various tissue banking organizations is broad and varied. Woll has described several goals of a tissue bank: (1) maximize the donation of organs and/or tissues to supply transplantation needs; (2) maximize the use of donated tissues; (3) ensure the safety of organs and tissues obtained for transplantation, and (4) support the donor family in its time of grief.[2]

Tissue banks differ in size, scope, and service area, ranging from smaller hospital-based programs to large regional or national tissue banking organizations involved with one or more types of tissues. They are usually established as nonprofit, charitable, tax-exempt organizations, whether part of a hospital, university, or an independent organization. Large regional tissue banks may be part of the local Organ Procurement Organization (OPO) or they may work in close cooperation with the local OPO. In some instances, the OPO and the tissue bank actively compete against each other for both tissue donors and tissue users. As discussed later in this chapter and in subsequent chapters, for-profit companies have increasingly entered the field—on their own or through alliances with these nonprofits.

The Donation System: From Donation to Aftercare

The primary tissue banking activities—donor referral, recovery, processing and distribution—may be handled by one organization or by multiple agencies (Fig. 1.1). The donation system includes the following steps:

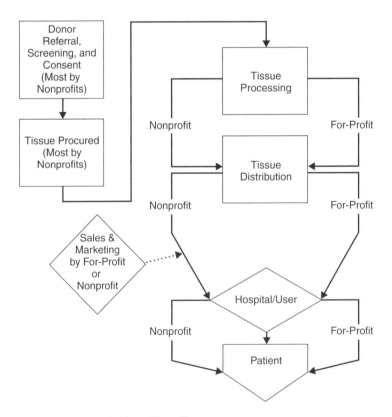

Figure 1.1. Tissue Banking Flow Chart

Donor Referral

In an effort to improve organ and tissue donation rates, the federal government requires that all hospital deaths be referred in a timely fashion to the OPO or its designee. Often, the OPO *is* the tissue procurement agency; otherwise, the appropriate agency is notified by the OPO or its designee of suitable deaths, based on general donor characteristics such as age and cause of death. Referrals of potential organ and tissue donors may also be made by the medical examiner or coroner, or the funeral home involved with the death, but these referrals are not mandatory.

Donor Screening

The tissue recovery agency or its designee (often a third-party telephone screening service) interviews hospital staff or other medical personnel attending the potential donors to evaluate the medical history (current and past) of all potential tissue donors. Additional medical and social history is obtained—often also by telephone—from the next of kin or other individuals who have knowledge of the donor's behavior or medical conditions that could have some bearing on suitability for donation. Conditions that would generally preclude tissue donation include: signs or symptoms of HIV or hepatitis infection or exposure; systemic infection; most cancers; or unknown cause of death. The general age requirement for musculoskeletal donors is 15–75, although some tissue banks have extended that.

Far more people meet criteria for tissue donation than for organ donation. Of the estimated 1.2 million people who die in hospitals each year, 11,000–14,000 of them die in circumstances that allow them to become organ donors.[3] In contrast, at least 100,000 meet criteria to donate tissue.

Consent

If donation criteria are met and the family wishes to consider donation, or the potential donor has designated his or her desire to be a donor, staff at the hospital, OPO, tissue recovery agency or the third-party telephone screening service discuss the process and the individual's wishes with the family. Typically, even if an individual has signed a donor card or other gift instrument, deference is given to the family if they oppose donation. Some states, however, including Virginia, Pennsylvania, and Colorado, have enacted legislation (Donor Directed Donation, First Person Consent laws) providing for a signed donor card or gift instrument expressing the donor's wishes to take precedence.

Tissue Recovery

Tissue recovery must generally be completed within 24 hours of the time of death. It is usually performed in the facility that referred the donor (i.e., the referring hospital), either in the operating room or in some other designated area. In some cases, the recovery is performed in a morgue or funeral home, especially if sterile conditions are not required. If the donor has also donated organs, the tissue recovery normally takes place immediately following the recovery of organs. Following tissue retrieval, the donor's body is reconstructed using various prosthetic devices and techniques, usually allowing the family to have an open-casket funeral if they so desire.

In the case of musculoskeletal tissue donation, the following bones are generally recovered: bilateral femurs (thigh bone), bilateral tibias (shin bone), bilateral fibulas (lower leg), bilateral humeri (upper arm), and bilateral iliac crest or hemi-pelvis (hip and pelvic bones). Soft tissues, such as tendons, ligaments, and cartilage, are also routinely recovered, including the patellar tendon, Achilles tendon, meniscus, fascia lata (tendonous sheath covering the muscles of the thigh), and rotator cuff. Cardiovascular tissues that are routinely donated include aortic and pulmonic heart valves, saphenous veins, and femoral veins.

Skin recovery can be more complex than bone recovery, and expertise in it varies among recovery agencies. Depending on a number of factors, either thin or thick skin may be taken. Each type has a range of uses. This is described more fully in Chapter 4.

Donor Review and Approval

Donated tissues are held in quarantine until all records can be reviewed by the tissue bank's medical director. This information includes the patient's medical record, autopsy report, and results of blood and tissue tests (to evaluate the presence of infection or contamination). In some cases, tissues may be processed prior to the complete review of all records, but they then must be held in a separate quarantine area until all required information is obtained. Fresh tissue, including skin and cartilage, is sometimes an exception. The time between donation and tissue processing ranges from a matter of days (with cardiovascular tissues and skin) to two to three months or more (with most musculoskeletal tissues).

Tissue Processing

Donated human tissue is processed in a variety of ways, depending on tissue type and the intended use of the tissues. Musculoskeletal tissues are generally cleaned with several different solutions, left whole or cut into different shapes, and then frozen or freeze-dried. In a very limited number of cases, knee tissue is refrigerated in a culture media to maintain the viability of the cartilage cells. Tissue is normally either sterilized or aseptically processed.

Tissues may be processed under three major scenarios:

1. by a recovering tissue bank with the capability to process tissues;
2. by a tissue processor that pays the tissue recovery agency an acquisition charge, processes and then distributes the tissue; or
3. by a contract processor (either nonprofit tissue bank or for-profit processor) followed by distribution by the recovery agency.

The vast majority of tissue processing is currently handled by a small number of large tissue processors, some nonprofit (np) and others for-profit (fp): AlloSource (np), Community Tissue Services (np), Cryolife (fp), LifeNet (np), Musculoskeletal Transplant Foundation (np), Osteotech (fp), and Regeneration Technologies, Inc. (fp)

Several types of tissue can be processed from each donor, depending on variables including the age and specific anatomy of the donor, and the specific demands for that type of tissue. Most tissue banks offer at least 200 different sizes, shapes, or types of tissues; others have upwards of 600 different grafts available. Approximately 50 pieces of musculoskeletal tissue are processed on an average donor, although some donors may yield as few as 10 or as many as over 100 pieces.

Tissue Distribution

Tissue is distributed by a variety of agencies or companies, including the recovering tissue bank, the tissue processor, or a third-party distribution entity. Until the end of the 1990s, most tissue was distributed by nonprofit organizations. Now an increasing amount of tissue is distributed by for-profit tissue processors and medical device companies, or by tissue brokers who sell donated tissue either as an alternative or adjuvant to traditional medical devices. Hospitals are charged a service fee for tissues that they use, and in turn typically pass those charges on to patients with a markup to cover their own costs.

Aftercare Services

A variety of aftercare services are provided by the recovery agency to donor families, including thank-you letters, general information about the recipients of their gift, support groups, and donor family recognition events.

Although the National Organ Transplant Act (NOTA) makes it illegal for any person to knowingly "acquire, receive or otherwise transfer any human [tissue] for valuable consideration if the transfer affects interstate commerce," tissue banks may charge "reasonable fees" for the services they render. NOTA left what constitutes "reasonable fees" open to interpretation, however. This ambiguity allowed for-profit companies to enter the tissue banking field, and set the stage for many of the ethical issues challenging tissue banking today. In addition to confusion over charges for services, the question of whether a company can "own" or "sell" tissue remains murky.

A Case Example

To better understand tissue banking, we will follow the process, using a hypothetical donor and following the financial transactions that occur at each step.

At 12:00 noon, Bob Jones, 35, is transported to St. Elsewhere Hospital following a motor vehicle accident. He has sustained multiple injuries and dies in the emergency room. In accordance with federal regulations governing all hospitals, the emergency room Registered Nurse notifies the local organ procurement organization, "Regional Donor Network" (RDN) of the death. The E.R. nurse provides Mr. Jones' age, sex, and cause of death, and information about his treatment at St. Elsewhere Hospital. She also tells the RDN coordinator about his next of kin (who have been informed of his death) and how they can be reached. Finally, the nurse informs the county medical examiner of Mr. Jones' death.

RDN's coordinator contacts Mr. Jones' wife by telephone about tissue donation. She explains that because of his injuries he does not meet the criteria for organ donation but he could be a tissue donor if Mrs. Jones so chooses. Although her husband has not signed a donor card, Mrs. Jones wishes to donate whatever tissues can be used. The RDN coordinator explains that his bone, tendons, ligaments, skin, heart valves, and veins can be donated. She explains the timing of the procedure and the uses of the donated tissue, and gives Mrs. Jones information affecting funeral arrangements and the involvement of the medical examiner. She might also be given information about the tissue processors (whether they are for-profit or nonprofit).

The RDN coordinator conducts a lengthy interview with Mrs. Jones about her husband's previous medical history, his overall health, and social activities that could influence his ability to be a donor (such as drug use, history of incarceration, sexual history, etc.). Finally, she provides Mrs. Jones with RDN's phone number should she or her family have further questions. The RDN coordinator then contacts the hospital nurse to obtain further information about Mr. Jones, including the extent of his injuries, results of blood tests performed, and so forth.

At 4:00 p.m., the RDN coordinator contacts the tissue recovery team, who are based at the OPO. She provides general information about Mr. Jones' death, his previous medical and social history, and which tissues Mrs. Jones has consented to donate. The tissue recovery team leader, who works as a per diem for the OPO, contacts the operating room supervisor of St. Elsewhere Hospital and is informed that an operating room will be available at approximately 9:00 p.m. The team leader contacts the other three members of the tissue recovery team, who agree to meet at RDN at 8:00 p.m. before driving to St. Elsewhere.

At 8:00 p.m., the tissue recovery team collects all of the recovery supplies and surgical instruments that will be necessary to perform the tissue recovery from RDN's offices and proceeds to St. Elsewhere's operating room, where Mr. Jones' body has been placed. They perform the tissue recovery using protocols established by the tissue processors with whom RDN has contracted. They recover the following tissues: bones (and attached tendons and ligaments) of the arms and legs, hip bones, Achilles tendons, fascia lata (the covering of the thigh muscles); heart; veins of the leg; and skin from Mr. Jones' back, torso, and thighs.

They reconstruct Mr. Jones' body using specially designed plastic prosthetic devices, wash his body, and return it to the hospital morgue. They clean the operating room and notify the supervisor that they have completed their work. At approximately 2:00 a.m., they bring several boxes containing the various tissues, blood samples, and cultures of the tissues

back to RDN's offices and prepare them for shipment to the three different tissue processors.

St. Elsewhere will charge RDN for the use of the operating room (between $500 and $3000) and any supplies the tissue recovery team needs.
The tissue recovery team members will be paid between $250 and $400
for their participation in the tissue recovery. If they have had to fly to
St. Elsewhere, the air charter company will charge between $1000 and $3000.
RDN (or their tissue processors) will have paid up to $550 for the supplies
needed for the recovery, including sterile drapes, packaging supplies, tissue storage solutions, protective gear, and reconstructive devices. Their tissue
processors will then pay for a courier to pick up or ship the tissues via air-
line and deliver them to the processing facilities. The RDN coordinator
receives no additional stipend or compensation, because Mrs. Jones agreed
to donation. Nor is Mrs. Jones compensated for her husband's donation.

Once the tissue is sent to the three tissue processors, RDN will bill
each of them a Standard Acquisition Charge (SAC). A SAC is intended to
cover the costs of tissue recovery, administrative costs, bereavement care,
and other costs associated with operating a tissue recovery program. SACs
also usually have a small percentage built-in that is intended to serve as
"margin" or excess revenue, to allow the OPO to build for the future, contribute to its savings, and so on. SACs vary throughout the United States,
but on average would be:

Musculoskeletal Tissues: $5500
Heart for Valves: $1400
Veins: $600 per vein (average four veins per donor)
Skin: $250–$500 per square foot (average 3.5 square feet per donor)

The tissue processors could be nonprofit or for-profit companies. Upon
receipt of the tissue, each begins the process of evaluating the tissue and
the donor's record for suitability. The blood samples will be sent to a laboratory for testing for hepatitis, HIV, and other infectious agents. The tissue
cultures will also be sent to a laboratory to determine if any bacterial contaminants are present on the tissues. In the case of the heart (for valves),
the tissues will be processed within three days and put in quarantine until
all necessary information is obtained and reviewed. The skin bank will
process the skin within ten days, some into skin that can be used for burn
patients and some acellularized for use in either urological, gynecological,
or reconstructive surgery (see Chapter 4). Skin that has not been frozen
but is kept "fresh" will be sent to a burn patient within several days; the

remaining skin for burns will be frozen for up to one year, as will the acellular skin. The process used for preparing acellular skin is more complex and requires significant technological resources.

The expenses incurred by the processor are part of the fees the processor charges to the hospital or other purchaser. Costs associated with testing the blood and tissue samples average approximately $400. Costs associated with processing tissues range from $3000 to over $6000, depending on the processor, the type of processing, and the amount of tissue being processed.

The musculoskeletal tissue bank will process Mr. Jones' tissue approximately 60 to 90 days following his death, after reviewing Mr. Jones' medical record, results from the medical examiner's autopsy, and the serological (blood) and microbiological (blood and tissue) test results. For any single tissue from Mr. Jones, the bank may have multiple options for its use in patient care. For example, a femur could be kept intact so that an orthopedic surgeon could use it to replace a femur. Alternatively, it could be processed into many smaller pieces for use in spinal and other surgeries or ground into a powder to be used as a void filler. (Chapters 2 and 3 describe various processed tissues, including highly machined pieces.)

The decisions may be based on many variables, including: (*1*) Mr. Jones' size and overall health; (*2*) the need for specific types of tissue at St. Elsewhere and other hospitals in the region served by the RDN, and (*3*) the need for specific types of tissue from other hospitals that normally obtain their tissue from the tissue bank. In some cases, the bank may be limited by a family's designation that no for-profit tissue processor be involved, since some processed tissues are available only through for-profit companies. A musculoskeletal tissue processor's choice of what to do with a recovered tissue may be purely financial: more revenue can be generated with the more sophisticated tissue forms than with a whole bone. For example, a whole femur used in oncology surgery is valued at $4000–$5000, whereas a femur that is made primarily into machined tissue grafts for spinal surgery can generate up to $15,000.

Tissue banks that offer highly machined or powdered bone products have formal relationships with one or more for-profit medical device partners, such as those that sell spinal instrumentation and metallic spinal devices. These relationships developed during the latter part of the 1990s, as spinal device companies found the value of combining their technology with human allograft tissue. Relationships between the nonprofit tissue bank and device company vary, but may include product research and development, development or funding of processing equipment and processing facilities, marketing support, tissue processing, and tissue distribution. Without these types of partnerships, many nonprofit tissue banks would have found the high costs associated with promoting tissue throughout the country, coupled with the high costs of new "product" development, to be prohibitive. A tissue bank's goal of maximizing the use of donated tissues can be better realized through these relationships.

In many cases, the for-profit device partner is responsible for selling these specialized tissues, including taking all orders from hospitals, shipping the tissue, and collecting the money charged for the tissues.

Table 1.1 provides examples of tissue fees charged to hospitals by several for-profit and nonprofit companies. An X indicates that the tissue is not available through that processor.

The fees charged for allografts include the direct costs associated with the tissue, such as recovery, transportation, testing, processing, shipping, and distribution, as well as the indirect costs associated with operating any business (payroll and benefits, rent, utilities, insurance, research and development, marketing, etc.). In the case of proprietary tissues (e.g., machined spinal spacers, bone fillers), they also include a percentage paid to the for-profit partner involved with that specialty graft. That percentage pays for their costs, including the development and FDA approval of surgical instrumentation, their sales and marketing efforts, administrative costs, and the use of the equipment the surgeon needs to place of the allografts. In many cases, hospitals are no longer willing to pay for surgical instrumentation that the device companies have spent millions of dollars developing—therefore, this part of their costs can only be recouped through the fees for the allograft. The money paid to the device company also contributes to their bottom line. In general, the percentage realized by the for-profit company ranges from 50%–80% of the total tissue fee charged to the hospital. Nonprofit tissue banks generally seek to generate 5%–10% revenues over costs, which allows them to build for the future, expand their facilities,

Table 1.1. Tissue Fees at Nonprofits and For-Profits

Tissue type	NP #1	NP #2	FP #1	FP #2
Cancellous Chips	$364	$375	$450	X
Patellar Tendon	$1335	$1395	$1595	$2875
Iliac Crest Wedge (12mm)	$580	$525	$690	X
Whole Femur	$5045	$4225	X	X
Machined Femoral "Spacer"	$2910	$1295	$2295–2495	X
DBM Defect Filler (10 cc)	$935	X	$950	X

perform research and development, and hold funds in reserve against any possible downturn in donor or transplant activity.

In the tissue marketplace that has emerged for these products, as in any commercial marketplace, price is not the only factor affecting sales. Surgeons in particular tend to develop loyalties to certain products or companies whose products they prefer. Therefore, although for-profit companies tend to charge more, they can often compete effectively with nonprofits if they establish close relationships with the end users.

The hospital passes the charges for the processed tissue on to the tissue recipient, often marking it up significantly. The surgeon who implants the tissue graft also charges the patient, although reimbursement for many kinds of allograft surgery—such as orthopedic oncology—is far below the surgeon's actual costs.

While it has been widely reported that the value of a human body can exceed $220,000, this would be the rare exception rather than the rule. On average, that amount could be expected to be approximately $30,000–$50,000, with an average of 50–60 grafts available per donor. The range is broad—from no money for donors from which no tissue can be used because of the contamination of tissue or new medical information obtained after the tissue recovery, to over $200,000 for donors from which tissue is processed into medical implants, demineralized bone matrices, or dermal implants in addition to traditional bone and skin grafts.

This road map of tissue transplantation—from identifying donors to transplanting tissue in a patient—reveals a complex and evolving process that includes many diverse stakeholders with various interests. Not surprisingly, these procedures are fodder for the many important clinical, ethical, and economic issues that are discussed in this book.

References

1. American Association of Tissue Banks. *Standards for Tissue Banking*. 1350 Beverly Road, Suite 220-A, McLean, Virginia 22101.
2. Woll JE. Ethics in tissue banking—recovery agency perspectives. Presented at Case Western Reserve University Ethics in Tissue Banking Symposium, October 5, 2000.
3. Association of Organ Procurement Organizations. *2000 Tissue Banking Survey of AOPO Members*. One Cambridge Court, 8110 Gatehouse Road, Falls Church, Virginia 22042.

2

Tissue Banking—Past, Present, and Future

MARTHA W. ANDERSON
AND SCOTT BOTTENFIELD

How did tissue banking grow from a cottage industry to a multimillion-dollar multinational enterprise? It is difficult to determine which was the chicken and which the egg: Did increased tissue availability spur expanded clinical use or did clinical demand promote increased procurement? What is clear is that as demand has grown, tissue banking has changed dramatically. Coupled with changes within the industry has been a growing interest from the government, media, and general public in tissue banking practices. This increased scrutiny has caused many tissue banks to reevaluate their practices in order to best assure their ability to serve their stakeholders, and ultimately, their very survival.

This chapter examines the history of tissue banking in the United States and the forces behind the changes that have transformed it over the past few decades. Although tissue banking encompasses a wide array of tissues, including skin, heart valves, blood vessels, and dura mater, our comments will pertain primarily to musculoskeletal tissues, which constitute the majority of tissues procured, processed, and transplanted in the United States. They also apply primarily to cadaveric donations; tissue donation by living persons occurs, but it is rare and declining.

We will consider the evolution of tissue banking operations and donation systems, including the entry of for-profit companies, advances in processing technology and safety concerns, and the impact of industry standards and government oversight. We will also look at future trends.

Tissue Banking Organization

Musculoskeletal transplantation can be dated back to around A.D. 287 when Saints Cosmas and Damian reportedly transplanted the leg of a recently deceased Moor onto the leg of a white nobleman. It was not until 1878, however, that MacEwan documented successful transplants of musculoskeletal tissue.[1] In 1908 Lexer reported transplanting a whole joint.[2] Carrell first promoted transplanting banked frozen tissues from cadavers in a seminal article in 1912.[3] In 1940 Albee described a broad variety of applications for bone transplants and the use of lathes and saws to create bone screws and dowels that have been implemented by tissue banks only recently.[4]

Although Inclan established a surgical bone bank (storing bone from living patients for allografts or autografts) in Cuba in 1942,[5] the U.S. Navy Tissue Bank in Bethesda, Maryland, established in 1949, marked the emergence of the modern tissue bank. It remained the primary tissue bank in the United States for much of the next 30 years. The Navy Tissue Bank was created to recover and preserve tissues to treat traumatically injured servicemen on the battlefield and at home, but it also advanced the science of tissue banking through ambitious research programs involving noted researchers and clinicians.[6] This new knowledge promoted wider acceptance of tissue transplantation as a legitimate treatment method. The Navy Tissue Bank's founder, Dr. George Hyatt, pioneered systems that remain in place today, including freeze-drying tissue for long-term storage, screening donors for transmissible diseases, obtaining informed consent for donation, and the concept of an independent, free-standing tissue bank that functioned outside of an individual medical center.[7]

Changes in Demand

The focus of tissue banks has always been to provide whatever tissues were needed by surgeons and clinicians in the form that they could best use. The organization and operations of tissue banks have changed over the past several decades, primarily in response to changes in surgical practice that led to different demands for human donated tissue.

Limited access to tissue throughout the 1960s and 1970s led many hospitals to maintain their own surgical discard bone banks, banking primarily femoral heads that were removed during hip replacement surgery. These tissues were usually frozen at the hospital until needed and then ground into a morselized form and used in various procedures. including traumatic bone repair and joint revisions. Often, the patients from whom these tissues were obtained were not informed that their tissue might be used for another patient, nor were the tissues or patients routinely tested for infectious diseases.

Advances in orthopedic oncological surgery were a driving force behind changes in tissue banking beginning in the 1970s. Orthopedic surgeons such as Enneking, Mankin, and Parrish began successfully transplanting large allografts (e.g., whole and partial femora, tibiae and humeri) to treat primary bone cancers, located mostly in the long bones of the arms and legs.[8-10] To meet their growing need for this type of specialized bone graft, orthopaedic departments of medical centers developed cadaveric tissue banks. sometimes storing surgical discard tissue as well.

In the 1980s, local tissue banks began to proliferate. They were often started by blood banks, eye banks, universities, or hospitals, but just as often by entrepreneurial individuals who saw either a need or an opportunity in tissue banking. At the same time, a few regional tissue banks began to operate, most notably Mile High Transplant Bank (now AlloSource) in 1980, the Virginia Tissue Bank (now LifeNet) in 1982, and the Pennsylvania Regional Tissue Bank (now part of the Musculoskeletal Transplant Foundation) in 1982. Most provided priority access to key surgeons or to selected local hospitals. Over time, tissue banks began to distribute outside of their traditional service areas, perhaps an indication of the growing uses of tissue or their willingness and ability to expand their market reach. Currently, many tissue banks have allocation systems that return high-demand tissue to the area that provided the donation, while distributing tissue broadly throughout the United States. Some tissue banks also actively distribute tissue to other countries.

As the proportion of older patients in the country grew, the 1980s and 1990s saw a dramatic expansion in the types of tissue used for joint-replacement surgery, which often requires allograft in combination with a metallic prosthesis. Continued expansion of limb-salvage surgery for orthopedic oncology patients also increased demand for large bone allografts. Sports medicine surgeons began using increasingly larger amounts of "soft tissues," primarily patellar and Achilles tendons used to repair damaged cruciate (knee) ligaments.

A major increase in spinal fusion surgery also caused rapid growth in the use of allograft, and became a driving force behind the growth of many tissue banks. Allograft tissue used in spinal fusion surgery accounts for about half of all allograft tissue transplanted in the United States.

Steadily increasing rates of back injury and serious back pain, successful outcomes in spinal surgeries, and enthusiasm for spinal fusion surgery among orthopedic surgeons all contributed to the growing use of allograft. The 1990s saw the development of proprietary processing technologies, patented tissue configurations, and advanced processing systems that result in tissue grafts with very specific dimensions and shapes designed by biomechanical engineers that are used primarily in spinal fusion surgery and sports medicine.

For most surgeons, however, autograft remains the "gold standard," especially for spinal fusion surgery. This is primarily because patients receiving autograft heal faster and because there is no risk of disease transmission. That risk, most notably from HIV or hepatitis, is small yet of understandable concern. On the negative side, autograft requires "harvesting" bone, generally from the iliac crest of the pelvis, which is then implanted into the patient's spine or other part of the body. This results in two surgical sites, a longer hospital stay, and often hip pain that far exceeds and outlasts the pain of the transplant site. When the patient's bone is unavailable, insufficient, or unsuitable, allograft is required.

According to one report, each year more than 200,000 U.S. patients receive allografts for spinal surgery;[11] another study estimates that 85% of spinal fusions use either allograft or autograft.[12] Some surgeons use synthetic materials in addition to, or in place of allograft. Exact national statistics for the use of allograft are not available, but industry estimates indicate that tissue used in spinal surgery alone accounts for up to $300,000,000 in revenue to U.S. tissue banks.

These new tissue forms and uses all contributed to a steadily expanding demand for tissues. One major tissue bank's experience, presented in Figure 2.1, illustrates the shift in types of tissue provided and the dramatic growth experienced by U.S. tissue banks over the past ten years.

The growth and shift in tissue demand resulted in a need to hire new and different kinds of personnel, the move by tissue banks to affiliate with traditional competitors in order to gain access to new technologies, the elimination of processing by smaller tissue banks who cannot provide technologically advanced tissues, and the consolidation of tissue banks into larger, stronger entities. It also facilitated the entry of for-profit companies.

Entry of For-Profits and New Strategic Alliances

One of the most dramatic and controversial changes in tissue banking came in the 1980s with the entrance of for-profit tissue processors into the field—

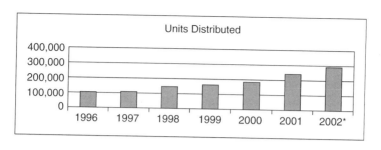

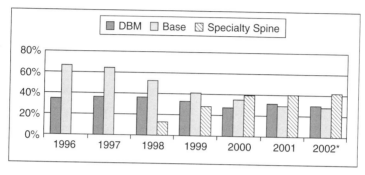

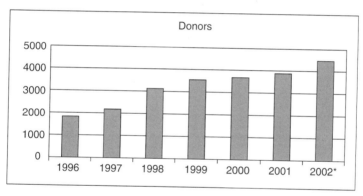

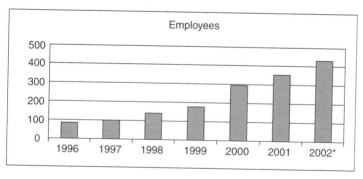

Figure 2.1a-d. Growth at Musculoskeleletal Transplant Foundation 1996–2002 (largest nonprofit tissue bank). DBM: demineralized bone matrix typically used as a defect filler or to promote bone healing. Base: standard musculoskeletal tissues (e.g., cancellous chips, tendons, femoral heads). Specialty Spine: highly-processed spinal implants.

Cryolife in 1982, Osteotech in 1987—and Osteotech's relationship to two nationwide nonprofit donor networks (Musculoskeletal Transplant Foundation and the American Red Cross). Tissue banking activities are generally regarded as a service for the benefit of the donors and tissue recipients. Many believed that the "crossing over" of this humanitarian effort into the commercial arena would have a lasting and adverse effect on all transplant organizations by creating a negative public image of the transplant community.[13]

In addition to prompting ethical concerns, for-profit tissue processing companies changed tissue banking by constructing advanced processing facilities and processes, and implementing traditional business activities such as advertising, sales, and marketing. They have been credited, fairly or not, with raising the bar on tissue processing techniques, thereby improving the quality of transplantable tissues throughout the U.S. Certainly, the use of clean-room technology did not exist prior to their involvement in the field. Nor would many of the new tissue forms currently in high demand have been developed without the capital provided by their investors.

It was in 1992 that the for-profit company Osteotech introduced Grafton demineralized bone matrix (DBM), the first tissue made available as a commercially promoted "product." DBM is made from demineralized cortical bone in combination with glycerol; its advantages are that it stimulates new bone formation and is in a form that is easily delivered to the surgical site. Initially designed for use in dental and periodontic applications, it rapidly spread to orthopedics and neurosurgery.

This new tissue form caused not a little consternation throughout the field of tissue banking. Issues raised with its development included branding the tissue, which seemed "too commercial," proprietary patents issued on the tissue process, and the publicly traded (on the NASDAQ) status of Osteotech. In addition, it was readily available throughout the United States, a departure from other tissues, which had been distributed primarily through a local or regional priority system. By 2000, at least five other demineralized tissues were available in various formats; all are either promoted or sold directly by for-profit companies, with demineralized tissues provided by tissue banks. This product set the stage for many changes the tissue banking industry would experience in the future.

By the 1990s, most larger tissue banks were moving toward a more traditional medical device/pharmaceutical sales and marketing system, using professionally trained sales representatives or agents to promote their tissue and their services, developing advertisements and brochures outlining their services, and implementing controversial market-driven practices such as consignment, discounting, and bundling. Even those banks that traditionally resided firmly in the nonprofit arena began to enter into relationships with orthopedic and medical device companies ranging from limited co-marketing to a relationship that allowed the device company to process, package, market, and sell the tissue.

Medical device companies became increasingly interested in allograft as an opportunity to expand their business and have remained very involved in tissue banking. Not only is human tissue often regarded as superior to synthetics, it is also less regulated than metallic or synthetic implants, so less time and resources are required to bring a new "product" to "market." Many of the new highly processed "machined" bone grafts have been developed in conjunction with these companies and are protected by U.S. and European patents. Medical device companies such as Johnson & Johnson/DePuy Acromed, Synthes and Medtronics/Sofamor Danek aggressively market them.

Strategic alliances between nonprofit tissue banks and for-profit medical device companies are now the norm. Nonprofit tissue banks as well as their for-profit partners are recognizing the financial advantages of these new relationships. The nonprofit sector has recognized the extensive resources of large companies that may be accessed through such partnerships. While these new affiliations may take any number of forms, it is clear that marketing strength, research and development capabilities, access to regulatory expertise, financial support, and other resources are attractive to the nonprofit sector. Table 2.1 provides a partial listing of the strategic alliances between the for-profit and nonprofit sectors for musculoskeletal tissues.

Tissue Donation Systems

The Impact of Organ Policies

Like tissue, most organ recovery and allocation activities were under local control in the 1970s and early 1980s. Organ transplant centers recovered organs from local hospitals and transplanted them into their own waiting patients, without any federal oversight for organ allocation or data compilation. But organ procurement and allocation began attracting the attention of policymakers, culminating in the passage of the National Organ Transplant Act in 1984.[14] Despite the fact that tissues are addressed in NOTA, a parallel system for the organization and operation of tissue banks was not developed, nor even discussed. But beginning in the latter part of

Table 2.1. Strategic Alliances Between Nonprofits and For-Profits

Nonprofit Tissue Bank	For-Profit Company	Relationship
American Red Cross	Osteotech	ARC provides tissues to OTI for processing into traditional and specialty tissue grafts and distribution of Grafton®
AlloSource	Wright Medical Technologies	AlloSource provides demineralized bone to Wright for a product containing bone
LifeNet	Johnson & Johnson/ DePuy Acromed	DePuy markets specialty spinal fusion grafts for LifeNet
LifeNet	Osteotech	LifeNet provides various bone tissue to Osteotech for products containing bone
Musculoskeletal Transplant Foundation	Synthes	Synthes co-develops and markets specialty spinal fusion grafts for MTF
Musculoskeletal Transplant Foundation	Howmedica	Howmedica markets tissue grafts for use in orthopedic procedures
Southeast Tissue Alliance (formerly Univ. of Florida Tissue Bank)	Regeneration Technologies	SETA provides tissue for processing and distribution by RTI and Medtronic/ Sofamor/Danek
Tennessee Donor Services	Cortek	Processes certain spinal tissue for distribution by Cortek
Tissue Banks International	Exactech	TBI distributes tissue-based products for Exactech
U. Miami Tissue Bank	Biomet/EBI	EBI markets tissue grafts for use in spinal procedures

the 1980s and continuing through the 1990s, changes in the organ donation system had a ripple effect on tissue banking. Some had positive effects on organ and tissue donation and transplantation; others had negligible results. At a minimum, their net effect was to raise the issue of donation to a higher level within health care, government, and the general public.

In 1986, the Omnibus Budget Reconciliation Act included so-called Required Request language, which was the first national effort aimed at addressing the growing organ shortage. It required all hospitals receiving Medicare or Medicaid funding to implement a system to identify potential donors and to offer their family members the option of donating organs, eyes or tissues. Although the results fell short of expectations, Required

Request marked the first time that hospitals were required to focus any resources or attention on organ and tissue donation.

In 1988, the Organ Procurement and Transplant Network (OPTN) was established to develop and manage a national system for organ allocation. Tissue, also a scarce resource, was not addressed. Regional Organ Procurement Organizations (OPOs) were established, often through the consolidation of multiple organ procurement and transplant programs that had previously been operated by individual transplant centers.

As the federally designated "donor network," OPOs were often seen as being ideally positioned to provide recovery services for all organs and tissues, thereby eliminating the need for multiple agencies. Hospitals looked to the OPOs to provide them with policy and procedure development, staff education, and donor family support services, regardless of the type of donation. When problems with tissue donation occurred, the family, hospital, medical examiner, or funeral home often blamed the OPO or looked to the OPO to resolve the problem.

Many OPOs saw great opportunities in tissue donation, including financial benefits. They found that adding tissue recovery to their operations could add many thousands of dollars to their bottom line, which allowed them to control rising organ acquisition costs, hire more staff, offer more services, or offset fixed expenses during times of low organ-donor activity. Others saw the organizational benefits of such vertical integration.

In some areas, tissue donation was implemented to fill an unmet need—if hospitals and medical centers were unable to obtain tissue grafts, they requested that the OPO begin this service. Some OPOs felt that this would allow them to offer the option of donation to more donor families. Other OPOs entered into tissue recovery, even though independent tissue banks already provided those services. This led to a competition for donors that continues today. By 2001, it was estimated that approximately 40% of all tissue donation was facilitated by OPOs.[15] Regardless of the motivation, tissue donation began to take on an increasingly important role within many OPOs, threatening the financial viability of some eye and tissue banks.

Tissue donor recovery rates increased dramatically in the 1990s. This was due in part to new federal regulations, improved systems of donor recruitment, expanded donor criteria, increased efficiencies of tissue and organ recovery agencies, consolidation of agencies, collaborative efforts encouraged through organizations such as the National Coalition on Donation (www.shareyourlife.org) and the active encouragement of donor-related efforts by federal, local, and state agencies. Public awareness of organ donation continued to increase rapidly through campaigns that included celebrity supporters (most notably, Michael Jordan) and the development of national slogans to convey a unified message ("Donate life"). HHS Secretary Tommy Thompson launched a national initiative in 2001 aimed at increasing workplace support of donation, and other national campaigns also promoted organ, tissue, blood, and bone marrow donation.

In 1997, new regulations known as "Conditions of Participation"[16] (COP) required that all deaths occurring in Medicare and Medicaid-supported hospitals be reported to the OPO that serves that hospital, or to an agency or entity designated by the OPO. The COP replaces Required Request systems in which hospital staff have the ability to determine suitability for donation and the responsibility to approach families about donation, with a process by which trained, designated individuals approach *every appropriate* family about organ, eye, or tissue donation.

Although organ donation rates did not increase markedly with the COP, the results for tissue banks were dramatic: within the first year, many tissue and eye banks experienced an impressive increase in donations. Donations to AATB-accredited tissue banks increased 62% between 1996 and 1999.[17] An unanticipated result of the COP was financial—over 1.2 million people die in U.S. hospitals every year, resulting in a huge volume of telephone calls that must be placed by overworked hospital staff and handled by organizations who were forced to either develop and staff telephone triage systems or to purchase those services from another organization. It has been estimated that OPOs, eye banks, and tissue banks spend well over $10,000,000 each year meeting the requirements of the COP.

Public Interest in Tissue Donation

Donor family activism also caused changes throughout the field. In 1992, the National Donor Family Council (NDFC) was organized with assistance and support from the National Kidney Foundation. Started by Maggie Coolican, a donor mother, the council was organized to give a voice and a home to donor families. Previously the silent and often unrecognized participants in the cycle of donation and transplantation, donor families began to gain significant power (see Chapter 7). OPOs, eye banks, and tissue banks began to provide better aftercare bereavement services to donor families, ranging from a follow-up thank-you letter to providing recipient information, donor family recognition events and commemoratives, bereavement counseling services, and peer support groups staffed by grief and counseling specialists.

In 2000 and 2001, a series of newspaper and television reports brought the public's attention to tissue banking.[18, 19] Following the articles in 2000, a thorough evaluation of the entire industry by the Office of the Inspector General (OIG) was conducted. Two reports were published in January 2001: "Oversight of Tissue Banking" and "Informed Consent in Tissue Donation."[20, 21] The National Donor Family Council developed guidelines regarding consent for tissue donation, which were broadly distributed and discussed.

In response to the newspaper articles and the OIG's report, many changes were made by the tissue banking industry, including the adoption of expanded informed consent guidelines developed by a joint task force of the associations most involved with this field (American Association of Tissue Banks, Eye Bank Association of America, and Association of Organ Procurement Organizations.[22] See Appendix A). The AOPO also developed a set of guidelines for OPOs to use when considering tissue processing partnerships.

Philosophical and operational changes related to the consent process are beginning to change the way that OPOs and tissue banks operate. In the past, consent was always obtained from the donor's next of kin, regardless of whether the donor had signed a donor card or indicated her or his wish to be a donor. In fact, to many people's surprise, family members were allowed to overrule that decision. In several parts of the country, new laws either allow or require an OPO to accept an individual's official, stated intent to donate (e.g., via driver's license, donor registry, donor card), and do not allow the donor's next of kin to override that decision. Donor registries are being developed throughout the country, allowing people to formally record their desire to donate. Donor registries exist in more than 28 states; in at least 10, an individual's donor registration is sufficient, requiring no further family consent for organ and in some cases, eye and tissue donation.[17]

These new laws pose unique challenges to tissue banks. Organ donation is well recognized by the general public; however, the public's sparse knowledge of tissue donation is worrisome. In some parts of the country, tissue banks must determine whether to accept the patient's "donor designation" for bone, skin, and other tissue donations, often without knowing whether he or she meant to consent to this type of donation. In addition, tissue recovery agencies must grapple with how to deal with a family who may be vehemently opposed to donation, yet who must provide significant amounts of personal and medical history about the potential donor. The agencies that have been most successful in implementing these new systems have worked diligently with the public, the media, and hospital staff to build consensus and understanding prior to implementation.

Tissue Processing and Graft Safety

Of paramount concern to all those involved in tissue transplantation is the safety of the graft. The elimination of potential infection has always been a guiding principle in tissue processing—not an easy task when one considers that tissue is removed from a dead body that may have been exposed to bacteria, viruses, or other pathogens prior to death or following death during the decomposition process. Tomford's thorough history of musculoskeletal tissue banking outlines the earliest types of tissue processing and preservation, including refrigeration, placement in tubes of Vaseline followed by cold storage, boiling, storage in plasma or Merthiolate, and freeze-drying.[6]

Until the late 1980s, processing techniques generally required sterilization of tissues due to non-aseptic tissue recovery techniques. Many tissue donors were recovered in non-sterile settings, such as hospital morgues, coroner's offices, and funeral homes. Many tissues were minimally processed immediately following tissue recovery. Lyophilization (freeze-drying) of tissues that were processed into various shapes (dowels, wedges, cubes) allowed the tissue bank to store tissues in vacuum-sealed bottles at room temperature for long periods of time.

In the late 1980s, a small number of for-profit tissue processing companies brought changes to tissue banking, notably with the construction of pharmaceutical-grade processing facilities, which eliminated the need for sterilization of tissue. This "aseptic processing" maintains the biomechanical and biological properties of the tissue. If, however, the tissue is contaminated with organisms that cannot be eliminated during aseptic processing, the tissue bank must discard, decontaminate or sterilize the tissue. The most common techniques for accomplishing this include gamma irradiation and gas sterilization with ethylene oxide. Both of these techniques can damage the tissue, however, leading to less than acceptable patient outcomes, so processors must strike a balance between the twin goals of maximal tissue safety and viability.

By the 1990s, many other tissue banks began to follow the lead of the for-profit companies, moving away from "terminal" sterilization techniques. In aseptic processing, tissue banks use "clean room" technology similar to that used by the pharmaceutical or computer industries. Clean rooms are classified in terms of the number of microorganisms present in a cubic foot: Aseptic tissue is generally processed in either a Class 10 or Class 100 environment, with fewer than 10 or 100 microorganisms per cubic foot. By way of comparison, a standard operating room, normally the "cleanest" space any of us will enter, is between Class 1000 and Class 10,000. In order to process tissues in these facilities, processing technicians must wear sterile attire designed to protect the tissue from them, and them from the tissue (Fig. 2.2). The tissue bank must filter the air (up to 10 times per minute), use copious amounts of sterile or purified water, install high-tech bone cleaning and cutting equipment, use advanced communication systems, and conduct in-depth, ongoing training programs.

In general, tissues are subjected to various chemical, ultrasonic, and mechanical cleansing treatments to remove unnecessary soft tissues, bone marrow, and blood. Then the tissues can be processed into many different sizes and shapes, depending on the individual donor's size, age, and anatomy, as well as on the tissue needs of the tissue bank. While this technology is broadly felt to be state-of-the-art, it comes at a great cost. The estimated cost for a six-room Class 10 clean-room facility that can process 1500 donors annually is $4,000,000.

Figure 2.2. Technicians aseptically processing bone for spinal procedures.

Disease transmission and infection concerns led to the development of new processing technologies in the late 1990s and early 2000s that offered surgeons and patients further levels of security with allograft tissues.

Disease Transmission

One key event of concern came in 1991 with the report of the transmission of HIV from an organ and tissue donor who had repeatedly tested negative for HIV.[23] This focused the public's attention for the first time on the potential for disease transmission through donation. On a positive note, this event also focused attention on donor screening and tissue processing techniques.

Donor screening practices, improved testing and documentation, and expanded interviews regarding medical *and* behavioral history with both family members and "significant others" were all implemented throughout the country. No further cases of HIV transmission through tissue transplantation have been documented. At the end of the 1980s, Malinan and Buck calculated the risk of HIV transmission through an allograft to be 1 in 1.67 million when the tissue and donor have been thoroughly screened using all available technologies, including PCR testing, in-depth donor family interviews, and autopsy.[24]

In 2001, safety issues resurfaced. The FDA and CDC reported several cases of infection stemming from allegedly contaminated tissues, including one that resulted in the death of a patient. The CDC issued a series of reports in 2002 on 54 tissue infections that occurred over several years, which included recommendations for culturing tissues to identify contaminants, sterilization of tissue when possible, and treatment of patients who are suspected of receiving contaminated tissues.[25] The CDC report also stressed the importance of allograft tissues for patient care, however, noting that out of an estimated 650,000 annual tissue transplants, bacterial infection is "a rare complication."[26] Compared to the estimated 44,000–98,000 hospital deaths due to preventable medical errors, the safety of donated tissue is noteworthy.[27]

Later in 2002, however, there were new reports of disease transmission involving six organ and tissue recipients who contracted hepatitis C (HCV) from a donor in the "window" period, and several organ transplant recipients who developed West Nile virus (WNV), including a number who died.[28] Although the West Nile cases have been linked to blood transfusion, they do elevate the concern about transmission through organ and tissue transplants. Creutzfeld-Jakob disease (CJD), the human variant of "mad cow disease," looms on the horizon, with the FDA evaluating new, stringent screening criteria to try to rule out those who could have been exposed to the disease.[29] New testing regimens for HCV, WNV, and CJD are anxiously anticipated by both the tissue banking and surgical communities, and will be no doubt be implemented as quickly as they can be made available.

Tissue Banking Standards and Regulation

Voluntary Standards

Safety concerns led the FDA to take more serious notice of the growth in tissue transplantation in the 1990s. Until then, tissue banks were subject to remarkably little oversight. The banks were left to establish their own policies and procedures on critical areas such as donor criteria, recovery, and processing systems.

In 1976, the American Association of Tissue Banks (AATB) was founded as a scientific, not-for-profit, peer group organization to help address some of these issues. Its stated goal is "to facilitate the provision of transplantable tissues of uniform high quality in quantities sufficient to meet national needs."[17] The AATB provides education to tissue banking professionals, and a network designed to link hospitals with tissue banks that have excess supplies of tissues.

AATB would go on to play a leading role in tissue banking, establishing voluntary standards and developing an accreditation system in the mid-1980s. It published its first *Standards for Tissue Banking*[22] in 1984 to promote adherence to acceptable norms of technical and ethical performance. Although voluntary, compliance with the AATB standards is intended to ensure that all activities related to the collection, processing, storage, and distribution of human tissues are carried out safely and professionally. In 1986, the AATB undertook a program of inspections and accreditation. Tissue banks may receive accreditation for retrieval, processing, storage, and distribution of tissues following a rigorous inspection of their operations. Their standard-setting and accreditation continues to be a significant element of tissue banking today.

As important as the AATB accreditation process is, however, it is strictly voluntary. Even in the rare case that a bank fails to be accredited or loses its accreditation, it is not prohibited from operating. In addition, not all agencies eligible for accreditation have applied for or received accreditation. As of 2002, AATB listed 73 accredited banks, including 14 that are either in Canada or are reproductive banks only. Based on the number of entities that have registered with the FDA, there are upwards of 300 banks in the United States. Many of these are involved solely with tissue donor screening and recovery, yet some of the country's largest tissue processors have resisted becoming accredited by the AATB.

Regulatory Oversight and Its Impact on Tissue Banks

Only four states have any type of tissue bank regulation: California, Florida, Maryland, and New York. Federal regulation of tissue banks by the FDA began in earnest in 1993, with the "Interim Rule for Banked Human Tissue" (see Chapter 5). The interim rule was intended to "require certain infectious disease testing, donor screening, and record-keeping to help prevent the transmission of AIDS and hepatitis through human tissue used in transplantation."[30] Some of the key changes associated with this new regulation centered on the medical and social history interviews that were required of the next of kin for all potential donors. These interviews are extensive, requiring the collection of information about an individual's sexual history and habits, use of illegal drugs, and exposure to infectious disease agents such as HIV and hepatitis. One tissue bank's questionnaire increased from three pages to nine pages of information to be gathered on the potential donor's medical and social behavior history.

These changes resulted in the need for in-depth training of tissue bank and hospital staff, a significant increase in the amount of time hospital staff must spend on each referral, and a lengthy interview (upwards of 30–60 minutes) with a grieving family member. Anecdotal statements from bereaved family members who anguished over the length and depth of the interviews included comments such as "if I had known you would have asked so much, or it would have taken so long, I wouldn't have said yes." The Interim Rule was finalized in 1997.

Over the past several years, the FDA has struggled with the definition of tissue—whether it is a biologic (like a pharmaceutical or blood), a medical device, or something else. The new tissues that are used in spinal and sports medicine applications look far more like their metallic cousins, and far less like the whole bones (femora, humeri or tibiae) from which they are processed. The use of advanced processing techniques has allowed tissue banks to produce tissues that are machined to exacting specifications, following rigorous testing for biomechanical strength and capability—not to the level that spinal implant manufacturers must go, but certainly farther than early-day tissue processors went. Tissues processed into screws, dowels, and tooth-lined wedges are designed specifically to integrate with surgical instrumentation. These tissues are currently considered to be "human tissue for transplantation," falling into a separate category that is neither device nor biologic.

The FDA did recently reclassify Grafton and other bone defect fillers (Osteofil, Allomatrix and DBX) as medical devices. Processors of these tissues (which by some reports account for over 30% of all tissues distributed in the U.S.) are therefore required to submit preclinical data ("510K") relating to safety and efficacy. In addition, quality systems will be required to comply with other FDA regulations. Costs associated with this ruling could run as high as $2,000,000 for each tissue bank that produces this type of tissue. Some within the field, including the AATB, continue to press their case against this new classification.

In 1998, the FDA published the proposed rule, "Establishment Registration and Listing for Manufacturers of Human Cellular and Tissue-Based Products," which requires all agencies and organizations involved with tissue banking to register with the FDA. The Agency published two more proposed rules in the late 1990s: "Suitability Determination for Donors of Human Cellular and Tissue-Based Products" (the "Donor-Suitability Proposed Rule"); and "Current Good Tissue Practice for Manufacturers of Human Cellular and Tissue-Based Products; Inspection and Enforcement" (the "GTP Proposed Rule"). They are expected to have a significant impact on the industry (see *The Future of Tissue Banking* below.)

The FDA now routinely inspects tissue banks, to learn about the industry and to insure regulatory compliance. In the course of these inspections, they have issued inspection reports ("483's") when a bank needs to make changes. Warning letters and mandatory recalls have been issued to a number of large tissue banks that have remained out of compliance.

The Future of Tissue Banking

Tissue banking and transplantation have a rich and important history, based on providing the best possible care for donors, their families, and tissue recipients. In the coming decade, dramatic changes will occur, hopefully allowing tissue banks to continue that history. Key among those changes will be new processing technologies, bioengineering and orthobiologics, the overall structure and operation of tissue banks, expanded governmental involvement, and increasing awareness of tissue donation by the public.

New Technology

Processing technology. Technologies to sterilize tissue or to prevent transmission of viral or bacterial infection will be a continuing priority. Advanced techniques and tools will also be used to process precision-shaped tissues, enabling a tissue bank to maximize the use of donated tissue and reduce the amount of donated tissue that is discarded. Much of the new technology will be patented or licensed from tissue banks and device companies that hold design or process patents.

Bioengineering and orthobiologics. Work on bone growth factors to improve bone, cartilage, and tendon growth will also continue. Known as bone morphogenic proteins (BMPs), these are naturally occurring signaling factors that initiate the "normal healing cascade leading to new bone formation."[31] BMPs were isolated in the 1960s and have been in development for decades. The combination of these bone growth factors with donated tissue (referred to as *orthobiologics*) shows great promise for regenerating healthy tissues in the recipient. In 2002, the FDA approved one such product made from a genetically engineered protein for use in patients with degenerative disc disease who would previously have been treated with an autograft. It also approved another growth factor to treat the delayed union or healing of a tibia. It is expected that in the future, these products and others like them will be combined with human allograft.

Another new technology to enhance new bone and tissue growth involves the use of the patient's own mesenchymal stem cells. The cells are removed and treated to change them into specific cell types, may be combined with donated tissue, and are then returned to the patient for treatment. This cellular technology relies on stem cells' unique ability to differentiate into bone, muscle, cartilage, and cardiac tissue. The technology is in its early stages. The use of stem cells for skin and cartilage is farthest along and has been commercial in the United States for a few years.

Yet another new technology involves the fabrication of cartilage tissue from juvenile cartilage cells (chondrocytes). The cartilage is being developed as an implant treatment for various cartilaginous defects including joint injuries, arthritis, and age-related degeneration.

Xenogenic tissue (from other species) as a source of organs and tissue is also an active area of research. Using a combination of cloning and DNA modification, workers in the United States and United Kingdom have modified pigs to reduce the tendency of their tissue to be rejected when implanted. Commercial or clinical use of this science is years away.

Tissue Banking Operations

New partnerships and alliances. Medical device companies, most notably those involved with spine surgery and other key areas of orthopedics, will play an increasingly important role in tissue banking. Their significant financial resources will allow them to increase the use of tissue, and promote technological advances, which may justify their involvement in expanding the supply of donated tissues. As OPOs and other nonprofit tissue recovery agencies become more comfortable with for-profit partners, their direct role in tissue-donor referral processes as well as tissue distribution may become more and more evident, possibly replacing nonprofit tissue banks in some areas.

Continued consolidation of tissue banks. Increasingly sophisticated tissue processing will require that tissue banks either gain access to this kind of processing or cease processing much or all of their tissue. It has been predicted that by 2010 only a few large tissue processors will remain, and that other tissue banks will have either merged with them or transformed themselves into solely tissue recovery or distribution agencies.

Protecting intellectual property rights. In 1999, 14 proprietary bone "products" were available, protected by patents issued for specific shapes, formulations or processing technologies.[32] By 2002, that number had easily grown to well over 100, and is expected to continue in this fashion. This trend could have an impact on the way tissue banks process and distribute tissues. It will probably lead to additional litigation as tissue banks are accused of infringing on patents. At the very least, it may lead to new partnerships between processors, or to licenses on technologies allowing other tissue banks access to new technologies or types of tissue.

Regulatory requirements. The FDA's "Good Tissue Practices" regulations, taking effect in 2004, coupled with new donor screening and tissue bank registration regulations, will no doubt have a dramatic impact on tissue banks and tissue recovery agencies. The GTPs pose major challenges to tissue banks, requiring the establishment and maintenance of a quality program that addresses most aspects of the tissue banks' operations. Those would include organization and personnel, facilities, environmental control and monitoring, equipment, supplies, and reagents. Controls over the agencies' processes, including validation, any changes to processes, labeling, storage, record maintenance, and reporting of internal nonconformance and customer complaints force all tissue banks to dramatically increase their staffing and resources. It is anticipated that the GTPs will add yet another layer of safety (and cost) to the United States' supply of tissue.

In addition, some tissue banks are beginning work on combining bone growth factors or other substances with allografts, or on combining allografts with other medical devices such as implants or sutures. These new products will no doubt be classified as medical devices, requiring extensive research and two-year clinical trials, which will cost upwards of $10,000,000 and seven years—a complex, expensive, time-consuming process that will challenge tissue banks as they have never been challenged before.

Preventing disease transmission. Infectious disease transmission will remain a significant concern in tissue banking, with HIV and hepatitis at the top of the list, but with Creuztfield-Jakob Disease and West Nile Virus looming. At present, no tests are available to readily detect CJD or WNV.

It is estimated that 3.9 million Americans have Hepatitis C (HCV) and that 2.7 million more are chronically infected and will develop it in the next decade, outstripping HIV prevalence.[33] Many patients who develop this life-threatening disease will no doubt be recipients of some type of allograft tissue, opening tissue banks up to litigation (founded or unfounded) and to increased concerns about the safety of allograft tissue.

Pre-transplant testing of tissue recipients may be indicated as a way to protect the tissue banks from unwarranted litigation. The growing incidence of Hepatitis C could also have an impact on the overall pool of available donors.

Increased demand for tissues. Allograft's portion of the overall spine fusion market is expected to grow as the market grows. This is not surprising when one considers that sometimes allograft bone implants have considerable biological advantages over metal and other synthetic devices, and tissue providers are producing allograft bone grafts that are highly machined and in some cases designed to mimic characteristics of their metal and carbon-fiber analogs. The American market for commercial demineralized bone was estimated at $141 million in 2001 and is predicted to grow to $342.2 million by 2005.[32, 34]

As surgeons, tissue banks, and their device partners find more and more new and innovative uses of tissue, the need for tissues will also increase. Competition for tissues (and subsequently, donors) will drive tissue banks and their partners to look for new sources of donors, and to continuously expand the pool of potential donors.

Summary

In just the last few decades, tissue banking in this country has grown from predominantly hospital-based surgical banks providing tissues to local surgeons, to a burgeoning industry in which highly sophisticated and proprietary tissues are provided to almost every hospital in the country. Since the late 1990s, large national for-profit companies have played an integral role in what was traditionally a nonprofit, altruistically motivated field. Tissues have become increasingly processed, often closely resembling synthetic or metallic devices, and their use has also rapidly grown and expanded. The industry continues to evolve in response to ethical concerns and various economic, clinical, organizational, and regulatory demands.

References

1. MacEwen W. Observations concerning transplantation of bone: illustrated by a case of inter-human osseous transplantation, whereby over two-thirds of the shaft of a humerus was restored. *Proc R Soc Lond.* 1881;32:232–247.
2. Chase SW, Herndon CH. The fate of autogenous and homogenous bone grafts: a historical review. *J Bone Joint Surg Am.* 1955;37:809–839.
3. Carrell A. The preservation of tissues and its application in surgery. *JAMA.* 1912;59:523–527.
4. Albee FE. *Bone Graft Surgery in Disease, Injury and Deformity.* New York, D. Appleton Century Company, 1940.
5. Inclan A. The use of preserved bone graft in surgery. *J Bone Joint Surg Am.* 1942;24:81–96.
6. Tomford WW. A history of musculoskeletal tissue banking in the United States. In: Tomford WW (ed.) *Musculoskeletal Tissue Banking.* New York, Raven Press, 1993. 149–180.
7. Hyatt GW. Fundamentals in the use and preservation of homogenous bone. *U.S. Armed Forces Med J.* 1950;1:8252–8481.
8. Enneking WF. A system for evaluation of the surgical management of musculo-skeletal tumors. In: Enneking WF (ed.). *Limb Salvage in Musculoskeletal Oncology.* New York, Churchill Livingstone, 1987. 145–150.
9. Parrish FF. Allograft replacement of all or part of the end of a long bone following excision of a tumor: report of twenty-one cases. *J Bone Joint Surg Am.* 1973;5:1–22.
10. Mankin HJ, Gebhardt MC, Jennings LC, Springfield DS, Tomford WW. Long-term results of allograft replacement in the management of bone tumors. *Clin Rel Res.* 1996;324:86–97.
11. Englehardt S. Personal correspondence. *Knowledge Enterprises 2001.* Available at: http://shirley@orthoworld.com.
12. Einhorn TA. Biological enhancement of skeletal repair. *Orthopaedic Trauma Association,* October 10–12, 2002.

13. Leslie HW, Bottenfield S. Donation, banking and transplantation of allograft tissues. *Nurs Clin North Am.* 1989;24:891–905.
14. National Organ Transplantation Act of 1984 (PL 98-507).
15. *2000 Tissue Banking Survey of AOPO Members.* Association of Organ Procurement Organizations, 1364 Beverly Road, McLean, Virginia 22101.
16. Anderson MA. Conditions of participation: the tissue bank perspective. Presentation at *North American Transplant Coordinator's Organization,* July 27, 1999.
17. American Association of Tissue Banks, 1350 Beverly Road, Suite 220-A, McLean, Virginia 22101. Available at: http://www.aatb.org.
18. Katches M. The body brokers. *Orange County Register,* April 2000.
19. Hedges SJ, Gaines W. Donor bodies milled into growing profits: little-regulated industry thrives on unsuspecting families. *Chicago Tribune.* May 21, 2000.1.
20. Office of the Inspector General. Oversight of tissue banking. January 2001.
21. Office of the Inspector General. Informed consent in tissue donation: expectations and realities. January 2001.
22. *Standards for Tissue Banking,* American Association of Tissue Banks, 1350 Beverly Road, Suite 220-A, McLean, Virginia 22101.
23. Simonds RJ, Holmberg SD, Hurwitz RL, et al. Transmission of human immunodeficiency virus type 1 from a seronegative organ and tissue donor. *N Engl J Med.* 1992;326:726–732.
24. Buck RE, Malinin TI, Brown MD. Bone transplantation and human immunodeficiency virus. An estimate of risk of acquired immunodeficiency syndrome (AIDS). *Clin Orthop.* 1989;240:129–136.
25. Statement of Marion A. Kainer, M.D., M.P.H. FDA/CBER Blood Products Advisory Committee, 72nd meeting, March 15, 2002. Available at: http://www.fda.gov/ohrms/dockets/ac/02/transcripts/3839t2.rtf.
26. Centers for Disease Control. Update: Allograft-associated bacterial infections—United States, 2002. *MMWR.* 2002;51;207–210.
27. "To Err is Human: Building a Safer Health Care System," Kohn LT, Corrigan JM, Donaldson MS (eds.), Committee on Quality of Health Care in America, Institute of Medicine, 2000; 1.
28. Blakesee S. 40 people unknowingly got tissue or organs from donor with hepatitis C; 5 died. *New York Times.* October 4, 2002. A20.
29. FDA draft guidance on preventive measures to reduce the possible risk of transmission of Cruetzfeldt-Jakob disease (CJD) and variant Creutzfeldt-Jakob disease (vCJD) by human cells, tissue, and cellular and tissue-based products. *FDA Draft Issue Summary,* June 26, 2002.
30. Interim Rule for Banked Human Tissue. *Public Health Service Act* (42 U.S.C. 264), December 14, 1993.
31. BMPs: Boom or Bust. *Medtech Insight.* 2001(November/December):278–294.
32. Bone grafts and bone substitutes. *Orthopedic Network News.* 2001;12:11–15.
33. CDC National Center for Infectious Diseases. Viral hepatitis C: fact sheet. Available at: http://www.cdc.gov/ncidod/diseases/hepatitis/c/fact.htm.
34. *DataMonitor 2001.* Available at http://www.datamonitor.com.

3

Clinical Aspects of Allograft Tissue

JOHN T. MAKLEY AND
RICHARD NICHOLAS

As clinicians who implant allograft tissues, our purpose in this chapter is to familiarize the reader with the potential benefits and the practical applications of human tissue transplantation. We will provide a brief overview and clinical examples illustrating the use of allograft tissue.

Allograft tissue is often necessary when adequate amounts of autograft are not available. Some surgical techniques require modifications of allograft tissues before they can be implanted into the recipient. Bone, for example, can be shaped, processed, or combined with other materials and then used as pins, screws, pastes, or putties in skeletal reconstruction. Intricate machining of bone yields tissue forms that are essential for certain types of spinal reconstruction.

In general, the long bones of the arms and legs (femur, tibia, fibula, humerus), iliac crest or pelvis, and associated tendons and ligaments (patellar tendon, Achilles tendon, tensor fascia lata, rotator cuff) are retrieved from musculoskeletal tissue donors. Radius and ulna (the bones of the forearm), ribs, vertebral bodies (from the lumbar spine) may also be procured and used for specialized reconstructions. Other non-musculoskeletal tissues commonly donated include skin, heart valves, veins and arteries and corneas.

Contrast with Organs

The extended storage of some tissue contrasts with the immediacy of organ transplantation. Once processed, allograft tissues can be stored up to five years in different forms. Many large grafts are deep-frozen at –70 degrees Centigrade, while smaller preparations are freeze-dried. A small number of allograft tissues are preserved in a fresh state. These grafts, prepared to preserve the cartilage on the joint surfaces, are usually put into chilled, sterile solutions and must be used within a short time, generally less than three to four weeks.

Another difference between organs and tissues is that skeletal reconstruction using bone and other allograft soft tissues is done in most medical centers, including many community hospitals, while organ transplants are performed only in about 240 transplant centers. Allograft tissues are also more plentiful than whole organs and are often used for life-enhancing procedures, in addition to life-saving ones, so the controversies surrounding the allocation of limited, but life-saving organ transplants are not wholly echoed in tissue transplantation.

Immunological rejection can be a problem with most organ transplants and some types of tissue transfers. Blood transfusions are an excellent example. Unmatched blood transfused into a patient results in an immunological response. The development of the ABO blood typing system and the ability to match blood types has enabled blood transfusions to become commonplace. Even so, a patient who receives multiple transfusions can still develop antibodies to a set of minor blood antigens and develop transfusion reactions with subsequent blood infusions.

Similarly, organ transplantation involves matching six major histocompatibility antigens. Even with a perfect or six-antigen match, continuous immunosuppression of the recipient is necessary in order to prevent the body from developing an immune response to the transplanted organ. The proteins on the surface of the transplanted organ are different enough from the recipient to elicit an intense reaction. Eventually the attacking immune system destroys the foreign cells, resulting in death or the rejection of the transplanted organs.

In contrast, allograft tissues, such as many of the bone preparations that have been processed or stored, have a minimal immunological response. Studies indicate that the freezing and other processing steps reduce the immunological potential of the tissue.[1] Few bone or tendon allograft procedures require immunosuppression for success. Some types of allografts that are not extensively processed, such as skin used for the temporary coverage of burns, do elicit an immune response, and the transplanted skin is eventually rejected by the host immune system. In this situation, the allograft skin is only intended as a temporary cover to prevent fluid loss and infection in the burn victim while a permanent method of skin coverage is developed. Later grafting with autologous skin (skin taken from an unburned location on the same individual) is often used to replace the rejected allograft skin. This procedure is usually done when the patient has been stabilized and the burned area is ready to accept the final graft. Additional information on skin transplantation can be found in Chapter 4 of this book.

Primary Types of Musculoskeletal Tissues

The typical tissue bank offers a wide variety of musculoskeletal tissues, in some cases over 600 different sizes, shapes, and types. The surgeon selects the specific type of tissue based on the type of surgery, the anticipated outcome and activity level of the patient, and the tissues available from the tissue bank. Whole bones can be used to reconstruct large skeletal segments in which a tumor and the bone containing it have been removed. Smaller cavitary defects, such as those that occur in several types of bone cysts and other benign tumors, trauma, and other degenerative orthopedic situations, can be filled with morselized chips of bone. Although there are several common uses for allograft tissues, some operations are individualized and innovative. The versatility of allograft tissues and the ability to modify them during a surgical procedure are major advantages of using allograft bones and tendons for reconstruction surgeries.

Osteoarticular and Intercalary Grafts

Osteoarticular allografts include the cartilage joint surface and are used to reconstruct joints without the use of internal joint prostheses. These allografts are carefully removed at the time of recovery and extra steps are taken to preserve the viability of the cartilage cells of the surface of the joint. The ligaments and capsular tissue are also preserved for use by the surgeon to secure the allograft to the patient's joint tissues. Using careful preoperative measurements, the surgeon must choose an allograft with an exact size match of the joint surfaces to ensure that the osteoarticular graft allograft will fit and move smoothly, and that the joint will be stable. With properly implanted grafts, these patients can have good to excellent functional results. Many primary musculoskeletal tumors occur in children and adolescents, and osteoarticular allografts are often used with this patient population to preserve the potential growth in the adjacent bones. Older patients may also benefit from select applications of osteoarticular grafting.

Reconstructions using large segments of graft that span a bone defect are called *intercalary* or *large segmental* allografts. They can be used successfully in a wide variety of applications, including bone cancers, total joint revisions, and for major traumatic injuries. These grafts are typically made from long shafts of the tibia, femur, or humerus. They usually function well and have the advantage of preserving the normal joints on either side of the graft (Fig. 3.1a–d).

Initially, surgeons who performed whole-bone transplantation would remove a bone from a cadaver or from an amputated limb and immediately transplant it into the recipient. Initial studies were single case reports or contained few patients with limited followup.[2, 3] Recent practice depends on

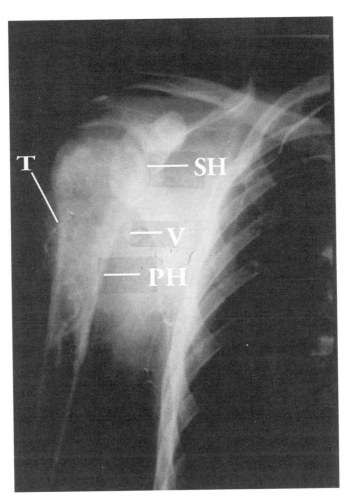

Figure 3.1a. X-ray of proximal humerus and shoulder joint with tumor. SH–shoulder joint. PH–proximal humeros. Infiltrated with tumor. V–vessels feeding tumor. T–tumor infiltrating soft tissues.

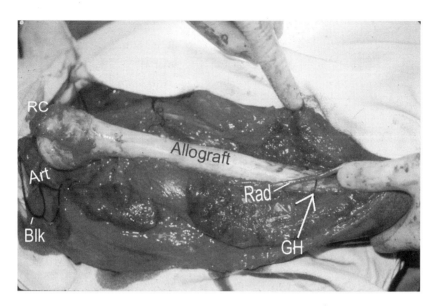

Figure 3.1b. Humeral osteoarticular allograft during surgery. ART—articular cartilage of proximal humeral allograft. RC—rotator cuff of the proximal humoral allograft still attached and preserved. Blk—black sutures attached to patient's rotator cuff that will be attached to the allograft rotator cuff that remains. Rad—radial nerve circling around humerus at the attachment of the allograft to the patient's humerus. GH—graft–host junction.

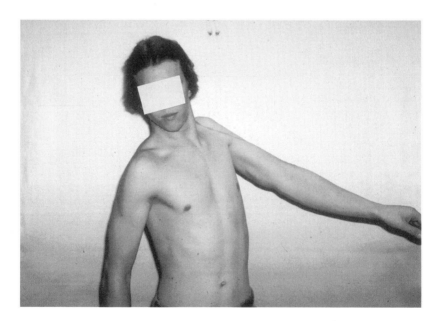

Figure 3.1c. Post-operative photograph demonstrating shoulder function.

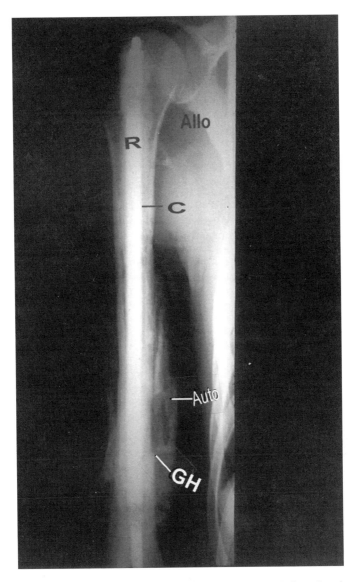

Figure 3.1d. X-ray one year after surgery. R—Metal rod in center of allograft and patient's bone. C—Cement used to hold allograft and rod. Auto—Autograft taken from patient's ilium to reinforce healing of allograft to patient's bone. GH—Well-healed interface of the allograft/host bone. Allo—Osteoarticular allograft.

improved banking techniques, use of deep-frozen bone grafts, and secure fixation methods. There now are reports of successful series with large numbers of recipients who have been carefully evaluated over long periods.[4-6]

Cancellous Chips

The most commonly used preparation of bone allograft tissue is cancellous chips. These are small cubes of woven bone—ranging in size from dice-sized cubes to granular preparations—that are cut from larger pieces of bone when the bone is processed (Fig. 3.2). The chips are used to fill holes or cavities created by degenerative processes, infection, benign tumors, trauma, or surgery. One common use is to fill and repair bone defects in conjunction with revision total-joint surgery. Cancellous chips are also used to supplement autologous bone graft for spinal fusion where large amounts of bone graft are often needed in multilevel spinal fusions. This type of graft has a large surface area of bone for scaffolding for the host bone to attach to and grow into. Living autologous bone replaces the allograft bone as the chips are slowly resorbed.[7] The new bone forms a solid block of viable bone that bridges the previously unstable area. This process of bone growing onto and over a matrix surface is referred to as *osteoconduction*.

Demineralized Bone Matrix

An alternative means of promoting bone formation uses a different preparation of allograft bone tissues. Removing all or most of the mineral from

Figure 3.2. Cancellous chips.

cortical bone using acid solutions produces demineralized bone matrix (DBM). This process leaves behind the bone proteins, including growth factors that can stimulate new bone growth. DBM can be combined, generally by the tissue bank, with a carrier material to improve the handling characteristics of the preparation. This allows the surgeon to pack the DBM into a bony defect, adjacent to surgical instrumentation or around other allograft materials. Like cancellous chips, demineralized bone has been shown to be osteoinductive—it can induce primitive host mesenchymal cells to form bone.

Tendons and Ligaments

Tendons, ligaments, and cartilage form a subgroup of musculoskeletal allograft tissues known commonly as "soft tissues" or "sports medicine tissues." These are primarily used to repair the cruciate ligaments of the knee, an injury common to athletes. The most common of these is the patellar tendon, or "bone-tendon-bone" which is attached to bone blocks from the femur and tibia. Others include the Achilles tendon, hamstring tendons, and tensor fascia lata, the tendinous sheath covering the quadriceps muscle, the major muscle of the thigh. These tissues are in very high demand, limited by the age of donors (generally less than 55 years old) and the limited amount of tissue available from each donor (two to four patellar tendons).

The Clinical Applications of Musculoskeletal Allograft

Bone allografts and soft-tissue allografts, such as tendons, have become indispensable for the orthopedic surgeon for reconstruction of a variety of bone and soft-tissue defects caused by disease or trauma. A wide range of other surgical specialists, including neurosurgeons, dentists, and trauma and burn surgeons, also use allograft tissue. A list of surgical specialties, the tissues that they commonly use, and clinical examples can be found in Table 3.1.

Orthopedic Oncology

The orthopedic oncologist, or specialist in soft tissue and bone cancers, is often confronted with large defects of bone and soft tissue after a tumor has been removed. The preoperative planning must anticipate the need for reconstruction, and precise measurement and preparation are essential for a

Table 3.1. Tissue Use by Specialty

Specialty	Tissue Use
Cardiothoracic surgeon	Heart valves for valve replacement/arteries and veins for cardiac artery bypass grafts
Plastic surgeon	Skin and components of skin for facial reconstruction and cosmetic use/bone for facial reconstruction due to trauma, congenital defects, cancer
Trauma and burn specialist	Skin for coverage of burns/bone, tendon and fascia for repair of traumatic defects
Orthopedic oncologist	Large bone graft, osteoarticular, fresh cartilage and menisci, patellar ligament, bone dowels, screws, bone wedges for spine, cortical struts, cortical cancellous chips, and demineralized bone to replace cancerous tissues, and to attach grafts to host bone
Foot and ankle surgeon	Bone dowels, screws, demineralized bone, cortical bone, cancellous chips, and tendon for reconstruction, bunionectomies, etc.
Spine specialist	Machined wedges, cortical cancellous chips, demineralized bone putty, cortical struts, dowels for spinal defects, herniated discs, etc.
Neurosurgeon	Pericardium, dura mater to repair dural defects
Dental surgeon/periodontist	Cortical cancellous chips, cortical struts, demineralized bone to rebuild jaws, provide support for dental implants
Urologist	Fascia lata, acellular skin, and tendons to reconstruct bladder and gynecological defects
General surgeon	Acellular skin for treatment of skin ulcers, non-healing skin/fascia for hernia repairs

successful and functional outcome. In some cases an internal metal component or implant may be used for reconstruction to avoid an amputation if sufficient tissues remain to provide a functional limb. Reconstruction of the affected limb may be also be accomplished using a variety of allograft tissues:

1. Osteoarticular grafts with tendons and ligaments attached
2. Intercalary grafts (segments of long bones)
3. Cortical/cancellous chips
4. Combination of a metallic prosthesis with allograft bone

Metallic prosthetic reconstruction has distinct advantages over allograft transplantation. Because most of these implants do not require healing to the host for their fixation, they are stable immediately, and the patients can mobilize and bear weight shortly after surgery rather than staying on crutches for long periods of time. But, allograft reconstruction offers the patient a biological alternative that, in theory, could provide a lifelong repair. At times, a combination of the two techniques, using an allograft bone in conjunction with a metallic implant for partial or total joint replacement, provides both the immediate stability and the long-term preservation of bone stock.[8]

Innovative use of whole-bone allografts can be life-enhancing even in a dying patient. The stability provided by solid reconstructions can provide marked pain relief as well as improved function, especially ambulation. The benefits of improved independence cannot be overemphasized. This point is exemplified in a case involving a 40–year-old woman who presented with breast cancer. Spread of the tumor, or metastatic disease, involved her entire femur. Despite a previous surgical intervention with a cemented total hip and other treatment, the cancer progressed. She became bedridden with a fracture of the bone below the tip of the metal prosthesis, creating pain and instability. She required hourly doses of 50mg of intravenous morphine to control her pain. She had a limited life expectancy, a grieving husband and several children at home, and could do nothing. Using a whole-femur allograft that matched her own femur in both length and diameter, the surgeon conducted a straightforward operation to remove the entire diseased femur and reconstruct the defect with an allograft femur incorporating both a metallic total hip and a metallic total knee. After her wounds healed, she was able to stop her morphine and walk with a cane. She remained functional at home with her family until she died from her disease.

Orthopedic Sports Medicine

Sports medicine specialists are frequent users of allograft tissues for repair in athletic injuries, especially ligament and cartilage damage to the knee joint.[9–11] Such soft-tissue injuries require specialized allograft tissues such as tendons, ligaments and fascia (the fibrous layer or sheath that covers large muscle groups) that are needed for strengthening or repair of torn and damaged ligaments in the athlete. The most commonly used allograft material in this field is the patellar tendon graft. Many surgeons will repair a torn or ruptured anterior cruciate ligament (ACL) of the knee using this tissue. Many of the estimated 102,000 ACL procedures in the United States each year are repaired with donated human tendons and ligaments.[12] Noyes and others have reported series of these surgeries, indicating that two-thirds of patients reported good to excellent results, allowing their return to an active lifestyle with a stable knee joint.[10]

Alternatives to allograft tissues for ACL repair include autograft (using a portion of the patient's own patellar tendon or hamstring tendons), xenograft (materials such as tendons taken from another species) or synthetic grafts made from carbon fibers, Dacron® or Goretex®. Disadvantages of allograft surgery for ACL reconstructions compared with autologous tendon repair include the slower healing and biological incorporation of the graft, a higher chance of knee swelling, and the theoretical possibility of disease transmission. Advantages of the allograft procedures are the elimination of second-site surgery, fracture of the patella, and potential instability of the knee, as well as relatively ready access to donated tissues. Because of their popularity, patellar tendons are at times in short supply and may be back-ordered, thus delaying surgery for some patients.

More recently many orthopedic sports specialists have used fresh cartilage grafts to replace areas of damaged articular cartilage caused by tumors, trauma, degenerative joint disease, osteochondritis dissecans, and osteonecrosis. These small joint grafts are specially treated and held in a culture medium designed to maintain cell viability. This process attempts to preserve viable chondrocytes, or cartilage cells, which can be placed directly into the damaged joint surface. Small plugs of cartilage are removed from the donated tissue and placed into areas on the patient's joint where the cartilage has been torn or damaged. The bony portion of these plugs heals underneath the cartilage. Within the joint, the transplanted cartilage cells continue to survive because they are bathed in joint fluid. The newly restored cartilage layer then aids in lubricating and maintaining the joint surface. For patient undergoing such allograft implants, McAllister has reported excellent results in 75% and 64% percent of patients at 5 and 10 years, as has Garrett, who reported that 16 of 17 grafts were a success at 2 to 9 years after surgery.[13, 14] The enthusiasm surrounding these grafts has been somewhat tempered of late with an allograft-associated clostridium infection that resulted in the death of a 23-year-old male in 2002. While the use of allografts for sports medicine and other applications remains high, this unfortunate episode certainly has drawn many surgeons' attention to the need for advanced tissue screening and processing technologies, and the need to carefully outline treatment options for the patient.

Orthopedic Reconstruction Surgery

Orthopedic surgeons primarily involved in total joint surgery (hip, knee, and shoulder) are faced with performing total replacements of many difficult deteriorating or failed joints. Such situations require careful planning if a new reconstruction or repeat total joint operation is required. Micromotion of the metallic implants or infections often lead to bone loss around the implant. Use of allograft material has allowed the surgeons to restore the deficient bone stock and accomplish a reconstruction in many difficult situations. In some cases, the patient's bone canal is expanded so that only a thin rim of bone remains. Because such weakened bone cannot support a new prosthesis, the surgeon will frequently use particulate or morselized grafts such as cancellous chips or cortical-cancellous granules to fill the canal. When packed tightly and properly prepared, the canal can often support a new prosthesis. When major structural weakness results from bone loss, the use of structural, load-sharing grafts such as proximal femurs or on-lay cortical strut allografts can provide needed support. These larger grafts heal more slowly but can eventually be incorporated into the host bone.[15]

Spine Surgery

Several clinical conditions of the spine are related to instability between levels of the vertebral bodies of the spine and lend themselves to fusion, or bridging of the unstable area with one solid "fused" mass of bone. The most common of these conditions is a herniated nucleus pulposus ("herniated disc"), in which the fibrous wall of the disc ruptures and the gelatinous material from the center of the disc protrudes through the defect. The extruded material and the associated inflammation caused by the disc fragment can impinge on adjacent nerve roots, causing pain and nerve dysfunction. Fusion types of operations are designed to stabilize the segment so the repeated stress will not cause additional nerve root damage.

Surgical procedures for spinal conditions requiring fusion grew dramatically in the late 1990s, resulting in a reported 300,000–380,000 procedures in 2001.[16, 17] This increase in procedures no doubt reflects both the large number of aging baby boomers who now require surgical intervention, as well as increased technology available to spine surgeons.

Allograft bone such as bone dowels, demineralized bone matrices, and newer, highly engineered wedges and dowels with teeth and threads are often used in this surgical setting, accounting for at least 50% of all musculoskeletal allografts used in the United States.[16] The dense cortical bone of femoral and tibial shafts is used for the production of these innovative types of tissue, which are designed to combine with spinal instrumentation, fit between the vertebral bodies, and replace the damaged disc. Some tissue banks process bone into multipiece constructs that fit together, forming an allograft that is designed to better approximate the space and curvature between the vertebral bodies, withstand the loads in the lumbar spine, provide stable bone-to-bone interface, and promote bone fusion (Fig. 3.3a–c). The healing of the bone above and below the allograft produces a fusion of the two segments and prevents further motion.

Foot and Ankle Surgery

Somewhat at the other end of the surgical spectrum, surgeons with particular interest in the foot and ankle are frequently faced with the need to stabilize or fixate small bones and joints. Recent advances in the machining of allograft bone into pins, dowels, and screws allow these surgeons to stabilize surgical osteotomies and fractures of small bones of the foot with a mechanized allograft screw or dowel. This not only provides stabilization, but also acts as a bone graft. The type of biological fixation often avoids the need for metal implants, which may need to be removed at a later time.

Ethical Considerations for the Surgeon

From an ethical standpoint, surgeons need to explain every surgical procedure to their patients in language that can be easily understood. With allograft transplantation, additional concerns and information must be included in these preoperative discussions. The surgeon is in the best position to have knowledge regarding not only the surgical procedure, but also the facts surrounding allograft transplantation. This includes enumerating the risks of both the surgical procedure and the allograft itself, and, often, an explanation of the postoperative rehabilitation requirements and possible methods used to address problems. With allograft reconstructions, certain types of complications occur and have been documented throughout the literature.[4, 18–20] These include potential fracture of the transplanted graft, infections, joint instability, and failure of healing to the host bone. Such complications may require a second operation or they could result in long-term disability. The extreme case of a complication of an allograft (and the first of its kind, to our knowledge) was reported in December 2001, in which a patient who received a fresh cartilage allograft developed a serious infection, possibly related to the allograft, and subsequently died.

In addition, it is the responsibility of the surgeon during these discussions to inform the patient that this type of surgery involves donated human tissues. As such, the graft is a gift from these anonymous individuals and families. Without individual generosity and the continued support of the

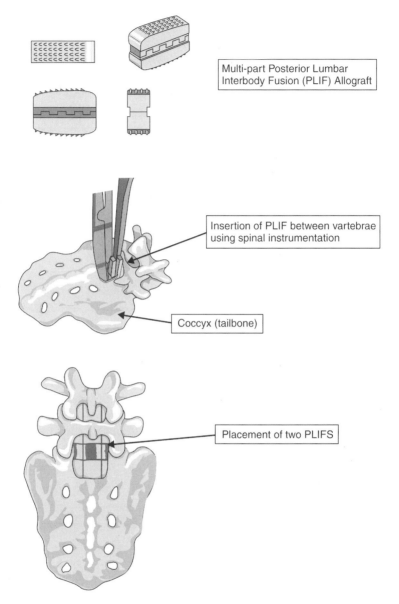

Multi-part Posterior Lumbar
Interbody Fusion (PLIF) Allograft

Insertion of PLIF between vartebrae
using spinal instrumentation

Coccyx (tailbone)

Placement of two PLIFS

Figure 3.3. Posterior lumbar interbody fusion (PLIF). Used in spinal fusion surgery.

donor organizations, no graft tissues would be available for reconstructions. Because the surgeons may be the best individuals to recognize this relationship, it is often their responsibility to promote organ and tissue donation to the community at large.

Following any operation, especially those involved in allograft reconstructions, followup of the patients is necessary to insure that no late complications occur. Some of the problems specific to allografts are known to occur several years following the original surgery. These can be best managed if they are identified early. Finally, in certain situations, especially teaching institutions, continued research on allografts and their applications is needed. Such institutions have the responsibility to report their results completely and honestly, and to promote a frank and straightforward evaluation of the surgical procedures and the ethical concerns of human tissue transplantation.

Conclusion

In summary, use of human tissue for reconstruction of musculoskeletal defects and other procedures continues to increase. Tissue banking and preservation techniques have increased the availability of allograft tissue and therefore enabled the development of new surgical procedures requiring allograft tissue. Allograft tissue has enhanced the lives of patients who could not be helped without these materials. At present, allograft tissues are necessary for many types of musculoskeletal reconstructions, particularly when nonbiological solutions such as joint replacement or artificial bone substitutes are inadequate, unavailable, or incompatible with good long-term results. The continued willingness of donors and their families to help other individuals through tissue donation is vital to the future use of allograft tissue. A sound ethical platform is necessary if we are to continue in the public trust and realize the full potential of allograft use.

References

1. Curtiss PH, Powell A, Herndon CH. Immunological factors in homologous bone transplants. *J Bone Joint Surg Am.* 1959;41(1):1482–1488.
2. Parrish FF. Allograft replacement of all or part of the end of a long bone following excision of a tumor. *J Bone Joint Surg Am.* 1973;55(1):1–22.
3. Albee FE. *Bone-graft Surgery.* Philadelphia, W.B. Saunders, 1915.
4. Mankin H, Gebhardt MC, Jennings LC, Springfield DS, Tomford WW. Long-term results of allograft replacement in the management of bone tumors. *Clin Orthop.* 1996;324:86–97.

5. Friedlaender GE, Mankin HJ, Sell KW. *Osteochondral Allografts*. Boston, Little, Brown, 1993.

6. Malinin TI, Martinez OV, Brown MD. Banking of massive osteoarticular and intercalary bone allografts—12 years' experience. *Clin Orthop*. 1985;197:44–57.

7. Stevenson S, Emery S, Goldberg, V. Factors affecting bone graft incorporation. *Clin Orthop*. 1996;324:66–74.

8. Makley JT. The use of allografts to reconstruct intercalary defects of long bones. *Clin Orthop*. 1985;197:58–75.

9. Jackson DW, Corsetti J, Simon TM. Biologic incorporation of allograft anterior cruciate ligament replacements. *Clin Orthop*. 1996;324:126–133.

10. Noyes FR, Barber-Westin SD. Reconstruction of the anterior cruciate ligament with human allograft. Comparison of early and later results. *J Bone Joint Surg Am*. 1996;78(4):524–537.

11. Olson EJ, Harner CD, Fu FH, Silbey MB. Clinical use of fresh, frozen soft tissue allografts. *Orthopedics*. 1992;15(10):1225–1232.

12. Owings MF, Kozak LJ. Ambulatory and inpatient procedures in the U.S. 1996. *Vital Health Statistics*. 1998;134:1–119.

13. McAllister D. Reported at Allograft Symposium. San Diego, California, 2001.

14. Garrett JC. Fresh osteochondral allografts for treatment of articular defects in osteochondritis dissecans of the lateral femoral condyle in adults. *Clin Orthop*. 1994;303:33–37.

15. Ghazavi MT, Stockley I, Yee G, Davis A, Gross A. Reconstruction of massive bone defects with allograft in revision total knee arthroplasty. *J Bone Joint Surg Am*. 1997;79(1):17–25.

16. Weighing the bone replacement market. *Medtech Insight*. March 2002:1,74–77.

17. Personal correspondence, Shirley Englehardt, *Orthoworld*, August 2002.

18. Buttermann GR, Glazer PA, Bradford DS. The use of bone allografts in the spine. *Clin Orthop*. 1996;324:75–85.4

19. Jackson DW, Grood ES, Goldstein JD. A comparison of patellar tendon autograft and allograft used for anterior cruciate ligament reconstruction in the goat model. *Am J Sports Med*. 1993;21:176–185.

20. Slooff TJ, Buma P, Schreurs BW, Schimmel JW, Huiskes R, Gardeniers J. Acetabular and femoral reconstruction with impacted graft and cement. *Clin Orthop*. 1996;324:108–115.

4

Skin Transplantation: Clinical Applications and Current Issues

GLENN GREENLEAF

As with musculoskeletal tissue, transplantation of allograft skin has expanded as a result of increased donor supply, technical advances in processing and preservation, and clinical innovations. These developments greatly enhance our ability to repair or replace diseased, damaged, or inadequate tissue, benefiting over 30,000 patients each year.

Although skin banking is closely tied to musculoskeletal banking, the field attracts a range of unique and sometimes controversial issues in areas such as recovery, supply, and clinical uses. This chapter provides an overview of the uses of allograft skin and some of the economic, social, and ethical issues surrounding skin banking.

The Skin and Wound Healing

The skin is the largest organ of the human body. In the simplest of terms, the skin comprises essentially two layers: (1) the epidermis, the superficial cellular layer that provides important protective barrier functions; and (2) the dermis, the extracellular matrix that provides strength, elasticity, and durability. This simple yet elegantly complex organ is responsible for the regulation of heat, fluids, and proteins. More important, the skin is a crucial component of the body's immune system, serving as the first line of defense against the hostile environment we live in. This environment is teaming with opportunistic organisms that, given the chance, would rapidly invade, proliferate, and devour our warm, nutrient-rich bodies. The importance of the skin is often taken for granted until the integrity of this protective barrier is compromised.

Under most circumstances, the human body possesses a remarkable ability to heal itself. When the skin is compromised as the result of disease or injury, the body quickly responds by contracting the surface area of the wound and increasing cell proliferation to restore the important barrier function. While rapid proliferation of the cells of the epidermis can quickly and effectively seal the wound, the highly organized matrix of the dermis is largely incapable of regeneration and is replaced instead by invading granulation tissue.[1] This granulation tissue ultimately matures to scar. While in most instances this "quick fix" provides appropriate restoration, the unfortunate consequence of the "repair" of extensive deep dermal injuries is often disfigurement and functional impairment. In these cases, the ability to use the patient's own tissue or to transplant donated tissues temporarily restores the physiological environment of the wound bed by providing the critical mechanical and barrier properties of intact skin. These improvements are particularly significant in the treatment of burn injuries.

Skin transplantation is not a new concept. The first well-documented cases describing the use of cadaveric allograft began to appear in the late 1800s when Reverdin, Pollack, and Innvanova published reports on the use of skin grafts for wound healing.[2–4] World Wars I and II underscored the limitations facing clinicians attempting to treat large surface area wounds and provided an impetus for the widespread use of allograft skin. In the 1950s, advances in the understanding of immunology and the principles of rejection provided valuable insights.[5] Today, the use of allograft skin in the treatment of extensive cutaneous injury is a widely accepted surgical modality.[6, 7]

Treatment of Burn Injuries and Other Forms of Skin Loss

More than 1 million people suffer burn injuries each year in the United States. Approximately 45,000 of them will require some form of hospitalization, and nearly 4,500 will die.[8] The chances of surviving a burn injury can depend on a number of factors, but two of the most important are the depth and extent of the burn injury. Many people have heard the terms *first*, *second* and *third degree* used to denote the severity of burn injury. First-degree burns are generally limited to the epithelial layer of the skin and usually heal spontaneously. Second-degree injuries are deeper and may involve not only the epidermal layer but also the upper portion of the dermis. Second-degree burns may require grafting. Third-degree burns are the deepest burns and involve not only the epidermis and the dermis but may extend to the underlying fat and/or muscle as well. Third-degree burns require excision and grafting.

Recently, more descriptive terms, such as *superficial*, *partial* (split thickness), and *deep* (full thickness) have tended to replace the use of first, second, and third degree designations. The extent of burn injury is most often indicated as a percentage of total body surface area (TBSA). As a generalization, burns can be characterized as small (<15% TBSA), moderate (15%–49% TBSA), large (50%–69% TBSA) and massive (>70% TBSA).

The presentation of a patient with severe burn injury represents a significant clinical challenge, and the treatment of these injuries requires an intensive, multi-disciplinary approach. It is interesting to note that in most deaths of patients with burn injuries, the trauma of the burn itself is not the primary cause of death. Rather, death results from the deleterious cascade of events that occurs subsequent to the initial injury.

Prior to the 1970s, the most common cause of death associated with burn injury was wound sepsis. This condition occurs as opportunistic organisms invade and colonize the nutrient-rich necrotic burned tissue. The proliferation of microorganisms and the progression of burn wound inflammation can alter physiological responses, impair immunity, and may contribute to distant organ and tissue damage.[9, 10] Many clinicians feel that the complete removal of the necrotic burn tissue is necessary to minimize the likelihood of this deleterious cascade of events. Early excision of burned skin followed by wound closure has increased survival rates and decreased the mortality associated with extensive burn wounds.[11, 12]

In full thickness injuries (those involving the dermis), the use of split thickness skin grafts (removing the upper layer and a small portion of dermis) taken from unburned areas of the patient can provide wound closure and improve the chances of survival. These autografts restore the barrier function of the epidermis and deliver a dermal component to the wound that would otherwise heal by intensive scarring and contracture. In extensive injuries, where there is insufficient non-burned autograft, allograft skin (or a suitable skin equivalent) must be used as a temporary biological dressing to provide a bridge between wound excision and permanent closure.

The traditional processing of allograft skin involves either short-term storage at refrigerated temperatures (fresh grafts) or cryopreservation for longer-term storage (frozen grafts). Physicians differ widely in their preferences for either fresh or frozen grafts. Citing rapidity and strength of adherence to the wound, control of wound microbial growth,[13,14] and acceleration of revascularization, some clinicians feel that fresh grafts are superior to frozen grafts in the treatment of full thickness burn injuries and would prefer to use it whenever possible or, more accurately, whenever available.[15] Two factors are primarily responsible for inconsistencies in the availability of fresh skin. One is the relatively short shelf life of refrigerated skin. Cryopreserved grafts have a shelf life of several years while fresh graft must be transplanted within 14 days (most within 3–7 days). Since it is not possible to time the admission of a burn patient with the availability of a tissue donor, it is often difficult to maintain a ready and available supply of fresh skin. This is particularly true in smaller communities or in areas with less active tissue recovery agencies. Larger burn centers such as the Shriners' burn hospitals have been able to ensure an adequate supply of fresh skin by either maintaining their own dedicated skin bank or developing a network of skin-recovery agencies that can funnel fresh skin to a few processing centers.

A second factor influencing the availability of fresh skin is the increasing regulatory requirements and the risk-management issues involved in the release of fresh skin for transplant. All tissue provided for transplantation must undergo extensive testing and screening prior to transplantation. This can be problematic in the case of fresh skin because often only preliminary results from microbiological and other testing (which may take up to 14 days) and autopsy results (which might take up to 6 months or more) are available by the time the fresh skin must be transplanted. When these results are not available, the tissue bank's medical director must agree to release the tissue on an "exceptional release" basis. Due to increasing regulatory requirements and heightened liability concerns, a number of skin-processing centers have made the risk-management decision not to allow exceptional releases and as a result have elected not to provide fresh skin.

The controversy of fresh versus cryopreserved allograft skin raises an interesting question regarding the future of tissue preservation. While cryopreserved skin maintains a degree of cellular viability, conventional methods of cryopreservation cause significant damage to the ultrastructure or "matrix" of the grafts. The damaged matrix may serve as a nidus for a nonspecific inflammatory response that may exacerbate or accelerate the ultimate specific immune response to the cellular elements of the graft. It is interesting to speculate that the positive characteristics attributed to fresh skin, which many attribute to the "viability" of the tissue, may actually be a surrogate indicator of the preservation of matrix structure and biochemical components of the grafts. The successful application of nonviable glycerol-preserved allograft as provided by the EuroSkin Bank can be cited in this continuing controversy.[16] The challenge facing the skin banking industry is to develop preservation technology that will enable long-term storage of skin grafts that provide the same clinical results that physicians have come to expect from fresh grafts.

While burn injury is the most familiar example of extensive skin loss or damage, there are other conditions in which the skin is compromised beyond its ability to effectively repair itself. Some of these conditions result in the sloughing or loss of skin from the total body surface area of the patient and are often lethal. Toxic epidermal necrolysis (TEN), Stevens Johnson syndrome (SJS), staphylococcal scalded skin syndrome (SSSS), and necrotizing fasciitis (flesh eating bacteria) are just a few of the conditions in which massive amounts of skin are compromised. These conditions may be brought on by systemic reaction to drugs or the rampant and invasive proliferation of bacteria. Any condition that results in significant skin loss requires extensive and aggressive treatment, including early replacement of the lost barrier function.

Limitation of Allograft Skin and Alternatives

The ultimate fate for most allograft skin grafts is rejection. Under normal conditions, a healthy adult will reject an allograft skin transplant in seven to ten days. Under extremely traumatic conditions such as a major burn, the body's ability to mount an effective immune response may become compromised. "Burn-induced" immunosuppression has enabled transplanted allografts to survive for several weeks at a time. It is somewhat ironic that this "window of opportunity" has decreased due to major advancements in burn patient care. Aggressive intervention to meet the metabolic needs and to maintain the physiological status of the burn patient has helped restore the immune status of these patients, and this in turn increases the body's ability to reject transplanted tissue. This presents a particular dilemma to patients with extensive burn injuries who require large areas of coverage with allograft: the return to immune competence requires that the donated skin be replaced with increasing frequency. This problem is further exacerbated by the development of increased antigenic sensitivity to the skin grafts with each new graft placement.

While the importance of allograft skin cannot be overemphasized, the ultimate rejection of these grafts has historically limited their use to that of a temporary biological dressing. As an alternative to traditional allograft skin, several burn centers have elected to use biosynthetics such as Biobrane or Dermagraft-TC as their dressings of choice. These synthetic grafts restore the barrier function[17] but may not optimally prepare the wound for the ultimate application of autograft. In the past several years, the use of composite grafts such as Apligraf and Integra have attempted not only to restore barrier function but to replace the missing dermal component as well. In the next 10 years we can expect to see bioactive dressings, which are combinations of growth factors and biological or synthetic matrices that actually accelerate wound healing.

Expanded Clinical Uses Using Acellular Dermal Grafts

Traditional methods of preserving allograft skin have focused on maintaining cell viability, yet it is the cellular components of the tissue that contain the antigenic signals that cause graft rejection. By removing the cellular or antigenic components and maintaining the integrity of the matrix of allograft skin, the tissue can be transplanted without being rejected as a foreign material.[18, 19] Processed acellular allograft can provide the dermal matrix required for competent wound healing, which is particularly important when the patient's own dermis is unavailable or when it is undesirable to perform the extensive surgery required to use the patient's own tissue.[20-22]

Acellular dermal grafts have greatly expanded the applications for donated human skin[23] beyond the role of a temporary biological dressing. While initially applied to the treatment of full-thickness burn injuries,[24] acellular dermal grafts are today used in a variety of surgical procedures to treat thousands of patients each year. These applications include surgical procedures such as scar revision and contracture release where the body's own healing process has resulted in a compromised outcome. In these procedures, the scar or contracture is surgically excised, and a layer of donated acellular dermis is placed over the excision, then covered with a very thin layer of the patient's own tissue. Additionally, acellular dermis can be used in soft tissue repair or replacement[24] to effectively restore form and function (e.g., tumor removal, facial reconstruction). Other procedures, such as replacing the covering of the brain (duraplasty),[25] repairing traumatic injuries of the eye socket by facilitating orbital reconstruction, and the repair of large abdominal hernias, have been described.

The expanded use of these grafts in periodontal and urogynecology procedures, two divergent surgical specialties, illustrate how far removed the use of allograft skin is from its traditional use as a temporary dressing. Over one half of all adults will suffer some form of periodontal disease. Many of these cases will require surgical intervention to repair or replace lost tissue. In fact, periodontal surgery is one of the most commonly performed surgical procedures in the United States. Thousands of acellular dermal allografts have been successfully used in periodontal applications to increase attached gingiva,[26] reduce gingival recession, and facilitate guided tissue regeneration.[27] By utilizing donated allograft skin, the patient is spared the extremely painful procedure of surgically removing autograft tissue from the roof of her or his own mouth. Additionally, since the acellular dermis is eventually populated with the cells of the native gingival tissue, the use of donated tissue results in a more aesthetic outcome.

On the other side of the surgical spectrum, the use of allograft skin in urological and gynecological procedures has increased dramatically. More patients receive donated skin for these purposes than for burn treatment, although because these grafts are relatively small (e.g., 1" × 3"), treatment of burn patients accounts for the largest quantity of transplanted skin. In the United States alone, over 13 million patients suffer from urinary incontinence. While this condition—a relatively common occurrence after childbirth—is not life-threatening, the psychological and emotional consequences can be devastating. Restoration of the original angle between the ureter and the bladder can be obtained by fashioning a bladder sling constructed of acellular dermis. This is a minimally invasive procedure that has been shown to be a very effective treatment for this condition. Additional urogynecological procedures include pelvic floor reconstruction and vaginal wall repair.

While the availability of acellular dermis greatly expands surgical options and increases the utility of allograft skin, there are some limitations to the use of this tissue. Acellular dermis is relatively costly in comparison with traditionally prepared allograft skin, and its application may not always be suitable or appropriate. In many instances, temporary coverage is all that is needed to bridge the gap between wound excision and final coverage, and traditional allograft skin is a relatively inexpensive and reliable method of achieving this. In less severe injuries, the amount of scarring and contracture may be minimal, unnoticeable, or in an area that does not affect functionality or mobility. In these instances the additional cost associated with the use of acellular dermis may not be justified. Acellular dermis lacks the barrier function of traditional allograft skin, and therefore it can not serve as a "standalone" biological dressing; it must be covered and protected while the patient's own cells repopulate and integrate into the graft.

The Rise (and Fall) of Skin Banks

The unexpected and random nature of burn injuries has historically dictated treatment options. Prior to the advent of cell and tissue preservation techniques, availability of allograft tissue was purely a matter of happenstance or fortuitous timing. With World Wars I and II demonstrating the importance of a readily available supply of allograft tissue, it is not surprising that the U.S. military took an early lead in establishing a ready supply of tissues for transplant.

In the early 1950s, tissue preservation pioneers working at the U.S. Navy Tissue Bank used advances in cryopreservation technology to successfully preserve skin and other tissues for transplant. In the early 1970s, Janzeckowic promoted the practice of early excision and grafting for the treatment of burn injuries, which required access to an extensive amount of allograft skin. Most major burn centers in the United States developed "in-house" skin banks to supply these grafts.

The American Burn Association (ABA) listed 40 skin banks in its 1986 *Directory of Burn Resources*. In 1999, that number had fallen to 24. This precipitous drop in the number of skin banks was due in large part to economics and increased competition.

The economics of operating a skin bank, or any tissue bank, include the costs of: maintaining staff, facilities, and equipment; recovery and processing of tissue; and hospital and donor development.[28] In most instances, these costs are passed on to the patients receiving the tissue grafts. In the case of small, regional skin banks, this may represent a considerable challenge. Employees of many regional burn centers have observed that a disproportionate number of burn patients are low-income, uninsured or underinsured people. This may be due in part to greater safety dangers in the home environment, including the use of highly combustible (and less costly) propane fuel and absent or inadequate smoke alarms.

Hospitals are required to provide emergency care to all patients, but reimbursements to health care facilities rarely cover actual costs. This presents an economic challenge to the existence of skin banks, which need either to receive additional hospital subsidies or to find alternative sources of revenue to continue operations. Many of these banks elected to offset the financial loss associated with providing allograft skin by incorporating the recovery of musculoskeletal (primarily bone) and cardiac tissues. In some of these cases, the lack of support from the burn center (as discussed later), coupled with a stimulated interest on the part of the orthopedic community, resulted in a shift of the primary focus of the tissue bank from supplying skin to supplying orthopedic surgeons with musculoskeletal tissue.

In the mid-1980s, the emergence of nationwide recovery agencies, which focused primarily on the recovery of musculoskeletal tissues, resulted in an increased competition for the limited donor pool. Many smaller skin banks found it impossible to compete with the significant resources of these large organizations. Additionally, the ever-increasing federal and state regulation of tissue banking has placed a significant financial burden on tissue recovery agencies; tissue banks are forced to add staff, expand the scope of their operations to include other tissues, merge with competing tissue recovery agencies, or simply close their doors. As the ABA's numbers indicate, many chose the later. Yet, the recent technical advances in the processing and preservation of allograft skin have greatly enhanced the surgical utility of these grafts and prompted many organizations to initiate or revive skin-recovery programs.

Factors Influencing the Decision to Recover Allograft Skin

Individual members of the Skin Council of the American Association of Tissue Banks have long been concerned with the tissue banking community's responsibility to meet the clinical needs for allograft skin, but this concern has not been universally shared outside of this small group of individuals. A recent survey found that only 70% of AATB-accredited tissue banks recover allograft skin. More important, although the acceptance criteria for allograft skin donors are much broader than for musculoskeletal donors, the AATB's 2000 *Annual Registration Survey of Accredited Tissue Banks* reports a staggering disparity of one skin recovery for every three musculoskeletal tissue recoveries. The success of any tissue bank is critically linked to its ability to serve the needs of its community, so it is apparent that many tissue banks do not recognize a compelling community need or desire to initiate or maximize the recovery of allograft skin. It is interesting that while many tissue-procurement agencies are willing to look beyond their local service areas when it comes to maximizing the recovery of musculoskeletal and cardiovascular tissue, for reasons discussed below, many will not do the same with skin. A number of factors account for the failure to initiate or maximize skin recovery. As the complexity of these issues is explored, it becomes apparent that tissue recovery organizations are faced with many difficult decisions.

Skin recovery programs may have limited local support. If a tissue bank is located in an area that is not served by a major burn center, there may be little or no local support for the recovery of skin tissue. Likewise, if the local burn center has an existing relationship with an outside allograft skin provider, the local tissue bank may not feel impelled to institute a skin-recovery program. The lack of support for skin-recovery programs can also be attributed to changes in the treatment practices of the local burn care providers. While many burn centers may have actively supported skin-recovery programs in years past, the lure of biosynthetics and skin equivalents, coupled with rising costs and the declining patient census, has lead many clinicians to abandon their support of their local skin program.

A burn surgeon's acceptance of alternatives to allograft skin may be a reflection of the skin bank's inability to adequately address the needs of the particular surgeon or the result of intense marketing campaigns designed to promote a particular product as a superior material to meet the surgical need. The hope or promise that biosynthetic products may offer greater flexibility for patient care, including longer periods between dressing changes or faster, more effective wound healing, may entice the surgeon to favor these types of dressings.

The American Burn Association reports that the rate of reportable burn injuries has declined from 10/10,000 in the 1960s to 4.2/10,000 in the 1990s. While specialized burn care centers now see over 50% of all burn injuries, as compared to only 13% in 1971, the number of acute admissions to burn centers throughout the country has stabilized or even declined in many areas. This may be due to increased efforts directed at burn prevention and education, including flame resistant or retardant clothing, fabric, and toys. It is interesting to note that with approximately 125 burn centers located throughout the United States, there are fewer than a dozen burn care physicians actively involved in the issues surrounding allograft skin banking, such as regulatory oversight, development of standards, and other critical issues. As a new breed of burn care providers reassesses the merits of allograft skin, many are surprised to find that local access to allograft skin has vanished.

The recovery of allograft skin is a technically challenging procedure. Unlike the surgical recovery of bone or ligaments, the procurement of skin is extremely donor-dependent and requires a great amount of skill and dexterity to obtain grafts of appropriate quality. In addition, since the skin cannot be subsequently sterilized like other tissue such as bone, meticulous attention to donor preparation and sterile technique may add a fair amount of time to the recovery procedure. Exacerbating the technical challenges, the equipment currently used to obtain allograft skin grafts was neither designed nor intended to withstand the significant demands of cadaveric skin recovery. The surgical equipment industry has been slow to address the limitations of the current recovery equipment. As a result, members of the skin banking community have taken matters into their own hands and are currently developing skin-recovery equipment designed to meet the specific challenges of cadaveric skin procurement.

Skin recovery is not always cost-effective. While reimbursement of the costs associated with the procurement and processing of musculoskeletal tissues such as bone and tendons have sky rocketed, the reimbursement for the costs associated with allograft skin have changed very little over the past 15 years.

In 1995, the service fees charged to hospitals by a national musculo-skeletal tissue bank were approximately $27,000 per donor. By 2001, this amount had increased to over $42,000. This dramatic increase is due to a variety of factors, including processing techniques that result in high-cost and sophisticated tissue forms that are delivered to the operating room with customized surgical instrumentation. In addition, more musculoskeletal tissues are now recovered from most donors, thereby increasing the total amount of tissues that can be processed and distributed. At the same time that tissue banks have been able to increase their revenue streams, recovery agencies such as organ procurement organizations have increased their costs and therefore reimbursement expectations. The bulk of reimbursement provided to an OPO involved with tissue recovery comes from musculoskeletal tissue banks or processors, primarily because they have been willing and able to bear the financial responsibility for tissue procurement costs.

In contrast, reimbursement for skin for burn patients has remained relatively flat, ranging from $800 to $1,000 per square foot. On average, two to four square feet of skin can be processed from one skin donor. Some skin banks have been able to increase their revenue by also providing skin for nontraditional uses such as burn scar revision, gynecological-urological procedures for urinary incontinence, and reconstruction procedures. In these cases, the service fees from one donor can range from $1,000 to $3,500. But, due to procurement issues that may have an impact on funeral arrangements, many recovery agencies have opted not to request this kind of donation from potential donor families. The disparity between the reimbursement potential for musculoskeletal tissues and skin becomes important because the costs associated with the recovery of tissues can be significant. Assembling and transporting a team of trained technicians and their surgical equipment can be very expensive. Many recovery agencies cover large service areas and are forced to fly recovery teams to various procurement sites. While including skin in the recovery of a musculoskeletal donor may appear to be an incremental cost, additional technician and aircraft standby time may be significant. While some banks may send a procurement team out on a local "skin only" recovery, very few would elect to send a team on a long-distance recovery if no additional tissues could be obtained to help defray the costs.

Skin recovery may jeopardize the recovery of other tissues. As discussed above, the recovery of musculoskeletal tissue represents a significant source of operating revenue for many tissue banks. Some of these banks feel that the incorporation of a skin-recovery program can present potential risks that could jeopardize their ability to recover musculoskeletal tissue. Perceived risks may range from third-party objections to the donation process, to the potential for negative media attention. All tissue banks must work in cooperation with personnel from funeral homes and mortuary services. In the best situation, tissue banks work collaboratively with these individuals to optimize the donation process while minimizing any additional efforts required by these professionals to prepare the donor for funeral or burial arrangements. Unfortunately, the relationship between the tissue bank and the aftercare professionals may not be so cordial in all areas. In some cases, there may be an underlying objection to tissue donation in general and skin recovery in particular. Whether this objection is based on personal beliefs or operational issues, or is merely a reflection of inexperience in dealing with the recovery process, the loss of support and, in some cases, actual antidonation sentiment, can severely compromise the entire tissue program. Tissue banks must walk the fine line of maintaining amicable working relationships while optimizing the donation process.

Public perception is another very important factor that can potentially jeopardize the success of a recovery program. As with any organization dependent on public support, tissue banks work diligently to obtain positive media coverage and maintain a high level of visibility within the community. Unfortunately, media attention can be a double-edged sword, and unfavorable or controversial coverage can jeopardize the success of the entire recovery program. Recent media attention regarding the use of allograft skin and the subsequent reaction by some of the nation's prominent tissue recovery organizations clearly illustrates this point. Concerned that unfavorable publicity regarding the use of skin for cosmetic procedures might negatively impact their programs and discourage tissue donation, several of these organizations simply elected to discontinue their skin-recovery efforts.

In summary, the success of a tissue bank depends on maintaining the support of the community that it serves. This support must be earned by meeting local needs and acting as a responsible member of the community. As many in the local community may know little about traditional uses, much less the advances in tissue transplantation, the need for a particular type of tissue may simply not be recognized. Without a clear mandate from its community or the local health care providers, many tissue banks have found it simpler not to be involved in the recovery of allograft skin.

One of the obligations that a tissue procurement agency has to its community is to facilitate the donation process. This includes providing the option of donation of all suitable tissues and then honoring the donor family's requests by making a reasonable effort to recover all of the tissues that the family has consented to donate. On the other hand, procurement agencies may be understandably reluctant to expend the time and resources necessary to recover tissues without a local demand. The apparent lack of a recognized need by many tissue banks and the communities they serve may lead one to question the extent of the current demand for allograft skin.

Current Trends and Controversies

Availability of Skin

Recent media attention has focused on the procurement, processing, and distribution of donated human tissues. Newspaper articles, most notably in the *Orange County Register* and the *Chicago Tribune*, have raised some issues about using allograft skin for applications outside of the traditional use in burn care. These articles suggest that burn patients received a lower standard of care due to a "shortage" of allograft skin caused by tissues being diverted to nontraditional uses. Describing nontraditional uses, reporters selectively focused on the cosmetic or vanity applications while failing to note that the vast majority of these grafts are being used in recognized clinical applications, improving the lives of thousand of patients each year. Nevertheless, these reports have sparked controversy about a possible skin shortage for critical needs and inappropriate diversions of donated skin.

The decision about how donated skin will be used begins at the procurement stage when recovery specialists determine whether to recover *thin skin* (approximately the thickness of four pages in this book) or *thick skin* (about 10 pages). This decision is based on a number of factors, including physiological characteristics of the donor (age, weight, body contour, skin quality), family directives, tissue needs, and, in some cases, contractual obligations. Procurement of thick skin also requires greater technical expertise, which is not always available at every skin bank. Reimbursement rates are also higher for thick skin.

Thin skin may be processed to either traditional cryopreserved allograft, which is used primarily as a temporary dressing in burn patients, or to acellular dermal allograft with its wider range of uses. Thicker grafts are almost always processed to acellular dermal allografts because physicians do not want to use the thicker grafts for temporary burn wound coverage. (They cite difficulty of use and delayed or inadequate adherence to the excised wound as reasons.) The thick grafts are ideally suited, however, for processing to acellular dermal allografts since the increased thickness means a thicker, stronger dermal matrix, which is important in procedures such as bladder slings and hernia repair. Most donation is thin skin. The recovered skin is forwarded to one of several skin-processing facilities. Most facilities can perform traditional cryopreservation of the allografts, but only a couple of processors have the ability to prepare acellular dermal allografts, because it is a proprietary process.

During the processing procedure, grafts are cut to the appropriate sizes and shapes to facilitate clinical application. In the case of traditional cryopreserved allografts, the cut edges and tissue remnants must be discarded. Fortunately, in the acellular dermal allograft process, these edges and tissue remnants can be further processed to an injectable form of the matrix. While developed to minimize the discard of donated tissue and intended to help meet a recognized clinical need, such as reconstruction and vocal cord repair, this form of tissue has been associated with controversial uses such as puffy lips and other vanity surgeries.

Most people are comfortable with the use of donated tissue to restore form and function, but many feel that the use of these tissues for so-called "vanity" procedures is contrary to the principles and altruistic nature of the donation process. The use of dermal injections to eliminate severe acne scars may be acceptable to some, while they find the use of the same tissue to remove facial wrinkles in an aging actress, or to enlarge the lips of an aspiring model, completely unacceptable. Some find it acceptable to utilize the tissue to correct hypospadias of the penis but quite offensive if it is used to increase the size of the same organ. While these examples may illustrate the obvious extremes, the fine lines between restorative, cosmetic, and vanity surgery may be clearer to the recipients of the grafts than to those judging the merits of, or the motivation behind, the procedures.

Given the relatively small number of burn patients requiring allograft skin each year (approximately 1,000), it is readily apparent that the tissue banking community should have little problem satisfying this critical need. With reports of over 20,000 tissue donors annually, there should be no reason that the allograft skin requirements for all patients should not be met. There is, however, no ongoing national monitoring system in place to determine whether there is a skin shortage.

Before the media recently became interested in the issues surrounding donated human tissue, the Skin Council of the AATB had begun to develop survey tools designed to determine the status of allograft skin recovery and usage. The Skin Council obtained the help of the American Burn Association for collection of this important data. The AATB's skin *recovery* survey targeted 69 tissue banks in the U.S. believed to recover skin (42 AATB-accredited tissue banks and 27 nonaccredited "skin banks"). The ABA's skin *usage* survey was distributed to 139 burn care providers.

Eighty-three percent (57) of the tissue banks surveyed responded. Seventy-five percent (43) of the 57 respondents indicated that they recover allograft skin, with most reporting that they can almost always meet the local need for allograft skin, although their ability to meet outside needs was somewhat less dependable. Most (93%) of those recovering skin indicated that they attempted to perform skin recovery on all donors, and 73% indicated they recovered "skin only" donors. These banks reported 6542 skin donors in 1999, a 40% increase since the survey performed in 1995. Cryopreserved skin was distributed by 85% of the banks, while 57% of them distributed "fresh" skin.

Of the 139 burn centers surveyed, 75% (104) responded. Eight-two percent stated that they used allograft skin within the past year, with the majority using cryopreserved skin. Fifty-two percent of the respondents indicated they had "experienced difficulty" in obtaining allograft skin. The degree of difficulty encountered is unclear from the present survey. This could mean that tissue was unavailable from the usual supplier and several phone calls had to be made prior to locating the tissue. (In one case, it was apparently the hospital's refusal to pay for allograft skin that resulted in the surgeon's difficulty in obtaining the grafts.) A followup survey has been proposed to clarify these issues and elicit more specific responses.

Despite several significant limitations of these two surveys, it is apparent that in some regions there may be a serious lack of communication between the tissue procurement and processing agencies and the allograft users. As previously discussed, the need for allograft skin varies tremendously. A burn care facility may go weeks or months without a significant need for allograft skin, only to be inundated at a moment's notice with massive injuries. The key to supplying this extremely variable need is rapid and accurate communications between burn facilities and tissue providers.

A case in point is the 2001 New Year's fire disaster in Amsterdam in which hundreds of people were injured in a nightclub fire. Over 60 patients received significant burn injuries. The need for allograft skin to treat these patients far exceeded the ability and available allograft supplies of European tissue banks. The EuroSkin bank placed an urgent request for help to the members of the AATB's Skin Council, which arranged for an immediate delivery of allograft skin and identified U.S. tissue banks that had sufficient inventory of allograft skin to assist if additional grafts were required. Of nine U.S. tissue banks contacted, all but two indicated that they had enough available reserves to comfortably supply grafts to Europe without jeopardizing their ability to meet local needs. In fact, it was learned that two tissue banks had reserve inventories of over 1000 square feet of allograft skin each.

In summary, contrary to recent media reports, there is little evidence to indicate that there is a national shortage of skin to treat burn patients. This is true even though not all tissue recovery agencies are maximizing skin recovery. It seems that some burn centers have not kept current with significant changes in the recovery and processing practices of their local tissue banks. To help burn care providers obtain the allograft tissues they need, the AATB's Skin Council established a National Allograft Skin Hotline to connect the suppliers of allograft skin with those in need. The AATB distributed literature at the annual meeting of the American Burn Association and directed a mailing to all burn units in the United States with information about the hotline. In the first 26 months of this program (data available as of March 2003), the AATB had yet to receive a single call for allograft skin.

Consent Issues

Concerns have also been raised about the consent process for tissue donation. Within the tissue banking community there is little argument that consent for the donation of tissues should be based on a decision made by an appropriately informed individual. It is apparent, however, that the term "appropriately informed" is vague and controversial. Certainly, the individuals making the decision to donate should be afforded all the information that they need regarding the procurement, processing, and ultimate use of the donated tissue. It is understandable that the extent or depth of this information may vary widely among individuals. What is the best way to present this information without offending or upsetting the individual? Is there a point where the information becomes "too much"? These issues are under discussion by the skin banking community and are discussed in several chapters in this book in Part II and Part IV.

The Future of Allograft Skin Recovery and Transplantation

Recent developments in the processing of allograft skin have unlocked an enormous potential for this versatile tissue graft. The potential for expansion of the surgical applications of this donated tissue could dwarf that of any tissue currently transplanted. Appropriately processed and preserved, allograft skin can be transformed into a truly universal transplant graft. Providing an immunologically inert yet biochemically and biomechanically intact matrix, these grafts could be combined with a number of components, resulting in innovative biological tissue forms. The combination of specific cell populations such as hepatocytes or islet cells could potentially produce an auxiliary organ such as a liver or pancreas. Seeded with stem cells, these grafts could possibly be used to regenerate any diseased organ or tissue. By combining acellular grafts with recombinant forms of delivery systems, clinicians might be able to provide sustained delivery of the desired substance—be it insulin, antibiotics, or neurotransmitters. Adding growth factors or other cellular mediators or modulators, properly processed skin grafts might be valuable tools in wound healing and the treatment of local or systemic disease. The incorporation of chemotherapeutic agents may provide clinicians with the ability to target the delivery of these drugs to aid in the treatment of cancer or localized infections. With the availability of a universal transplant graft, the possibilities are limited only by the bounds of clinical innovation.

This chapter is dedicated to the memory of John F. Hansbrough, M.D., a compassionate clinician, gifted surgeon, and innovative researcher. Ever challenging those around him to rise to their full potential, Dr. Hansbrough was an inspiration, a mentor, and a friend.

References

1. Rudolph R, Klein L. Healing process in skin grafts. *Surg Gynecol Obstet.* 1973; 136:641–654.
2. Reverdin JL. De la greffe epidermique. *Arch Gen Med.* 1872:276.
3. Innvanova SS. The transplantation of skin from dead body to granulating surface. *Ann Surg.* 1890;12:354–355.

4. Freshwater MF, Krizek TJ. George David Pollack and the development of skin grafting. *Ann Plast Surg*. 1978;1:96–102.

5. Briggaman RA, Wheeler CE. Epidermal-dermal interactions in adult human skin: role of dermis in epidermal maintenance. *J Invest Dermatol*. 1968;51:454–465.

6. Spence RJ, Wong L. The enhancement of wound healing with human skin allograft. *Surg Clin North Am*. 1997;77:731–745.

7. Peters WJ. Biological dressings in burns–a review. *Ann Plast Surg*. 1980;4:133–137.

8. American Burn Association. Burn incidence and treatment in the U.S.: 2000 fact sheet. Chicago, Illinois 2000. Available at: http://www.ameriburn.org/pub/Burn Incidence Fact Sheet.htm.

9. Hansbrough JF. Allograft skin. In: *Wound Coverage with Biologic Dressings and Cultured Skin Substitutes*. Austin, Texas, R.G. Landes Co, 1992; 21–40.

10. Sparks BG. Immunological responses to thermal injury. *Burns*. 1997;23:106–113.

11. Janzekovic Z. A new concept in the early excision and immediate grafting of burns. *J Trauma*. 1970;10:1103–1108.

12. Munster AM. Burns of the world. *J Burn Care Rehabil*. 1996;17(6 Pt 1):477–484.

13. Greenleaf G, Cooper ML, Hansbrough JF. Microbial contamination in allografted wound beds in patients with burns. *J Burn Care Rehabil*. 1991;12:442–445.

14. Rose JK, Desai MH, Mlakar JM, Herndon DN. Allograft is superior to topical antimicrobial therapy in the treatment of partial-thickness scald burns in children. *J Burn Care Rehabil*. 1997;18:338–341.

15. Greenleaf G, Hansbrough JF. Current trends in the use of allograft skin for burn patients and reflections on the future of skin banking in the United States. *J Burn Care Rehabil*. 1994;15:428–431.

16. Richters CD, Hoekstra MJ, Van Baare J, Du Pont JS, Kamperdijk EWA. Morphology of glycerol-preserved human cadaver skin. *Burns*. 1996;22:113–116.

17. Hansbrough JF, Morgan J, Greenleaf G, Underwood J. Development of a temporary living skin replacement composed of neonatal fibroblasts cultured on Biobrane, a synthetic dressing material. *Surgery*. 1994;115:633–644.

18. Grillo HC, Mckhann CF. The acceptance and evolution of dermal homografts freed of viable cells. *Transplantation*. 1964;2:48–59.

19. Livesey S, Herndon D, Hollyoak M, Atkinson Y, Nag A. Transplanted acellular allograft dermal matrix. *Transplantation*. 1995;60:1–9.

20. Cuono C, Langdon R, Mcguire J. Use of cultured epidermal autografts and dermal allografts as skin replacements after burn injury. *Lancet*. 1986;1:1123–1124.

21. Cooper ML, Hansbrough JF. Advantages of a dermal component in designing a cultured skin substitute. *J Cell Biochem*. 1990;14:251.

22. Rennekampff HO, Kiessig V, Griffey ES, Greenleaf G, Hansbrough JF. Acellular human dermis promotes cultured keratinocyte engraftment. *J Burn Care Rehabil*. 1997;18:535–544.

23. Wainwright D, Madden M, Luterman A, et al. Clinical evaluation of an acellular allograft dermal matrix in full-thickness burns. *J Burn Care Rehabil*. 1996;17:124–136.

24. Jones FR, Schwartz BM, Silverstein P. Use of a nonimmunogenic acellular dermal allograft for soft tissue augmentation. *Aesthetic Surg Quarterly*. 1996;16:196–201.

25. Desai MH, Dziewulski P, Trier TT, Chen JW, Barret JP, Herndon DN. Dural reconstruction of a class IV calvarial burn with AlloDerm. *Proc Am Burn Assoc.* 1998;19:243.
26. Schulman J. Clinical evaluation of an acellular dermal allograft for increasing the zone of attached gingiva. *Pract Periodont Aesthet Dent.* 1996;8:201–208.
27. Callan D, Silverstein L. An acellular dermal matrix allograft substitute for palatal donor tissue. *Post Grad Dentistry.* 1997;3:14–21.
28. Freedlander E, Boyce S, Ghosh M, Ralston DR, MacNeil S. Skin banking in the U.K.: the need for proper organization. *Burns.* 1998;24:19–24.

5

The View from the Food and Drug Administration

JILL HARTZLER WARNER
AND KATHRYN C. ZOON

The Food and Drug Administration's goals with regard to the regulation of human tissue are to prevent the spread of communicable disease, assure that manufacturers of cellular and tissue-based therapeutic products demonstrate safety and effectiveness (where appropriate) and encourage the development and availability of these products through a risk-based, rational, and comprehensive regulatory framework. The FDA's new regulatory approach, when completed, will apply to a broad range of human cells, tissues, and cellular and tissue-based products, including the subject of this book, musculoskeletal tissue and skin. The FDA's Center for Biologics Evaluation and Research has lead responsibility.

FDA Begins Regulation of Tissues

The FDA's first efforts to regulate human skin and musculoskeletal tissue for transplantation began in 1993, following reports that brokers offering to sell tissue from Russia, Eastern Europe, and Central and South America had contacted U.S. tissue banks. In many cases, the brokers were unwilling or unable to identify the actual source of the tissue or provide documentation of cause of death, donor medical records, results of donor screening and testing, or samples of donor serum for testing. The FDA immediately launched its own investigation in September of 1993, and documented that these tissues, which did not meet even minimal standards for preventing transmission of infectious disease, were being offered for importation and distribution. In one case, the FDA was able to obtain donor-cadaver blood samples from a broker, accompanied by documentation of previous infectious disease testing, including alleged testing for hepatitis B indicating negative results. The FDA's retesting confirmed that the sample was markedly positive for hepatitis B surface antigen.

Acting swiftly to respond to an immediate need to protect the public health from the risk of transmission of HIV and hepatitis through human tissue, the FDA, under Commissioner David Kessler, M.D., published an interim final rule, effective immediately, entitled "Human Tissue Intended for Transplantation."[1] Because the overriding public health objective was to prevent the transmission of communicable disease, the FDA relied on Section 361 of the Public Health Service Act (PHS Act).[2] This section authorizes the Secretary of the Department of Health and Human Services to make and enforce such regulations as judged necessary to prevent the introduction, transmission, or spread of communicable diseases from foreign countries into the states or from state to state. Intrastate transactions may be regulated under authority of this provision, as appropriate.[3] These regulations are codified in 21 CFR Part 1270.

The 1993 regulations were a focused, immediate response to a specific public health threat, and, as such, were never intended to provide comprehensive regulation of human tissue for transplantation. The regulations require that tissue banks conduct basic infectious disease testing and donor screening for HIV and hepatitis, follow written procedures for testing and screening, and maintain testing records. Establishments that recover, process, store, or distribute banked human tissue are subject to FDA inspection. The FDA may order recall or destruction of any tissue found to violate the regulations.[4]

Incidents Prompt Increased Scrutiny

With the increased use of human tissue has come a heightened public awareness of the need for appropriate regulation to minimize the potential risks. Several incidents during the 1980s and early 1990s prompted the FDA to examine the scope and elements of an appropriate regulatory approach. More recent reports have caused growing concern and highlight the challenges in a public health response:

- In the 1980s, there were reports of multiple incidents of Creutzfeld-Jakob disease (CJD) transmission by dura mater allograft. The disease appeared to have spread to multiple recipients due to the practice of commingling products from different donors during processing.[5]

- A 1992 report documented that seven people were infected with HIV through transplantation of organs and tissue from a single donor.[6] Although the donor had tested negative for HIV, the incident illustrated the need for better testing methodologies and tracking mechanisms to identify recipients of implicated tissue.
- In the 1990s, possible transmission of CJD through corneas and eye tissue was reported.[7]
- In 1999, a patient died from cardiac arrest during surgery to remove an infected corneal transplant. The probable source of the infection was contamination of the media that had been used to store the cornea.[8]
- In 2001, a healthy 23–year-old male patient who had undergone elective knee surgery that involved implanted tissue died. Subsequent investigation confirmed that the tissue was contaminated with the bacterium *Clostridium spp.*[9]
- As of July 2002, the Centers for Disease Control had received reports of 54 allograft-associated bacterial/fungal infections occurring since 1997.[10]
- In 2002, West Nile virus was thought to have been transmitted by blood and organ donation.[11, 12]
- As of October 2002, three organ and five probable tissue recipients had been determined to be infected with hepatitis C from a single donor. The donor appeared to have been in the "window period" in which the test used could not detect evidence of infection.[13]

The number of musculoskeletal tissue transplants nearly doubled during the 1990s, from approximately 350,000 in 1990 to 650,000 in 1999.[14] While the overall risk of disease transmission through tissue transplantation is thought to be very low, more tissue transplants are taking place and reports of contaminated tissue have increased. Because over 100 tissue transplants can come from a single donor, many potential recipients may be at risk when communicable disease risk is inadequately assessed. The public expectation for safety is high, as tissue transplants are often elective in nature—life-enhancing rather than life-saving.

It may be difficult to ascertain the scope of a problem from a single incident, as current tissue regulations do not require that establishments track tissue from an infected donor to the recipients or from a recipient back to the original donor. Moreover, we may not have a clear picture of the incidence and prevalence of infectious disease transmission by human tissue, because infections are not routinely reported. While facilities may voluntarily report adverse incidents through the FDA's MedWatch system, current regulations do not require such reports.

A further challenge stems from the limits of current testing methods. For some agents of concern, there are no validated donor-screening tests. For others, tests are available but not foolproof. Over the last several years, the agency and the public have become increasingly concerned about reports of transmission of bacteria, yeast, and fungi from tissue transplants. Many of these infections have resulted in permanent disability and, in the case of the 23-year-old man noted above, even death. Of particular concern, and the cause of the fatality, is *Clostridium*, a spore-forming anaerobe that can be difficult to detect and remove from tissue using current testing and processing methods. Half of the transplant-associated instances of bacterial infection have been *Clostridium* species.[15]

Emerging infectious diseases such as West Nile virus and new variant CJD pose particular challenges as risk factors may not be completely understood and screening tests unavailable. The agency has encouraged development of adequate screening and testing methodologies while knowledge of the scope of the risk is still evolving.

The FDA's New Regulatory Framework

In addition to the FDA's increased awareness of the type and scope of infectious disease risks that are potentially associated with human tissue transplants, the industry itself was changing. By the mid 1990s, the use of conventional, banked musculoskeletal tissue and skin was increasing to meet demand, industry was applying new techniques for processing and manipulating human cells and tissues, and the future held the promise of novel therapeutic approaches involving human cells and tissues, such as "tissue-engineered" products for skin repair and hematopoietic stem cells derived from umbilical cord blood and peripheral blood.

From Fragmented to Comprehensive Regulatory Approach

The existing FDA approach to the regulation of human cellular and tissue-based products was perceived as highly fragmented. If a product was regulated as a tissue, it was subject to minimal FDA oversight that focused primarily on HIV and hepatitis screening and testing. If a product was considered a biological product, it was subject to comprehensive premarket and postmarket requirements, including demonstration of safety and effectiveness. If a product was considered a medical device, different premarket and postmarket requirements applied. Industry members were concerned that it was not always possible to predict how the FDA would regulate a particular human cellular or tissue-based product. Concerns about the current state of tissue and cell product regulation led Congress to consider enacting new legislation. Meanwhile, the FDA began to reexamine existing statutory authorities and explore alternatives to a legislative response.

The FDA met with representatives of industry, academia, and patient and consumer groups in December 1996 and again in January and February 1997. After intensive work within the FDA and extensive public engagement on the issues, the FDA announced the "Proposed Approach to the Regulation of Cellular and Tissue-Based Products" in February 1997.[16] The "Proposed Approach" was also selected as a "Reinventing Government" report—"Reinventing the Regulation of Human Tissue"—produced in conjunction with (then) Vice President Al Gore's "National Performance Review."[17]

The 1997 "Proposed Approach" provided for the first time a comprehensive, risk-based framework for the regulation of a wide range of human cells, tissues, and cellular and tissue-based products. In crafting the "Proposed Approach," the agency began with a set of basic questions and principles:

- What are the risks that FDA regulation can and should address?
- What product characteristics affect risk?
- The level and type of regulation should be commensurate with the risk posed by the product characteristic.
- Like products should be treated alike.
- The FDA should exercise regulatory oversight only to the degree necessary to protect the public health.

The FDA included a wide range of human cells, tissues, and cellular and tissue-based products in the scope of the "Proposed Approach." The new framework would apply to conventional musculoskeletal tissue and skin, ocular tissue such as corneas and sclera, reproductive tissue such as semen and ova, cellular therapies (including therapies derived from adult and embryonic stem cells), hematopoietic stem cells derived from umbilical cord blood or peripheral blood, human heart valves, dura mater, as well as combination products such as cells combined with a matrix for wound healing.

The agency faced a number of practical limitations and challenges in reinventing tissue regulation. First, because the approach would rely on existing statutes, the agency worked within the boundaries of the Food, Drug, and Cosmetic Act (FDCA),[18] which provides authority to regulate drugs and devices (including biological products); section 351 of the PHS Act,[19] which requires licensure of biological products; and section 361 of the PHS Act,[20] which authorizes the FDA to promulgate regulations to control the spread of communicable disease.

Second, the agency did not include within the scope of the "Proposed Approach" a number of product areas that raise related regulatory issues. One could certainly characterize organs for transplant, blood for transfusion, and xenotransplantation products[21] as "cellular and tissue-based products," and they share many of the same infectious disease concerns. The FDA, however, has not traditionally regulated vascularized organs for transplant or minimally manipulated bone marrow. Within the Department of Health and Human Services (DHHS), the Health Resources and Services Administration (HRSA) and the Centers for Medicare and Medicaid Services (CMS) provide federal oversight of the organ transplant system under the National Organ Transplant Act of 1984.[22] The National Heart, Lung, and Blood Institute, within the National Institutes of Health (NIH), administers the contract for the National Marrow Donor Program, for which the Transplant Amendments Act of 1990[23] established standards. Accordingly, organs and minimally manipulated bone marrow are excluded from the "Proposed Approach."

The FDA actively regulates blood and blood products, but because the infrastructure and regulations are longstanding and highly developed, the agency decided not to bring blood products under the umbrella of the "Proposed Approach." For different reasons, the FDA excluded xenotransplantation products from the new framework. Xenotransplantation raises broad public health concerns that differ in some ways from concerns about human cells and tissues. For example, the threat of introducing new pathogenic agents into the human species must be carefully assessed. The FDA is actively developing a regulatory approach to xenotransplantation products in conjunction with other DHHS agencies and public review.[24] In addition, the FDA excluded from the new regulatory approach secreted or extracted human products (such as milk, collagen, and cell factors), ancillary products used in the manufacture or preparation of the cell or tissue product, and in vitro diagnostic products.[25]

Finally, the new framework would need to be developed using the limited resources available to the agency.

The regulatory framework focuses on three general areas: (1) Preventing unwitting use of contaminated tissues with the potential for transmitting infectious disease, (2) preventing improper handling or processing that might contaminate or damage tissues, and (3) ensuring that clinical safety and effectiveness is demonstrated for tissues that are highly processed, are used for non-natural purposes, are combined with non-tissue components, or that have systemic effects on the body.

The agency would require that infectious disease screening and testing be done for cells and tissues transplanted from one person to another. The agency would also require that cells and tissues be handled according to procedures designed to prevent contamination and to preserve tissue function and integrity. The agency would recommend, but not require, that screening and testing procedures be followed when tissues are transplanted back into the person from whom they were obtained. In general, there would be no agency submissions required regarding infectious disease controls and handling requirements. Thus, most conventional tissues would not be subject to premarket approval requirements. The agency would impose no requirements on cells and tissues transplanted within a patient's body in a single surgical procedure.

Cells and tissues that were manipulated extensively, were combined with non-tissue components, or were to be used for other than their normal functions would be regulated as drugs, devices, and/or biological products requiring premarket approval by the FDA. Metabolic cells and tissues, unless minimally manipulated and used for their natural function in close relatives of the person they were obtained from, also would be regulated as drugs or biological products requiring premarket approval by the FDA.

The agency would require that all tissue establishments register with the agency, and list their products, via a simple electronic system. And the agency would require that all labeling and promotion be clear, accurate, balanced, and not misleading.

For certain products requiring FDA premarket approval, the agency would call on industry and researchers to submit clinical data and manufacturing and product standards designed to ensure their safety and effectiveness. The agency would phase in the product licensure requirements as the standards were formulated. If such standards could be developed for a certain product and were adopted by the agency, applicants could certify that they met the standards, and would not have to submit individual applications containing clinical data to receive licensure.

Industry, academia, and other stakeholders applauded the announcement of the FDA's "Proposed Approach." Although some could (and would) disagree with certain details, commentaters recognized the significant effort to develop a thoughtful, comprehensive strategy for the regulation of both traditional and new products.[26]

New Regulations to Implement Approach

The "Proposed Approach" relied on the FDA's existing statutory authorities. Much of the framework, however, would require development of regulations before it could be implemented. The FDA planned to issue new regulations under the communicable disease provisions of the PHS Act (Section 361). Some human cellular and tissue-based products would be regulated only under these new regulations, while others would also be regulated under existing requirements as drugs, devices, and/or biological products. Accordingly, the FDA formed the Tissue Action Plan (TAP) to develop the policies, regulations, and guidance documents needed to implement the "Proposed Approach." In order to provide direction and coordination, a TAP Core Team was created with representation from the FDA's Center for Biologics Evaluation and Research, Center for Devices and Radiological Health, Office of Regulatory Affairs, and Office of the Commissioner. In addition, several task groups report to the TAP Core Team on specific issues and documents. One of these task groups is the Tissue Reference Group (TRG), which provides a single reference point for product-specific questions. The TRG responds to inquiries from cellular and tissue-product manufacturers, makes recommendations on the appropriate review pathway, and interacts with the FDA's ombudsman on product jurisdiction requests.[27]

The FDA is in the process of completing rules to implement the "Proposed Approach." Three rules, to be contained in 21 CFR Part 1271, will form the platform for regulation of all human cells, tissues, and cellular and tissue-based products. For some products, these regulations will be the sole regulatory requirements. For other products—those regulated as drugs, devices, and/or biological products—the new regulations (donor eligibility and good tissue practice) will supplement good manufacturing practice requirements.

Establishment registration rule. In May 1998, as a first step toward accomplishing this goal, the agency published the proposed rule, "Establishment Registration and Listing for Manufacturers of Human Cellular and Tissue-Based Products."[28] That rule proposed to require cell and tissue establishments to register with the FDA and submit a list of their human cellular and tissue-based products. The agency also proposed modifications to current registration and listing requirements for drugs (including biological products) and devices to create a unified registration system for all human cell and tissue establishments regardless of the level of regulation applied.

The "Establishment Registration" proposed rule was also significant in that it set out the criteria that the FDA would apply in determining whether a tissue or cellular product would be regulated solely under the communicable disease provisions and new regulations, whether it would be exempt from the new requirements, or whether additional premarket and postmarket requirements would apply. The FDA issued the "Establishment Registration" rule in final form in January 2001.[29] A human cell, tissue, or cellular and tissue-based product (HCT/P) will be regulated solely under Section 361 of the PHS Act and the regulations in Part 1271 if it meets all of the following criteria:

- The HCT/P is minimally manipulated[30];
- The HCT/P is intended for homologous use[31] only, as reflected by the labeling, advertising, or other indications of the manufacturer's objective intent;
- The manufacture of the HCT/P does not involve the combination of the cell or tissue component with a drug or device, except for a sterilizing, preserving, or storage agent, if the addition of the agent does not raise new clinical safety concerns with respect to the HCT/P; and
- Either:
  - The HCT/P does not have a systemic effect and is not dependent upon the metabolic activity of living cells for its primary function; or
  - The HCT/P has a systemic effect or is dependent upon the metabolic activity of living cells for its primary function, and:
    - Is for autologous use;
    - Is for allogeneic use in a first-degree or second-degree blood relative; or
    - Is for reproductive use.

Establishments that engage only in certain types of activities using HCT/Ps are not subject to the Part 1271 regulations if they:

- Use HCT/Ps solely for nonclinical scientific or educational purposes
- Remove HCT/Ps from an individual and implant such HCT/Ps into the same individual during the same surgical procedure
- Accept, receive, carry, or deliver HCT/Ps in the usual course of business as a carrier

- Receive or store HCT/Ps solely for implantation, transplantation, infusion, or transfer within their facility
- Recover reproductive cells or tissue and immediately transfer such tissue into a sexually intimate partner of the cell or tissue donor.

The "Establishment Registration" rule also clarifies that if you are an establishment that does not meet the criteria set out above for regulation solely under Section 361 and the regulations in Part 1271, and you do not qualify for any of the exceptions, your HCT/P will be regulated as a drug, device, and/or biological product under the FDCA, Section 351 of the PHS Act, and applicable regulations in Title 21, Chapter I.

Donor suitability rule. In September 1999, the FDA published the proposed rule, "Suitability Determination for Donors of Human Cellular and Tissue-Based Products."[32] The proposed rule would require donor screening, consisting of a review of a donor's medical records for information about the donor that might indicate infection or risk factors for communicable disease, and donor testing for infectious agents. Consistent with the "Proposed Approach," the requirements would apply to a broader range of human cells, tissues, and cellular and tissue-based products than are covered in the current regulations. Moreover, in addition to HIV, hepatitis B, and hepatitis C, all donors would need to be screened and tested for syphilis and screened for transmissible spongiform encephalopathies. Donors of viable cells and tissues rich in leukocytes would require screening and testing for additional relevant cell-associated agents.

An important element of the "Donor Suitability" proposed rule is a provision that would require establishments to implement screening and testing for diseases identified in the future. When certain criteria are met (e.g., the disease is prevalent among potential donors, there is a risk of transmission, significant health risks may occur, and appropriate screening measures and/or tests have been developed), the proposed rule would require establishments to begin screening and testing donors without delay.

"Good Tissue Practice" rule. The FDA published the third proposed rule, "Current Good Tissue Practice for Manufacturers of Human Cellular and Tissue-Based Products; Inspection and Enforcement," in January 2001.[33] Good tissue practice differs from the good manufacturing practice that drug and device manufacturers are familiar with in that it focuses on the methods, facilities, and controls aimed at preventing infectious disease contamination. In order to permit maximum flexibility for establishments to tailor

the requirements to their needs, the regulations would set forth broad goals that could be accomplished in a variety of ways. This rule would require that establishments develop and maintain a quality assurance program, manufacturing controls, a system for tracking HCT/Ps, complaint files, and records. Establishments regulated solely under the communicable disease requirements would also be required to submit adverse reaction and product deviation reports (drugs and devices, including biological products, already file similar reports), and follow labeling requirements. The proposed rule includes inspection and enforcement provisions to monitor and enforce compliance with the requirements.

The FDA received many comments to the proposed rules for donor suitability and good tissue practice, and it is likely that the final rules will differ in some respects from the proposed rules as these comments are taken into consideration.

The Future of Tissue Regulation

When the FDA's new approach to the regulation of human cells, tissues, and cellular and tissue-based products is fully implemented, it will provide a rational, comprehensive, and comprehensible framework under which cell and tissue establishments can develop and market their products. It will support innovation and product development in this rapidly growing medical field by providing clear, appropriate, risk-based regulations. At the same time, it will provide physicians and patients with the assurance of safety that the public has come to expect from drugs, biologics, medical devices, and other medical products overseen by the FDA.

It is clear that the public expects greater assurance of safety in transplanted tissue. The recent reports of serious bacterial contamination in tissues and West Nile virus being transmitted through blood and organ donors, against the backdrop of a nation concerned about the threat of bioterrorism, underscore the need for a swift public health response. The FDA's new regulations will enable a rapid response in the following ways:

- Complete database of human cell, tissue, and cellular and tissue-based product establishments and products will increase the efficiency of FDA inspections, monitoring, and communication about risks.
- Clear requirements directed at preventing bacterial and fungal contamination of tissues through appropriate manufacturing methods, facilities, and controls will enhance industry compliance.

- The requirement to screen and test donors for "relevant communicable diseases" will permit rapid implementation of new tests to detect emerging disease threats.
- Clearer, more comprehensive requirements will permit timely and appropriate FDA enforcement action.
- An added enforcement tool—the order to cease manufacturing—will provide additional protection in cases where the recall of products may be insufficient to protect the public health.

As the future brings new technology and new products, further refinement of the FDA's regulatory approach can be expected. The agency continues to hold workshops and public meetings on issues affecting human cellular and tissue products, develop guidance to assist in complying with the regulations, and participate in meetings with professional organizations, industry, researchers, clinicians, academia, and consumers.

New screening assays for diseases such as West Nile virus and transmissible spongiform encephalopathies (CJD and variant CJD) could enhance the safety of tissues. Manufacturers are also investigating new approaches for pathogen inactivation and end-product sterilization, and we can expect to see these tactics applied to tissue in the near future. The FDA plays an active role in encouraging the development of new tests and methods to minimize the risk of communicable disease transmission through tissues. The agency works closely with sister agencies such as the Centers for Disease Control and Prevention (CDC), CMS, HRSA, and NIH as well as test manufacturers and tissue establishments to explore strategies for obtaining data on transmission risks and bringing needed tests and methods to market.

The future is likely to bring increased coordination and cooperation among international stakeholders. As vividly illustrated by the Eastern European imports that drove the FDA's first tissue regulations and by the recent spread of West Nile virus in the United States, infectious diseases do not respect national boundaries. International trade in tissue-based products can be expected to increase. The FDA anticipates continued work with international regulatory bodies to explore opportunities for sharing information and coordinating regulatory policy.

The authors would like to thank Mary A. Malarkey, Director, Division of Case Management, Office of Compliance and Biologics Quality, CBER, FDA; and Ruth Solomon, M.D., Director, Division of Human Tissue, Office of Cellular, Tissue, and Gene Therapies, CBER, FDA, for their assistance in the preparation of this chapter.

References

1. Human tissue intended for transplantation. Interim Rule. December 14, 1993;58 *Fed Reg*. 65514.
2. 42 U.S.C. 264
3. See State of Louisiana v. Mathews, 427 F. Supp. 174 (E.D. La. 1977).
4. The December 1993 interim rule was issued in final form in July 1997 [Human Tissue Intended for Transplantation; Final Rule, 62 Fed. Reg. 40429 (July 29, 1997)], with some clarifications.
5. Advisory Committee (transcript). FDA transmissible spongiform encephalopathies. Available at: http://www.fda.gov/ohrms/dockets/ac/97/transcpt/3345t.rtf.
6. Simonds RJ, Holmberg SD, Hurwitz RL, et al. Transmission of human immuno-deficiency virus type 1 from a seronegative organ and tissue donor. *N Engl J Med*. 1992;326:726–732.
7. Hogan RN, Brown P, Heck E, Cavanaugh HD. Risk of prion disease transmission from ocular donor tissue transplantation. *Cornea*. 1999;18:2–11.
8. Statement by Kathryn C. Zoon, Ph.D., Director, Center for Biologics Evaluation and Research, Food and Drug Administration, Department of Health and Human Services, Before the United States Senate Permanent Subcommittee on Investigations Committee on Government Affairs. Available at: http://www.fda.gov/ola/2001/humantissue.html.
9. CDC. Update, unexplained deaths following knee surgery—Minnesota 2001. *MMWR*. 2001;50(48):1080.
10. CDC. Presentation by Marion A. Kainer, M.D., M.P.H., June 19, 2002.
11. CDC. West Nile virus infection in organ donor and transplant recipient—Georgia and Florida, 2002. *MMWR*. 2002;51(35):790.
12. CDC. Investigation of blood transfusion recipients with West Nile virus infections. *MMWR*. 2002;51(36):823.
13. CDC. Hepatitis C Virus transmission from an antibody-negative organ and tissue donor—United States, 2000–2002. *MMWR*. 2003;52(13):273.
14. Statement of Marion A. Kainer, M.D., M.P.H., FDA/CBER Blood Products Advisory Committee, 72nd meeting. Available at: http://www.fda.gov/ohrms/dockets/ac/02/transcripts/3839t2.rtf.
15. CDC. Presentation by Marion A. Kainer, M.D., M.P.H., June 19, 2002.
16. *Proposed Approach to Regulation of Cellular and Tissue-Based Products*. Available at: *http://*www.fda.gov/cber/tissue/docs.htm. See also *Proposed Approach to Regulation of Cellular and Tissue-Based Products*, Availability and Public Meeting. Notification of proposed regulatory approach. Public Meeting. March 4, 1997;62 *Fed Reg*. 9721.
17. Reinventing the regulation of human tissue. Available at: http://www.fda.gov/cber/tissue/rego.htm.
18. 21 U.S.C. 301 *et seq*.
19. 42 U.S.C. 262.
20. 42 U.S.C. 264.

21. The Public Health Service has defined "xenotransplantation" to include any procedure that involves the transplantation, implantation, or infusion into a human recipient of either (*a*) live cells, tissues, or organs from a nonhuman animal source or (*b*) human body fluids, cells, tissues, or organs that have had ex vivo contact with live nonhuman animal cells, tissues, or organs. "Xenotransplantation products" include live cells, tissues, or organs used in xenotransplantation.

22. Pub. L. 98-507, 42 U.S.C. 273 *et seq.*

23. Pub. L. 101-616.

24. PHS guideline on infectious disease issues in xenotransplantation. Availability Notice. January 29, 2001;66 *Fed Reg.* 8120.

25. The FDA regulates many of these products under existing laws and regulations.

26. FDA open public meeting on the Proposed Approach (Transcript). Available at: http://www.fda.gov/cber/tissue/min.htm.

27. *Manual of Standard Operating Procedures and Policies.* Regulatory–General Information: Tissue Reference Group; SOPP 8004. Available at: http://www.fda.gov/cber/regsopp/8004.htm.

28. Establishment registration and listing for manufacturers of human cellular and tissue-based products. Proposed Rule. May 14, 1998;63 *Fed Reg.* 26744.

29. Human cells, tissues, and cellular and tissue-based products; establishment registration and listing. Final Rule. January 19, 2001;66 *Fed Reg.* 5447.

30. The FDA has defined "minimal manipulation" as:

    1. For structural tissue, processing that does not alter the original relevant characteristics of the tissue relating to the tissue's utility for reconstruction, repair, or replacement; and

    2. For cells or nonstructural tissues, processing that does not alter the relevant biological characteristics of cells or tissues.

31. The FDA has defined "homologous use" as the replacement or supplementation of a recipient's cells or tissues with an HCT/P that performs the same basic function or functions in the recipient as in the donor.

32. Suitability determination for donors of human cellular and tissue-based products. Proposed Rule. September 30, 1999;64 *Fed Reg.* 52696.

33. Current good tissue practice for manufacturers of human cellular and tissue-based products; inspection and enforcement. Proposed Rule. January 9, 2001;66 *Fed Reg.* 1508.

II

DONOR FAMILY PERSPECTIVES

If the journey along the tissue "chain of distribution" makes us think of human body parts as commercial "products," the essays by John Moyer and Ellen Kulik are a powerful reminder of why we should resist that tendency. Moyer and Kulik tell us that tissue for transplant comes as a gift from people in the midst of tragedy and that the gift-giving is both very important and highly personal. Their stories are also compelling arguments against making it too easy for recipient families and transplant surgeons to "forget" or ignore the source of their treatment.

Yet many persons may find denial more convenient. For example, *Time* magazine wrote that, "When most of us are rolled into an operating room, the last thing we want to think about (if we are conscious at all) is what the doctors are putting inside us. We don't want to know who donated the leg veins sometimes used for our coronary bypass operations or where the ligaments needed to hold a wobbly knee together were found." A similar sentiment was expressed less artfully by Mo Vaughn, a major league baseball player who was interviewed by the *New York Times Sunday Magazine* about his recent tendon transplant. When asked about the source, he replied, "I don't know what it means, but they said it's from the bank. It's somebody else's damn Achilles' tendon."

Moyer and Kulik also give us insight into the dilemma of informed consent. Their wish for donor families to be empowered by fully informed consent is tempered by their personal experience, in which shock and overwhelming grief compromised the ideal of autonomy. Their ambivalence provides an important insight to those responsible for making informed-consent policy in tissue donation and strengthens the argument, made later in this volume by Fost, Campbell, and Youngner, that the moral model of "stewardship" must play a central role in tissue transplantation.

Finally, Kulik emphasizes the important role for the National Family Donor Council—an influential consumer group that represents and advocates the interests of donor families. The Council members are dedicated, as Kulik so convincingly explains, to making sure that market values are balanced by the meaning of their gifts.

6

Andy's Gift: A Donor Family's Perspective

JOHN P. MOYER

Writing this has caused me to revisit a very painful incident that occurred in our family in 1992. We lost our older son in a skiing accident.

On a bright sunny Colorado day in December 1992, Andy was skiing with four of his closest friends when he fell and struck his head. Another skier found him, alerted the patrol, and life-saving measures were initiated. He was flown to a nearby trauma center where he was determined to be brain dead 24 hours later, despite expert and caring neurosurgery and intensive care. At that point we became a donor family.

My profession in medicine from 1962 to the present has brought me close to the field of transplantation on many occasions. As a first-year medical student I witnessed the performance of one of the nation's first renal transplants. As a pediatric resident, I worked closely with liver transplantation, which in the mid- to late sixties was very experimental.

Then on Christmas Eve of 1992, my wife, younger son, and I faced the horrific reality of losing a son and a brother. Organ and tissue donation was the decision we made, giving the ultimate gift to others who could use our son's heart, liver, kidneys, corneas, skin, bone, and connective tissues.

Our son Andy was a senior in college majoring in physics. Ironically, he planned a career in medicine or bioengineering. His friends tell me that he was a brilliant student who rarely had an equal in his academic endeavors. Our son would stop and come to the aid of those who didn't catch on quite as quickly and spend quality time with them as a tutor. He seemed to have very positive influences on people's lives. His friendships were genuine and cemented.

I keep reliving our last hike together in late September of 1992, three months before he died. It was in the Colorado high country. Picture an autumn morning with an overnight dusting of snow on the summits of the peaks. The tundra was brilliant orange as we passed it on our way to our destination up a beautiful alpine valley. I asked Andy to set the pace and find the route to the top. It was a rite of passage, as I had always led the way up the mountain. I saw his massive, powerful legs kicking steps in the steep ice field as we inched our way up to the final ridge that spilled onto the top. Victory! Little did I know that the tissue from those powerful legs would bring strength or new life to someone who couldn't walk or climb.

I often reflect on that image and think of the gifts of connective tissue, skin, and bone we donated in his honor. Just imagining the quality of life that Andy's bone might have given a dental patient or that his patellar tendons might have given someone suffering from a chronic knee disorder is so very healing to our grieving and to getting by this loss. I'm so hopeful that skin we donated might have brought comfort and healing to a burn victim or postoperatively to a cancer patient. Andy would have wanted that. He was so giving and caring.

The very intense feeling of finality gripped me after a call to the hospital about 6:00 a.m. on Christmas Eve. Critical care nurses are skilled in assessing very subtle changes in their patient's status. The status of our son turned from critical to grave, and it was at that time I let go and knew we had lost him. His brain was dead. He would never be a bioengineer or a physician. Today he would die.

About noon we began the process of firmly deciding to become a donor family. Very trustworthy and gentle nurses, social workers, and procurement coordinators began doing what they needed to do to set this donation into motion. We began saying our good-byes.

Then, not far from the intensive care unit, we met with more people who began explaining in great detail what would happen to Andy in the next several hours as they took his solid organs and granted them to perilously ill patients somewhere.

I was certain we were doing the correct thing by allowing someone else in dire need of healthy organs and tissues to receive these gifts. I remain certain to this day that the decision was right. Donation in some mysterious manner has assuaged our grief, and the gift has ended the suffering of another family.

Was I given full disclosure about what was going to happen to Andy's tissue? Did it matter? I hurt so badly leaving him there on life support. Would I have understood more than the compassionate and caring transplant coordinator told my wife and younger son and me? She assured us his tissues would be used for life-saving applications, life-enhancing applications and research. I remember that statement so clearly. I felt that that was how I wanted it to be. Andy wanted to be a health care provider or a scientist, finding a better way of life for many people who hurt. His best friends told me that in the many condolence cards I have read and reread recently.

I remember so vividly the Christmas tree and visitors bringing wrapped gifts to their loved ones in the hospital. Our gift was Andy. Writing this has compelled me to look at several deep topics that I faced on that Christmas Eve in 1992. I was so very grieved and overwhelmed that maybe I missed the issues.

Our choice to donate Andy's organs and tissues was a powerful means to give some spark of sense to the tragic loss we incurred. There was little comfort that we could glean in our bereavement until a thank-you note arrived one day from a gracious family whose husband and father had received one of our son's kidneys. How often I wish Andy could read this note, which we have kept and reread often.

The day we met Dave, Andy's heart recipient, was a triumph. That was six months after Andy's death and Dave's beginning of recovery from irreversible heart disease.

That letter and that meeting boosted us over a big hump in our bereavement.

Meeting or wanting more specific information about tissue recipients at that time would have been an impossible burden. The tissues went in so many directions, and, after all, we released them unconditionally.

Powerful new developments using gifted skin give the body power to restore its own tissue. Nowhere is this more applicable than in the treatment of burns or in the post-op cancer or trauma patient. What a coup for the bioengineers who toil hours to develop these marvelous medical tools to benefit many. Development of products like these costs money, for marketing and research and development programs. There is profit and loss involved, but is this something a grieving family needs to hear? Maybe, or maybe not.

I felt that I had received enough information to allow our family to make an informed decision that day we gifted Andy's organs and tissues. We were told at the time that the tissue was to be used for life-saving and life-enhancing surgery. No mention was made of purely aesthetic usage but we would have consented had we been told this. I have since come to realize that so very little donor skin is used in cosmetic surgery.

Would large amounts of information at the time of donation be overwhelming to the donor family? While they may be commodities, these tissues are very valuable to the tissue companies and to the patients who receive them. How much disclosure is needed to make informed consent? How much detail can a profoundly bereaved family comprehend and process?

I believe there is a point where too much disclosure is going to be detrimental to the family and perhaps the entire donation process itself. For those of us in the health care professions and ministering to donor families, the dilemma is somewhat easier to travel through. But what goes through the minds and hearts of those without the radical background and in a state of profound grief? This is the struggle, and the answer lies out there in unexplored territory, needing to be determined. That is the challenge lying ahead of us.

7

The Gift of Tissue: A Donor Mom's Perspective

ELLEN GOTTMANN KULIK

This chapter is an outpouring of a conflict that arose within me as I began to analyze informed consent and related issues on an intellectual level. On one side, I am an attorney by training; my legal mind tells me that there must be a definitive standard for obtaining consent for donation from families. But I am also a donor mother and a member of the Executive Committee of the National Donor Family Council; my heart calls for compassion and sensitivity to the family's grief. The crux of the issue is striking a delicate balance between informing families about the donation process and providing appropriate bereavement care to families. I do not claim to know the answers. I only know that resolving the issue is not as cut-and-dried as my legal mind wants it to be.

The Gift

For many families, the world has been shattered with the death of their loved one. Life as they knew it will never be the same. I cannot describe the physical, heart-wrenching pain I experienced when the doctor told me that my less than one-hour-old son's "condition is acute, his chance of surviving even the night is grim, and he has no brain activity." As I heard these words, I felt as if I were spiraling backwards down a long, dark tunnel with nothing to grab onto. I came to the hospital to give life, and now I was staring into the face of death. It would have been so easy to fall down that black tunnel of death, never again to emerge. Only by divine inspiration did I think, "If my son is going to die, I want to do something to spare some other parents from this pain." The answer came to me: organ and tissue donation.

My husband and I were exasperated and frustrated when the doctor and medical professionals did not want to discuss this end-of-life option with us. After being told about our son's likelihood of imminent death, we told the neonatologist that if our son was going to die, we wanted to donate his organs and tissues. With a startled, wide-eyed look, the doctor raised both of his hands in a double stop sign and said, "We don't need to talk about that right now." Well, we needed to talk about that right now. Our world was shattered. We needed something to hold onto, something to help us through this tragedy. I suspect that if my husband and I had not pursued discussions about organ and tissue donation, the matter would have been dropped.

At a time of utter despair, I was thrown a lifeline, a ray of hope. Hope because my precious child's death would not be in vain. If I could not have my son, perhaps some other mother could have her son. If my child would never see my face, perhaps some other child would see his or her mother's face for the first time through a corneal transplant. Nothing could take away my pain and grief, but perhaps others could be spared from this despair and utter darkness.

Organ and tissue donation can be a very healing end-of-life option for a family experiencing this magnitude of sadness and grief over the death of a loved one. Like my husband and me, families often choose to donate to "make something good come from the senseless death of our loved one," to "have some hope," to "give another person a chance at life that our loved one would not have," to "know that part of our loved one lives on." This is a truly altruistic gift to a stranger at a time of intense pain for a grieving family. Most donor families want or expect nothing in return for the gifts. In reality, however, many families are helped by the generous gifts of their loved ones. Knowing that our loved ones' deaths were not in vain helps us to hold onto hope. We learn that there can life after death, both for the recipient of our loved one's gifts and for ourselves.

The decision to donate tissue is an extremely personal decision that should be left to the donor and her family. The donor or her family has the right to choose whether and what to donate. Health care professionals and tissue procurement professionals should not take any part of this decision away from the family. To the contrary, through appropriate care and adequate information, they should do everything in their power to enable the family to make the decision.

The Market and the "Product"

In stark contrast to this altruistic gift is the tendency by professionals, fueled by the growing involvement of for-profit companies and new technologies, to treat donated tissue as a commodity. High-tech tissue forms come at a high price, and there is money to be made in processing and distributing tissue. The increased commercialization of the field is changing the way tissue is processed, stored, and distributed.

Elements of the for-profit business, like marketing, finance, and packaging, have been introduced into the tissue industry. With growth come increased sales forces and professionals far removed from contact with families and the donation process. The result is the tendency by some professionals to lose sight of the beauty and dignity of the gift, and to market donated tissue in the same fashion as medical products and devices. Donated tissue that has been modified for a special use is now referred to as a "product." Tissue is packaged in glossy, colorful boxes consistent with packaging for medical products, and designed for ease of use by the end-user. The promotional materials accompanying the packaged tissue hail the benefits of the special shapes of the "product" without even mentioning the gift.

This was dramatically driven home for me when I toured a tissue bank facility with a group of ethicists and others studying tissue donation. I work extensively with my local organ procurement office, and I am a regular at the hospital. I am well versed in organ and tissue donation. I am not meek at heart, overly sentimental, easily moved to tears, or squeamish. But in no way was I prepared for the emotional impact of my visit to the facility.

Upon our arrival, we were ushered into a large conference room with a long conference table in the center. Laid out on the table were several versions of glossy, colorful brochures describing the medical uses of the "products"; why this company's "products" were better than the competitor's "products"; and how to order the "products." At first glance, I didn't think these materials applied to us—we were here to discuss donated tissue. There was no mention of the gift or that these "products" were derived from donated human bone and tissue. A closer review barely revealed that these brochures were, in fact, referring to human tissue.

An employee of the tissue bank came into the room and proceeded to show us the brochures. He spoke of milling, machining, and packaging. I recall that he showed us how tissue was formerly packaged in dry ice (though I have since been told that that is not correct), but now could be shrinkwrapped and packaged in small, individual, easily stackable boxes with clear windows. He took pride in the fact that the packaging and brochures were akin to other medical products.

I was uncomfortable. I felt strangely out of place, at odds with my surroundings and the professionals gathered in the room. Then, he picked up the "screw" and callously tossed it down the table for us to view. My discomfort mounted and I am certain that my faced flushed. My mind screamed out, "that 'screw' is human bone—holy, human bone. That 'screw' came from someone's loved one!" I thought about the unknown family who, at a time of disbelief, great sadness, and death, made an incredible, selfless decision to give a gift, a "gift of life," to an unidentified stranger. I was horrified at the callous disregard for, and cheapening of, the gift of life.

As I reeled in disbelief, we were escorted downstairs to the storage room. While they marveled about the size of the room and capacity of the generators, I wistfully thought about the donors. Back upstairs, we approached the processing rooms. Our guide warned that bone and tissue would be visible and the squeamish should not look. Judging by my discomfort downstairs, I stayed back. I was surprised as I felt tears begin to well up in my eyes. I detested the talk of human bone, precious loved ones' gifts, as "products" to be milled, machined, and sold.

Looking back on my experience, I am surprised by my intense emotions on that day, and its continued impact on me. I cannot adequately describe the emotions that I experienced. I cannot stress enough that the emotions I experienced resulted from the lack of respect for the donors and the gift, *not* from the amount or type of information I received. I suspect that non-donor families cannot grasp these emotions or the importance of respecting the donors and their gifts. The use of the word *product* triggers a red flag for me that the professional has lost sight of the gift, of the indisputable fact that someone's loved one donated that tissue. The use of the word *product* and the increased marketing and packaging moves the industry away from the dignity and beauty of a selfless gift. This is a disservice to the donors and their families.

The National Donor Family Council Recommendations

Donor families have addressed various concerns about tissue donation since the National Kidney Foundation and Maggie Coolican, a donor mother, created the National Donor Family Council in 1992. The Council was founded as a "home for donor families" at a time when they were not consulted on issues concerning donation. The Council and Maggie Coolican, who served as Council chairperson from 1992–1998, became a voice for donor families.

The Council's mission is to enhance the sensitivity and effectiveness of the organ and tissue procurement process, to provide an opportunity for donor families to grieve and grow, and to utilize the unique perspective and experience of these families to increase organ and tissue donation. The Council supports the needs of all organ and tissue donor families and assists health care professionals who work most closely with these families. In addition to advocating for and supporting donor families, the Council develops programs to meet the ongoing needs of families, and of professionals involved in their care. The Council also has published numerous resources for families and professionals, including the "Bill of Rights for Donor Families," an informed-consent policy for tissue donation, and a tissue donation brochure.

Today, the Council represents over 10,000 members, including organ and tissue donor families, living donors and their families, and professionals. The Executive Committee membership has changed over the last decade, but has always included several donor families and grief and donation experts. At times the committee has also included educators, clergy, authors, recipients, scientists, researchers, ethicists, and physicians. All members are volunteers who give countless hours to develop and implement the projects and resources of the Council and to support families throughout the country.

From its inception, the Council recognized tissue donors and their families as equal to organ donors and their families. Its bill of rights (Appendix B) defines the standard of care that potential and actual donor families should expect to receive throughout the donation process. It states that potential tissue donor families have "the right and legitimate expectation to receive a full and careful explanation of the process and to be cared for in a sensitive manner by specially trained individuals."

In the mid-1990s, the Council recognized the need to increase the information provided to tissue donor families as a result of the great number of them coming to the Council for information and answers. Hence, the Council began writing and then published its "Tissue Donation" brochure. The development of this brochure was a natural segue into a discussion of the tissue donation consent process. The Council was concerned that some families were not being provided with the necessary information to make the decision whether to donate. Due to the variation in the amount and type of information provided to families, the Council felt it was necessary to expound upon the information provided to families as set forth in the bill of rights.

After preliminary discussions with donor families and Council members, the Council began the arduous task of writing a policy on informed consent for tissue donation. As with all its other work, this policy was formulated after consulting with the experts on donation—the donor families. As an attorney on the Council and a donor mother, I drafted a broad and far-reaching document policy document aimed at generating a discussion among the Executive Committee members. This began a series of discussions, which continued over many months, about the consent of donor families.

As we analyzed the issue, we discussed how consent should be obtained when a family is in a heightened emotional state and what that consent should look like. We pondered questions like, "How much information does the family hear when the professional talks to them about tissue donation?" "Do families want more or less information?" There were as many experiences and opinions as the number of people sitting at the table. It became obvious that a delicate balance must be struck to ensure that the family is provided with enough information to make a knowledgeable decision, but not so much information that it would completely overwhelm the newly bereaved family.

The "Informed Consent Policy for Tissue Donation" (Appendix C) was unanimously approved after extensive debate. The guiding principal of the policy, like all Council policies, is that the family is the expert regarding issues that affect them. The family has the right to be offered the option of donation and must be given adequate information to make a decision that is right for them and their loved one. This policy is a "work in progress" that may be revised to reflect the needs of donor families.

Adequate Information

Many of the ethical concerns raised by the clash between a family's altruism and the market dimensions would be eliminated if families were provided adequate information to make the donation decision. Contrary to many professionals' opinions, families need more information than is currently provided by some professionals. Health care professionals and tissue procurement professionals should strive to help the family accept their loved one's death and understand this option. This includes providing a family, in a caring and sensitive manner, with adequate information to make their decision and to understand what donating tissue entails.

As every family is different, each must be given a baseline amount of information, with additional information provided based on the needs or requests of each individual family. (A concern here was that some families do not even know what questions to ask to get the information necessary for making the decision.) Written information, which can be reviewed later, is needed. The family should be sufficiently informed so that after the death and the donation, they are not confused about their loved one's gifts or surprised to learn how the process works. For example, families would know that when heart valves are recovered, the heart is removed from the donor's chest and sent to a processing center where the valves are removed. A failure to provide enough information places the integrity of the tissue industry and families at risk. The risk to donor families is the unacceptable complication of their grief. The risk to the tissue industry is the backlash of angry families who feel they have been misled and the possible decline in donation rates.

The Dignity of the Gift

Another crucial component of balancing the market forces is the preservation and protection of the dignity and the beauty of the gift. There is no denying that the donor family is the industry's constituent—there is no industry without the donor families. As laid out in the Council's statement, the tissue industry should invest in the donor community through support and education and take a more active role in promoting awareness and sensitivity within the industry. The tissue industry must strive to educate the tissue professionals, physicians, and the funeral industry about the donor families' perspective and the important nature of the gift. To this end, package materials should include a statement indicating that the package contains donated tissue, which is a gift of life. The industry should resist the tendency to treat the gift of donated tissue as a commodity. Donated tissue is not a "product." Life is far more precious.

The End Use of the Gift

With full disclosure, donor families would understand the specific nature of their loved ones' gifts. For instance, while tissue is aptly called a "gift of life," most often the donated tissue does not save a life. But that does not diminish the gift of life. It is a "gift of life" in the sense that one life gives to another so that the stranger's life will be remarkably improved. There is a danger in using broad terminology like *cosmetic* since, for example, repair of deep facial scars may be cosmetic to some, but not to others. Tissue should be used in a way that promotes healing for the people with the greatest need. Families would have the option of restricting the use of donated tissue for specific uses consistent with their reasons for donating.

Armed with the knowledge that donated tissue may be modified and stored for long periods of time, families might not be so disappointed when they do not get information about the recipient or recipients fail to communicate with them.

Tissue donation can be a gift, not only for the thousands of patients in need, but for grieving families looking for a small glimpse of hope. The implementation of these changes would serve as a starting point for balancing the competing interests of altruism and market values. As with other health care organizations, tissue banks and their affiliates would be able to derive a profit from their efforts without risking additional harm to families caused by after-the-fact disclosures or irresponsible and sensational reporting by the media. Donor families could rest assured that just as their loved one was precious, their gift of life is precious.

III

COMPARISON WITH OTHER TISSUES AND ORGANS

In the introduction to the book, we identified its focus as the transplantation of human tissue donated by families upon the death of a loved one—specifically musculoskeleletal tissue and skin. We noted, however, that this is but one piece of the expanding topography of the tissue industry.

The next two chapters address the broader topography. They look at whether discussion of the ethical, legal, and policy approach to musculoskeletal tissue and skin transplantation can extract any lessons from the treatment of organs and other tissues. Put another way: what is the context for our consideration of the tissues discussed in this book?

Alta Charo considers the history and legal status of post-mortem markets of tissues, ranging from hair and blood to gametes and cell lines. She concludes that the law's view of the various human body parts as property is both ambivalent and inconsistent. Jeffrey Prottas focuses on the transplantation of solid organs. He compares similarities and differences between organ and tissue transplants, arguing that organ transplantation has benefited from collective action (albeit with considerable government prodding). He recommends a similar course for the tissue transplant industry if it wants to remain "master of its own house."

8

Legal Characterizations
of Human Tissue

R. ALTA CHARO

> Immediately the human corpse rises to a dignity and importance
> in the commercial world which it may not have possessed in its
> lifetime. It is a commercium, a thing of value, a subject of political
> economies, perhaps to be bought, sold, and exchanged, and sub-
> ject to the rules of supply and demand. . . . The whole foundation
> of law and custom is shaken. It becomes a serious question how it
> shall be rebuilt. A new civilization calls loudly for new definitions
> of the rights and duties of society to the dead body. Up to the present
> writing they have not been satisfactorily given.[1]
>
> —Francis Carey, 1885

This rather modern-sounding cry for examining the market for human tissue
actually comes from an article by Francis Carey in the late nineteenth century, when the supply of cadavers for medical education was dwindling.
But whether one dates the transformation to the nineteenth or twentieth
century, it is certain that, as Carey wrote, "[f]or better or worse, we have
irretrievably entered an age that requires examination of our understanding of the legal rights and relationships in the human body and the human
cell."[2] Where once the value of the human body was seen exclusively in
terms of its ability to perform labor or produce offspring or bring sensual
and other personal satisfaction, the potential of the human body as a source
of transferable physical material has led some to see its value in medical[1]
and, if made available for sale,[3] economic terms as well.[4]

  Human tissue is obtained in a variety of ways. Blood may be donated
or sold by living persons for use in transfusion or basic research. Hair may

be sold by living persons for wig makers, or placental tissue collected after childbirth for cosmetics manufacturers. Surgical procedures may result in pathological samples taken both for diagnostic purposes and for long-term storage for clinical uses related to the patient and research uses going far beyond the patient's lifetime. These tissues may also be manipulated to create replicating cell lines that have characteristics resulting both from the underlying tissue and from the laboratory manipulation. Gametes (sperm and eggs) and fetal tissue from abortions and miscarriages can be collected from donors and transferred to others, usually with reimbursement, although technically not with payment that would transform the transaction formally into a sale. While each of these forms of tissue transfer is interesting, this chapter will focus on a selection of human tissues—specifically, corneas, gametes, and cell lines—in order to illustrate some of the legal and market phenomena typically associated with tissue transfers.

Interestingly, there is relatively little law at either the state or the federal level governing tissue transfers, whether with regard to how tissue is obtained, how it is transferred, or how it is manipulated and transplanted. In part this may be due to the low economic value of most human tissue; in the absence of financially significant disputes, fewer cases come to courts for resolution and there is less pressure for legislative bodies to anticipate and regulate future disputes. In part it is due, as well, to the complexities of property law—the primary area of law applicable to the recovery and transfer of human tissue—and its historical inability to reconcile the concerns of the market with the more emotional and spiritual concerns associated with the legal characterization of personal control over one's body, both before and after death. Thus, while there is a growing interest in health- and safety-based regulation of tissue manipulation and transplantation, and a body of rules governing the distribution of whole organs from cadavers, there is only spotty legal coverage of other areas of what might be termed "tissue law."

This chapter provides an overview of existing legal frameworks for several non-organ tissues, whether obtained from living or deceased donors, so that markets in bone, skin, and other tissues can be better situated within the context of the American market for tissue generally. (Organ donation is discussed in Chapter 9.) It begins with a look at the interplay of property law and personal autonomy, and at the origins of the law's rather inconsistent treatment of the corpse, as it is here that one finds the beginnings of still lively discussions about the relationship between ourselves and our bodies that, in turn, inform discussions about the laws and regulations governing markets in human tissue. It then turns to some specific examples of markets in tissue, some in which people know they are releasing tissue for the use of others, and some in which that knowledge may be absent.

Property and Personal Autonomy

Depending on which basis is chosen to explain notions of personal autonomy, the removal of cadaver tissue without consent—a frequent proposal in the area of "presumed consent" laws to foster greater availability of transplantable organs and tissue—may or may not violate notions of personal autonomy that run deep in the American legal system.

The value of the body is intimately linked to the question of personal autonomy. Such autonomy can be achieved through many legal regimes. In one, autonomy is premised on the notion that one's body is one's personal property, and that uninvited removal of tissue is a form of theft or trespass. In another, the body is not "property," but personal autonomy is premised on liberty interests of the person within, and uninvited removal of tissue is a form of injury and a deprivation of liberty. The question of personal control over one's body is highlighted throughout civil and criminal law. An unwanted touching—whether by a criminal attacker or by a doctor who exceeds the scope of consent to surgery—is a battery. Bodily integrity is a highly protected legal and cultural value in the United States, and informed, uncoerced consent is necessary before any bodily invasion. This conclusion can be reached whether or not one views the body as a form of personal property.

But while it is clear that a living, competent person's body parts generally cannot be removed without his or her consent, the law of bodily integrity is less clear after someone has died. Here, the question of whether the body is property becomes pertinent, as the liberty interests that support an alternative theory of personal autonomy are usually considered to have died with the person. By characterizing the body as property, personal control over the removal of tissues can continue even after one's death, by virtue of testamentary wishes in a will or ownership interests in heirs and next of kin. Thus, courts and legislatures have struggled with the question of decision-making authority for research and clinical uses of organs and tissue. In general, the trend is to recognize that the source of the tissue has decision-making authority—even over interventions that will occur after death, or after the tissue has been removed—but at the same time to eschew a clear jurisprudence of "the body as a form of property." The result is legal confusion in the market (and quasi-market) for human tissue.

Furthermore, the issue of control is distinct from the issue of commercialization. Thus, in most cases, the donor of a cadaver organ for transplantation cannot be paid for the organ,[5] but the living donor of certain types of tissue (blood, sperm, eggs, genes) may be compensated. And doctors or researchers who claim intellectual property rights in altered versions of other people's cell lines or genes can earn millions.[6]

Historical Origins of the Legal Status of Corpses

The earliest Anglo-Saxon cases to consider ownership of human tissue, specifically corpses, were decided almost 1000 years ago by special ecclesiastical courts in England that were given complete jurisdiction over all matters concerning burials and the disposition of corpses.[7] With few exceptions, control of dead bodies remained within the exclusive jurisdiction of the church courts until the nineteenth century, when the growth of medical schools and their need for cadavers for dissection created a challenge to the ecclesiastical dominion over bodies.[8]

In the earliest recorded treatise on the subject of property rights in the human body, Lord Edward Coke wrote: "the buriall [sic] of the cadaver (that is caro data vermibus) is nullius in bonis [the goods of no one] and belongs to ecclesiastical cognizance,"[9] a statement that became the foundation for the Anglo-American law that human body parts cannot be property.[10]

In colonial America, the absence of ecclesiastical courts resulted in civil jurisdiction over bodies and the application of common-law principles. There were no commercial rights in cadavers, no rights for a decedent to direct the manner of burial, and no burial rights enforceable by the next of kin. The absence of property rights led to the other rules, as common-law courts were more focused on commercial disputes than on sentimental concerns.

During the 1800s, however, common-law doctrine was increasingly viewed as incapable of managing the real emotional distress associated with the mismanagement of bodies, and courts began assigning to the next of kin an enforceable right to possession of a body for burial. To preserve the continuity of common-law principles, this right was sometimes characterized as a "property right."[7] This right became so well established that in 1891, a court suggested that the "fact that a person has exclusive rights over a body for the purposes of burial leads necessarily to the conclusion that it is his property in the broadest and most general sense of the term."[11]

Judicial references to property rights in corpses were misleading, however.[12] While common-law property rights generally include the right to possess and use, to transfer by sale or gift, and to exclude others from possession,[13] few of these rights were applied to bodies: the theft of a cadaver was not larceny, the sale of a cadaver was not a common-law crime, the heirs had no right to repossess a body wrongfully taken from them, and a cadaver could not be the subject of a lien. Recognizing the limited applicability of property law to corpses, twentieth-century American courts retreated from the broad pronouncement of "bodies as property" and began referring to more limited "quasi-property rights" vested in the next of kin and arising out of their legal duty to bury the dead. These rights include the right to possession and custody of the body for burial, the right to have it remain in its final resting place, and the right to recover damages for any outrage, indignity, or injury to the body of the deceased.[14]

The family's interest in the dead body was subject to various interests of the state government, including concern for the public sensibility, promotion of public health, identifying cases of murder, and protecting the economic interests of undertakers and insurers. Quasi-property analysis became the prevailing rule in both the United States and England during the early twentieth century and continues to be applied to disputes over funeral arrangements.[15]

In the 1930s, American jurists and legal scholars began questioning the applicability of property law concepts to cases involving wrongful conduct toward corpses. Gradually, the newly developing tort law framework of intentional infliction of emotional distress (also called *outrageous conduct*) was viewed as a more appealing theoretical basis for a legal claim against anyone who wrongfully removes, mutilates, or operates on the body of a dead person, or who prevents its proper interment or cremation.[16] The cause of action is a personal right of the survivor rather than a right of the decedent or his estate, since the courts are not primarily concerned with the extent of the physical mishandling or injury to the body per se, but rather with the effect of such improper activities on the emotions of the surviving kin.

Even these rights, however, are tempered by the public interest. In American jurisdictions, a person may dictate the disposal of her or his remains through a will, and if she fails to do so, the decedent's family may exercise the power.[17] This power, however, is subject to limitation by rights of coroners and medical examiners. If the state interest is compelling enough, the relatives of the decedent may lose any quasi-property right.[18] Courts have shown recognition of quasi-property rights by allowing damages for interference with the corpse or by awarding damages for the infliction of emotional distress.[19] On the other hand, they discussed and rejected conversion claims (a tort concerning the unauthorized taking of someone else's property)[20] with respect to corpses,[21] in part because the partial remains of a human body have no inherent value.

The Law of Cadaveric Tissue Donation

In the mid-twentieth century, scientific advances led to an increasing need for transplantable tissue. From 1947 until 1968, forty states enacted statutes permitting anatomical donations from cadavers for transplantation or scientific research.[8] Variations among the statutes led to the formation of a special committee of the Commissioners on Uniform State Laws to draft a uniform donation statute. The result of this effort is the Uniform Anatomical Gift Act (UAGA), which has been adopted throughout the 50 states and the District of Columbia.[22]

The UAGA permits any competent adult to make a gift—to take effect upon death—of all or any part of his or her body for purposes such as medical education, research, and transplantation. Donations for research purposes may only be made to hospitals, physicians, medical and dental schools, and tissue banks. Post-mortem donations of human tissues and cells to noncommercial biomedical researchers are therefore permitted, although transfers from noncommercial researchers to commercial researchers are not addressed by the model law.[23] It has been argued that the UAGA recognizes rights in the human body that may be classified as property rights, but the UAGA does not discuss inter vivos ("during life") gifts, nor does it say anything about the sale of organs or other body parts. The chairman of the committee that drafted the UAGA has written that it was intended neither to encourage nor to prohibit sales.[24]

In 1984, Congress enacted the National Organ Transplant Act (NOTA; Public Law 98-507). NOTA prohibits the sale of a human kidney, liver, heart, lung, pancreas, bone marrow, cornea, eye, bone, and skin. Although the act makes it a felony to purchase specified human organs for transplantation, reasonable payments for a living donor's expenses (e.g., travel, housing, and lost wages) are permitted.[25] But despite this prohibition, there is a quasi-market in organs by virtue of reimbursement practices, as exemplified by corneal transplants.

Presumed-Consent Statutes and Corneal Transplantation

Corneal transplants have been done since 1905, and the Eye Bank Association of America estimates that 45,000 people around the world need such transplants each year.[26] The EBAA has 110 member eye banks operating in over 100 locations in 43 states, the District of Columbia, Puerto Rico, Canada, Europe, the Middle East, and Australia.

Corneas are considered "organs" under NOTA and many state statutes. Many corneas are acquired by ordinary, voluntary donation practices, such as prior authorization from the deceased or donation by next of kin. There is, however, an additional, lesser-known process for gathering corneas for transplantation: Statutes in approximately twenty states permit a coroner to remove the corneas of a cadaver on which an autopsy is performed if there is no known objection from surviving relatives.[27] Commonly referred to as "presumed-consent" laws, these statutes were enacted in the 1960s, 1970s, and 1980s in order to ward off shortages.[28]

Procuring cornea tissue under presumed-consent laws has resulted in several challenges to the constitutionality of state laws that would remove dispositional control over corneas from the next of kin. In a number of cases, the state courts found first, that the laws were valid under the state constitutions and second, that there was no property interest in the deceased person's body. Several courts held that the next of kin of the deceased has *no* property right in the dead body.[29] One of these courts also rejected the argument that presumed-consent statutes invade a fundamental privacy right in a person's body. The court held that a right of privacy deals with the right to make decisions about one's own body and that that right dies with the person.[30] At the same time, however, these courts have acknowledged a quasi-property right in the surviving relatives of the decedent to possession of the body for purposes of burial. Two more-recent cases in the federal courts have suggested, on the other hand, that the next of kin may have a stronger property interest in the dead body of a relative than these state cases would suggest, and that their dispositional authority might go beyond mere control over burial; the cases, however, do not develop this point enough to make it possible to generalize to other tissues or other forms of more purely voluntary donation.[31] In 2002, the influential Ninth Circuit Federal Court of Appeals determined that if a state enacts statutes that appear to endorse the notion that kin have property rights in the body of deceased relatives, then it may not remove that tissue (in that case, corneas) without adequate notice to kin of their right to refuse donation.[32]

According to Professor Julia Mahoney of the University of Virginia:

> The ability of coroners to harvest the corneas of corpses entrusted to them creates opportunities for market transactions, as coroners' offices sell the retrieved corneas to tissue "banks," [*who*] serve an intermediary function, in turn reselling usable eyes to corneal transplant programs. Late in 1997, press reports documenting a series of such exchanges appeared in the *Los Angeles Times*. From 1992 to 1997, reported the *Times*, the Los Angeles County coroner's office delivered corneas to the Doheny Eye and Tissue Transplant Bank in exchange for total payments of over $1,000,000. Doheny paid the coroner's office $215 to $335 per cornea, then resold the corneas for significantly more. Eye banks generally pay money to obtain corneas, whether obtained from morgues, hospitals, or otherwise, and in turn receive money from corneal programs. Corneal transplant programs in turn sell transplant services—which, of course, include a cornea as part of the deal—to patients.[27]

The Law of Gamete Sales

An example of another large-scale market for human tissue is the area of reproductive medicine, where sperm and ova are routinely obtained from donors whose reimbursements for the service of providing gametes strongly resemble a payment for the sale of their gametes. Gametes are retrieved from thousands of Americans every year for use in assisted reproduction. In many cases, the gametes are transferred to someone other than the gamete-provider's partner, a phenomenon commonly referred to as egg or sperm "donation," even where the donors are reimbursed for the gametes. The Centers for Disease Control, for example, estimate that donor eggs were used in approximately 10% of all assisted reproduction technology (ART) cycles carried out in 1998, or 7756 cycles.[33] A 1987 study by the Congressional Office of Technology Assessment estimated the frequency of sperm donation as considerably higher.[34]

Sperm and egg donors are sought by advertisement, sometimes as low-key as a flyer stuck on a billboard in a medical school, and other times as noticeable as an advertisement in a major national newspaper. Ron's Angels website bills itself as "the most visited egg and sperm site in the world."[35] Whether or not that is true, the Internet site offering to auction sperm and ova from physically attractive people has generated much greater public awareness of the market for human gametes.

Unlike citizens of most other developed countries, Americans can buy and sell gametes, although the transactions are sometimes labeled as something other than a "sale"—for example, where provision of a semen sample is rewarded with a cash payment for "services" as opposed to "a product." Similarly, recipients will pay for a fertility service that includes the provision of the necessary gametes, thus avoiding the need to consider the transaction strictly as a purchase of gametes. Indeed, the American Society of Reproductive Medicine condemned the Ron's Angels site in these terms:

> The ASRM Ethics Committee states that reasonable compensation is justified for the time and trouble of both sperm and egg donors. Compensation should not vary based on attributes that a child may have. The "Ron's Angels" website is essentially a donor egg "auction" to sell human eggs to the highest bidder in the hopes of providing potential parents with more attractive—and therefore desirable—children. We believe that the "Ron's Angels" website violates the ethical principles outlined by the Committee, promotes unrealistic expectations to potential parents, commercializes what is otherwise a voluntary donation process, offers undue enticement to potential donors, and has great potential to exploit highly vulnerable people.[36]

The amount offered to reimburse gamete donors has varied over the years. At the time of the 1987 congressional survey, men who met selection criteria (for health, absence of transmissible disease, freedom from family history of significant heritable disorders, and minimum height and physical fitness) appeared to receive between $30 and $50 for each semen sample provided, while egg donors (who must undergo a more arduous, unpleasant, and risky retrieval) would receive up to several thousand dollars. In 1998, however, an announcement by a New Jersey fertility clinic of plans to double the compensation offered to egg donors from $2,500 to $5,000 demonstrated that prices for egg donation were rising[37] and generated extensive press coverage and commentary. In the words of the *New York Times*, accounts of the price increase "put a spotlight on what is perhaps the touchiest issue in the egg donation process: are the eggs a gift or a free-market commodity?" In March 1999, the price offered for usable ova increased by an order of magnitude when an advertisement placed in the campus newspapers of several Ivy League schools offered a $50,000 "financial incentive" to an "Intelligent, Athletic Egg Donor."[38]

But gametes can also be retrieved from the dead, and a few instances of requests for sperm retrieval by widows, fianceés, girlfriends, and parents of men who had recently died has raised the question of who has dispositional authority over gametes. Hecht v. Superior Court[39] concerned the validity of a provision in a man's will that his companion of five years be permitted to use his semen. The appellate courts upheld the provision, treating the semen as if it were the property of the deceased and therefore eligible for disposition by testamentary provision. The status of sperm—and, by extension, other tissue—as the subject of property rights or personal rights also arises in cases where there is no testamentary wish. In the mid-1990s, a newly married young man was killed by the police, and his widow requested his semen even though there was no prior indication of his wishes, in a will or by other means.[40] Physicians acceded to her wishes, as they have on several other occasions to requests from girlfriends and parents.

In her analysis of the Hecht case, philosopher Bonnie Steinbock writes:

> [But] ownership does not settle the question of the scope of control—that is, what the owner may legally do with the stored sperm. Under certain circumstances one can own something one is not permitted to sell. For example, the Queen of England owns a great deal of land and many art treasures that she may not sell. However, since ordinarily one may sell one's property, the identification of sperm as property creates a presumption that it may be donated, stored, sold, and bequeathed.[41]

Whether ownership of something, whether of a pet or a piece of land or one's own tissue, should also convey the right to *sell* the property is not answerable merely by calling the item one's "property." As Stephen Munzer writes, "Too many incidents are lacking to say that persons own their bodies. Restrictions on transfer and the absence of a liberty to consume or destroy, for example, indicate that persons do not own their bodies in the way that they own automobiles or desks."[42]

Looking at the question of personal control over one's body, it is helpful to distinguish between property rights in one's body and personal rights over its treatment. Munzer notes: "Property rights are body rights that protect the choice to transfer. Personal rights are body rights that protect interests other than the choice to transfer. To note that someone has dispositional authority over a body or body part is thus not necessarily to acknowledge a property right; dispositional authority may indicate a personal right instead."[42]

At the same time, the law's tolerance of our decisions to donate or sell some of our body parts does suggest that some property rights clearly exist. Whether these property rights include the right of sale hinges on a more complex analysis of the social ramifications of such sales. Steinbock concludes:

> [*One should distinguish also*] between weak property rights, which involve only a choice to transfer gratuitously, and strong property rights, which involve a choice to transfer for value. Most countries permit the donation of organs, but forbid their sale. In these countries, people have weak property rights in their organs. In countries where the sale of blood and semen is legal, individuals have strong property rights in these bodily fluids.[41]

The question of whether sperm and ova should be available for sale in the United States—that is, should they be the subject of strong property rights on the part of the adult progenitors—is periodically revisited whenever controversies arise over the scale of such sales or the connection of such sales to purportedly eugenic goals, such as the sale of gametes from intellectually or physically "superior" adults.

The Law of Tissues and Cell Lines for Research

Many human tissues are obtained for use in research, commerce, and clinical care. While most of these tissues are obtained with the knowledge of the tissue source (if he or she is alive) or at least the consent of the kin (when the tissue source is dead), the use of tissues for research is characterized by a mix of both witting and unwitting "donation" for use.

But while individuals in the United States may be seen to have a strong property right in their gametes, no such strong property right has been identified in the other tissues of their bodies, even when these tissues are taken while the individual is alive. Human tissue is routinely excised in medical procedures and stored for both clinical and research purposes. Once stored, the tissues are then transferred among laboratories and researchers for work on such things as genetic epidemiology, but there is virtually no tradition of compensating the individuals from whom the tissues came. Indeed, in many cases these individuals have no knowledge that they have unwittingly made a gift of their human biological materials to the research world.

The medical and scientific practice of storing human biological materials is more than 100 years old. Human biological collections, which include DNA banks, tissue banks, and repositories, vary considerably, ranging from large collections formally designated as repositories, to blood or tissue informally stored in a researcher's laboratory freezer. Large collections include archived pathology materials and stored cards containing blood spots from newborn screening tests. Tissue specimens are stored at military facilities, forensic DNA banks, government laboratories, diagnostic pathology and cytology laboratories, university- and hospital-based research laboratories, commercial enterprises, and nonprofit organizations. Archives of human biological materials range in size from fewer than 200 specimens to more than 92 million. Conservatively estimated, at least 282 million specimens (from more than 176 million individual cases) are stored in the United States, and the collections are growing at a rate of over 20 million cases per year.[43]

The most common sources of human biological materials are diagnostic or therapeutic interventions in which diseased tissue is removed or tissue or other material is obtained to determine the nature and extent of a disease. Even after the diagnosis or treatment is complete, a portion of the specimen routinely is retained for future clinical, research, or legal purposes. Specimens also are obtained during autopsies. In addition, volunteers donate organs, blood, or other tissue for transplantation or research, and some donate their bodies after death for transplantation of organs or anatomical studies. Each specimen may be stored in multiple forms, including slides, paraffin blocks, formalin-fixed, tissue culture, or extracted DNA. Repositories provide qualified commercial and noncommercial laboratories with access to specimens for both clinical and research purposes.

In addition to its future clinical use, a specimen of human biological material can be used to study basic biology or disease. It can be examined to determine its normal and abnormal attributes, or it can be manipulated to develop a research tool or a potentially marketable product. Just as a clinician chooses biological materials appropriate to the clinical situation at hand, a researcher's choice of such materials depends on the goals of the research project. The selected tissue may be used only once, or it may be used to generate a renewable source of material, such as by developing a cell line, a cloned gene, or a gene marker. In addition, proteins can be extracted, or DNA isolated, from particular specimens.

There is substantial research value both in unidentified material (i.e., material that is not linked to an individual) and in material linked to an identifiable person and his or her continuing medical record.[44] In the former, the value to the researcher of the human biological material is in the tissue itself and often in the associated clinical information about that individual, without any need to know the identity of the person from whom it came.[45] In such cases, beyond knowing the diagnosis of the individual from whom the specimen was obtained, researchers may not require more detailed medical records, either past or ongoing. Sometimes, however, it is necessary to identify the source of the research sample, because the research value of the material depends on linking findings regarding the biology of the sample with updated information from medical or other records pertaining to its source.[46]

By using the power of new DNA technologies and other molecular techniques, scientists potentially can turn to millions of stored human biological materials as sources of valuable scientific, medical, anthropological, and sociological information.[47] Indeed, these technologies are so powerful—even revolutionary—that they also hold the ability to uncover knowledge about individuals no longer alive. In 1997, for example, scientists at the University of Oxford announced that they had compared DNA extracted from the molar cavity of a 9000-year-old skeleton (known as Cheddar Man) to DNA collected from 20 individuals currently residing in the village of Cheddar; this resulted in the establishment of a genetic tie between the skeleton and a schoolteacher who lived just half a mile from the cave where the bones were found.[48]

Other scientists have used enzyme-linked assays to analyze tissues more than 5000 years old and to track the historic spread of diseases such as malaria and schistosomiasis, obtaining knowledge that can enlighten current efforts to control infectious disease.[49] And in early 1999, a U.S. pathologist and a group of European molecular biologists announced that they had found DNA sequences in the Y chromosome of the descendants of Thomas Jefferson that matched DNA from the descendants of Sally Hemings, a slave at Monticello. The data establish only that Thomas Jefferson was the most likely of several candidates who might be the father of Eston Hemings, Hemings' fifth child, but also have raised a storm of controversy.[50]

In light of these new uses for stored human tissue, academics and government bodies have begun to ask whether the tissues may be used only with permission of the individuals they came from—a position consistent with the notion that these tissues are the property of those individuals—or whether the tissues are a kind of public resource that can be used with impunity, provided that no undue harm befalls these individuals by virtue of a release of tissue information to employers, insurers, or family members who might misuse the information or misunderstand its import. To date, it is this latter position; i.e., that the tissues do not "belong" to the

these individuals; that has guided federal policy, even while, in other respects, professional societies have called for recognizing that individuals
do have an interest in the uses their body tissue is put to.[51] In addition, the
AMA Code of Ethics requires that patients' consent must be obtained before
their tissue is used for commercial purposes.[52]

While federal human-subjects-research regulations and the 1999 report of the National Bioethics Advisory Commission (NBAC) both call for
a practice of seeking consent from individuals in most cases, this practice is
premised on the view that information revealed by studying the tissue ren-
ders these individuals research subjects who ought to have the privilege of
declining participation if they wish. Indeed, where risks are minimal and
obtaining consent is unwieldy, both current regulations and the NBAC's
proposals for revised practices would permit use of stored tissue without
any authorization from the person whose body provided the materials, a
sure sign that the tissues are not the subject of strong property rights. This
is consistent with the leading common-law case on the question of property rights in excised tissue, Moore v. Regents of the University of California,[53] in which the influential California Supreme Court held that a patient
whose cells had been removed and used by his physicians and others to
construct a valuable cell line did not have a cause of action for conversion,
citing the lack of any precedent holding that an individual has a property
interest in excised cells.

Summary

Human tissue is obtained from those who are dead and those who are alive.
At times the tissue is obtained with the full consent of the tissue source or
kin, especially in the context of organs and other tissue for transplantation;
at times, it is taken without their knowledge, let alone their consent, as is
often the case for corneas or tissue taken for research samples. In general,
tissue sales are discouraged, as is evidenced by some of the national laws
in this area, but tissue such as gametes, hair, and blood can be sold, albeit
not always because of a coherent view of these tissues as the property of
the people from whom they came.

This lack of consistency in the treatment of human tissues has made
it difficult to propose models for comprehensive regulation of the human
tissue market. In part this is due to underlying jurisprudential concerns about
treating the body and its parts as property, whether of individuals or of the
state. In part it is due to concerns that important scientific endeavors, such

as research on banked tissue samples, would be slowed or halted should the samples be considered the property of the people they came from, and their use subject to voluntary and informed consent in all cases. And in part it may be due to the low economic value of most human tissue, at least in its raw form, resulting in relatively few conflicts' arising to judicial or legislative attention.

Outside whole-organ donation, the only area in which comprehensive market regulation is appearing concerns the safety of the tissue transfers, especially with regard to transplantation. Here an evolving federal policy has resulted in a new, comprehensive regulatory system that would set federal standards to ensure that transplanted tissue is adequately screened for infectious disease and competently handled and manipulated by the tissue banks that act as intermediaries between those who collect the tissue and those who use it (see Chapter 5).

A more robust form of national control over the market in human tissue, then, will probably depend on resolving political and legal views of the body, so that its treatment—whether as property or as some other thing—will be consistent with underlying political and legal views concerning personal autonomy and the appropriate respect to be paid to our bodies, whether living or dead.

References

1. Francis K. Carey, "The Disposition of the Body After Death," 19 Am. L. Rev. 251 (1885).

2. Moore v. Regents of the Univ. of Cal., 249 Cal. Rptr. 494, 504 (Ct. App. 1988), modified, 793 P.2d 479 (Cal. 1990).

3. For the past few decades, advertisements and schemes have appeared offering the sale of various parts. See, e.g., Michael Finkel, "This Little Kidney Went to Market," *The New York Times Magazine*, May 27, 2001; Russell Scott, *The Body as Property*, Allen Lane Publishing, Camberwell, Victoria, Australia (1981); Jesse Dukeminier, Jr., "Supplying Organs for Transplantation," 68 Mich. L. R. 811, 811 n.1 (1970); Will Bennett, Advert "Offered Sterling 10,000 for a Kidney," *The Independent*, Jan. 10, 1990, at 2; Andy Riga, "Man on Dole Offers Kidney for a Job," *The Gazette* (Montreal), March 12, 1994, at A3; David Adams, "The Organ Theft Scandal," *The Times* of London Nov. 18, 1993, at 18; Tim McGirk, "India's Poor Sell 'Bits of Their Bodies' to the World's Rich," *Independent*, Aug. 13, 1994, at 8; Charles P. Wallace, "For Sale: The Poor's Body Parts," *L.A. Times*, Aug. 27, 1992, at A1.

4. See Russell Scott, *The Body as Property* (1981). Identifying a market value for the sum total of all human tissue is a popular intellectual exercise. In the early 1970s, for example, one student wrote on the possible tax consequences of organ sales,

and relied on the figure of $653.50 as the market value of the constituent minerals in the body, including blood serum. See Note, Tax Consequences of Transfers of Bodily Parts, 73 Colum. L. Rev. 842, 860 (1973) (citing *Chemical and Engineering News*, Nov. 13, 1972, at 60, col. 2). Today that figure would need radical adjustment to account for the potential economic value of gene sequences, rare tissue types, and reproductive material. See Lori Andrews and Dorothy Nelkin, *The Body Bazaar* (2001).

5. The federal National Organ Transplant Act prohibits payment for organs in interstate commerce when those organs are being used for transplantation: 42 U.S.C. § 274e (2000). Under the California Anatomical Gift Act, however, the donor can be paid, but a middleman cannot: Cal. Health & Safety Code § 7155 (2000). Pennsylvania passed a law allowing a modest compensation—up to $3,000 to pay for funeral expenses of organ donors: 20 Pa. Cons. Stat. Ann. § 8622(b)(1).

6. *Genetic Engineering News* publishes an annual list of "molecular millionaires." Prominent among them are researchers who have patented patients' genes. Brian O'Neill, "Biotechnology: Bay State Has Its Share of Molecular Millionaires," *Boston Globe*, April 21, 1999, at D4.

7. Jackson P. *The Law of Cadavers and of Burial and of Burial Places*. New York, Prentice-Hall, 1936.

8. Sideman R, Rosenfield E. "Legal Aspects of Tissue Donations from Cadavers." *Syracuse Law Review*. 1970;21:825.

9. Edward Coke, Institutes of the Laws of England 203 (1644).

10. See Griffith v. Charlotte, C. & A. R.R. 23 Supreme Court 25, 32 (1884). The Court noted that "Coke was understood to say that 'a dead body was the property of no one.' No matter what he did say; this understanding, or misunderstanding, has come down to us as law."

11. Larson v. Chase, 50 N.W. 238 (Minn. 1891).

12. Property is generally viewed, not as a single indivisible concept, but as a bundle of legally protected interests, including the right to possess and use, to transfer by sale or gift, and to exclude others from possession. Although the property concept can be invoked to protect various legal interests, one's right to use property is commonly limited to uses that do not offend public safety or sensibilities. For example, a person may own a car but not have a right to use it without first obtaining a driver's license.

13. Brown Ray, *The Law of Personal Property*, 34th ed. Callaghan and Co., Chicago, 1975. Section 15.

14. 22A American Jurisprudence 2nd, "Dead Bodies" (Lawyer's Cooperative Publishing Company, 2001).

15. William Boulier. "Sperms, Spleens, and Other Valuables: The Need to Recognize Property Rights in Human Body Parts," 23 *Hofstra L*. Rev. 693, 705 (1995); Matthews, "Whose Body? People as Property," 1983 *Current Legal Problems* 193 (1983).

16. American Law Institute, Restatement 2d of the Law of Torts, Section 868.

17. Monique C. Gorsline and Rachelle L.K. Johnson, "The United States System of Organ Donation, The International Solution and The Cadaveric Organ Donor Act: 'And The Winner Is . . .'," 20 *J. Corp. L.* 5, 10 (1995).

18. See State v. Powell, 497 So.2d 1188 (Fla. 1986) (holding that the state interest in providing sight to blind citizens is compelling enough to allow the removal of corneas from a corpse without notice to the next of kin).

19. Michelle Bourianoff Bray, Note, "Personalizing Personality: Toward a Property Right in Human Bodies," 69 *Tex. L. Rev.* 209, 231 (1990).

20. The essence of the tort of conversion is interference with the owner's right of possession or control. The plaintiff in a conversion suit must therefore show a right to possess the property or the suit will fail. Historically, establishing a property interest in a body part has been quite difficult. As discussed earlier, the sale or disposition of cadavers, cadaver tissues, or the cadaver's organs has generally been restricted. In addition to demonstrating a property interest in the tissue, a successful suit for conversion must show that the plaintiff has suffered some injury through interference with the property. One form of injury is a diminution in the availability (and hence the value) of the property to the plaintiff. But "raw" tissues and cells have little pecuniary value in themselves.

21. Shults v. United States, 995 F. Supp. 1270, 1272 (D. Kan. 1998).

22. The UAGA supersedes only the areas of the common law of cadavers that are addressed by the act.

23. Gifts may be made either by will or by a gift document such as a donor card. In the absence of contrary instructions by a decedent, the next of kin may authorize a gift.

24. Stason EB, "The Uniform Anatomical Gift Act," 23 Bus. Law 919 (1968).

25. The statute's organ sale prohibition was based primarily on congressional concern that permitting the sale of human organs might undermine the nation's system of voluntary organ donation. It was also driven by concern that the poor would sell their organs to the rich, to the detriment both of poor people who might feel economically coerced to become organ suppliers and of those who need but cannot afford transplantable organs. It may also reflect congressional distaste for sales of human body parts generally.

26. Available at: http://www.restoresight.org/pubsct.htm.

27. Julia D. Mahoney, "The Market for Human Tissue," 86 *Va. L. Rev.* 163 (March 2000).

28. Alexander Powhida, "Comment: Forced Organ Donation: The Presumed Consent to Organ Donation Laws of the Various States and the United States Constitution," 9 *Alb. L.J. Sci. & Tech.* 349 (1999).

29. Tillman v. Detroit Receiving Hospital, 360 N.W.2d 275 (Mich. Ct. App. 1984); State v. Powell, 497 So.2d 1188 (Fla. 1986); and Georgia Lion Eye Bank, Inc., v. Lavant, 335 S.E.2d 127 (Ga. 1985).

30. Tillman v. Detroit Receiving Hospital, 360 N.W.2d 275 (Mich. Ct. App. 1984).

31. Whaley v. County of Tuscola, 58 F.3d 1111 (6th Cir. 1995); Brotherton v. Cleveland, 923 F.2d 477 (6th Cir. 1991).

32. See Newman v. Sathyavaglswaran, 9th Cir., No. 00–55504, 4/16/02.

33. Available at: http//www.cdc.gov/nccdphp/drh/art98/section3.htm#Section%204%20fig.%2023.

34. Office of Technology Assessment, "Artificial Insemination Practice in the United States: Summary of a 1987 Survey," US GPO, Washington, D.C. 1988.

35. Available at: http//www.ronsangels.com.

36. Available at: http//www.obgyn.net/infertility/articles/asrm_pr.htm.

37. Gina Kolata, "Price of Donor Eggs Soars, Setting Off a Debate on Ethics," *New York Times*, Feb. 25, 1998, at A1; Sharon Lerner, "The Price of Eggs: Undercover in the Infertility Industry," *Ms.*, Mar./Apr. 1996, at 28.

38. Sydney Leavens, "Yale U. Students and Professors React to Egg Donation Ad," *Yale Daily News*, Mar. 4, 1999, available in LEXIS, News Library (describing various reactions among members of the Yale community), as cited in Mahoney, supra.

39. 16 Cal. App. 4th 836 (1993), discussed in John A. Robertson, "Posthumous Reproduction," 69 *Ind. L.J.* 1027, 1036–37 (1994), and reported in David Margolick, "15 Vials of Sperm: The Unusual Bequest of an Even More Unusual Man," *New York Times*, April 29, 1994, at B18.

40. Beth J. Harpaz, *Times Union*, Jan. 20, 1995, at B2.

41. Bonnie Steinbock, "In the absence of a compelling argument against reproduction, individual autonomy should prevail," 6 *Stan. L. & Pol'y Rev* 57 (1995).

42. Steinbock, op. cit, Stephen Munzer, *A Theory of Property*, at p. 56, 1990.

43. National Bioethics Advisory Commission, "Research Involving Human Biological Materials: Ethical and Policy Guidance," US GPO, Washington, D.C., 1999.

44. Human biological materials also may be used for quality control in health care delivery, particularly in diagnostic and pathology laboratories. In addition, these materials are used to identify an individual, such as in paternity testing and in cases of abduction or soldiers missing in action, as well as in other forensic matters for which biological evidence is available for comparison. The advent of technologies that can extract a wide array of information from these materials has generally increased the potential uses in research and otherwise of human biological materials that are unrelated to individual patient care.

45. For example, investigators may be interested in identifying a biological marker in a specific type of tissue, such as cells from individuals with Alzheimer's disease or specific tumors from a cancer patient.

46. Federal Register 82477. The recently published regulations designed to protect the privacy of medical records and other health information do not appear to affect tissue banks. The regulations, published by the U.S. Department of Health and Human Services (DHHS) on December 28, 2000, address not only medical records but also other individually identifiable health information maintained by health plans, health care clearinghouses and certain health care providers. They give consumers access to their health information and control the inappropriate use of that information. They limit non-consensual use and release of private health information and give patients new rights to access their records and to know who else has accessed them. The regulations specifically exempt tissue banks, organ procurement organizations, eye banks and blood banks because they are not considered "health care providers" within the meaning of the regulation.

47. The demonstrated use of these technical capabilities suggests that human tissue and DNA specimens that have been sitting in storage banks for years, or even a century, could be plumbed for new information to reveal something, not only about the individual from whom the tissue was obtained, but possibly about entire groups

of people who share genes, environmental exposures, and ethnic or even geographical characteristics. Clearly, the same is true for materials that may be collected in the future. DNA, whether already stored or yet to be collected, can be used to study genetic variation among people, to establish relationships between genes and characteristics (such as single-gene disorders), or, more generally, to conduct basic studies of the cause and progression of disease, all with the long-term goal of improving human health.

48. DiChristina M., "Stone Age Kin: A Briton's Relationship with a 9000-year-old Skeleton Is Established Through Mitochondrial DNA," *Popular Science*. 1997;250(6):90.

49. Egyptian Mummy Tissue Bank. Available at: http://www.mcc.ac.uk/Museum/General/mummy.htm.

50. Foster EA, Jobling, MA, Taylor PG, et al., "Jefferson Fathered Slave's Last Child," *Nature*. 1998;396:27–28.

51. Ethical opinions, professional guidelines, and court decisions are increasingly recognizing the importance of an individual's control over his or her tissue outside of the body. A workshop of the National Institutes of Health and Centers for Disease Control developed a protocol for the collection of tissue samples that recognizes the personal and religious implications of tissue donation and allows people to control what use is made of the tissue removed from their bodies. Clayton et al. Informed consent for genetic research on stored tissue samples. *JAMA*. 1995;274:1786–1792.

52. AMA Code of Ethics, E-2.08.

53. 793 P. 2d 479 (Cal. 1990).

9

Ethics of Allocation: Lessons from Organ Procurement History

JEFFREY PROTTAS

For those of us who live in it, human tissue has always been valuable. In the last thirty years of the twentieth century, however, this tissue has also become valuable as a medical treatment for illness and injury. The transformation of the human body from sui generis—whether as abused or sacred object—to medical raw material has not always been easy in organizational, legal, or ethical terms.[1] But, in our century, technological change waits on no consideration, and our organizational and legal tools have shown themselves able to adapt. Our ethical tools struggle to keep up with their more robust cousins.

It is now the turn of "tissue banking" (in the narrow sense used in this volume) to develop its structural and ethical solutions to the implacable advances of technology. It is tissue banking's good fortune that it is not the first field to do so. In the related field of organ transplantation, these issues have been addressed with some success over the last 25 years.[2] The purpose of this chapter is to consider if and how the experiences of the organ transplantation system can provide any guidance for the tissue banking system.

The similarities of the two systems are more striking than their differences but it does not follow that they are more important. Organizational as well as technological and ethical factors will influence the applicability of the lessons learned in one sphere for the other. For this reason I will begin with an abbreviated history of how the organ transplantation and procurement system developed into the present system of organ allocation.

Organ Allocation

Until 1985, organ transplantation was, like tissue banking today, largely un-regulated. Each organ procurement organization (OPO) and associated trans-plant services made their own policy and resolved whatever ethical issues arose by themselves. Most of these OPOs served a single transplant hospital and functioned as a supply service to that transplant service. The few alloca-tion or procurement issues that arose were resolved among the immediately affected surgeons. Even when an OPO served a number of transplant hospi-tals—as, for example, in cities like Boston, New York City, Dallas, and Los Angles—clinical and allocation issues were resolved locally and privately.

Few of the issues that had to be addressed were formulated in ethical terms. The most pressing issue was organ supply. Shortages were then, as now, chronic. OPOs were seen almost wholly as a sort of medical supply service to provide the material for transplantation. Relationships with donor families were understood to have an ethical component, but these were of sorts familiar to medical institutions—informed consent, sensitivity to grief, and so forth. Only the new definition of death as determinable by brain function tests—called, most unfortunately, "brain death"—broke new ground. But even here the organ transplant system understood this to be a clinical matter, not a social or ethical one.

Issues of organ allocation were also defined in clinical terms. Allocation schemes were debated, but in terms of the clinical outcomes alone. The superior allocation model was one that insured that organs went to patients likely to have longer graft survival rates. Issues of access, equity, or statistical uncertainty rarely intruded into the debates among clinicians. For the mi-nority of organs that were shared across OPO lines, rules were resolved by agreement among transplant services. Interorganizational sharing was man-aged by professional associations and informal understandings.[3]

This proved to be such a stable arrangement that it lasted with little alteration for well over a decade. By the early 1980s, however, a number of forces combined to threaten this informal, self-directed system of organ allocation. One factor was success. Over the prior decade, organ trans-plantation and procurement had prospered. The number of donors grew steadily, the success rates of the procedures improved markedly, and pub-lic awareness increased apace—indeed, more than apace. Demand for transplants grew much faster than supply.

Increased visibility meant an increase in the numbers and kinds of interests that wanted input into the process. The media raised issues of the

fairness of allocation practices and asked for justifications of regional variations in what was, in effect, a Federally funded system. (At this time—in
the early 1980s—95% of all organ transplants were of kidneys and all of
them were paid for via the End-Stage Renal Disease Program, a sub-section
of Medicare.) The media and the public found differences in waiting times
among different hospitals hard to understand and found assertions that
only clinical criteria were used in deciding who should be transplanted
to be unpersuasive. Members of Congress began to take a skeptical
interest.

The entrepreneurial spirit of America made an additional contribution to skepticism. As organ shortages become more visible—the number
awaiting a transplant grew far more rapidly than the number of donated
organs—organizations emerged that offered to obtain organs and transplants for those able to pay. These efforts never had very much reality,
but their existence helped spur the decision to address issues of organ
procurement and allocation explicitly and in a consistent, publicly acceptable manner.

The prestige of the medical profession and the highly esoteric nature of
the issues might still have kept outside involvement to a minimum if the transplant community had presented a united front. They could not, however.
Several important disputes divided them. As the number of transplant centers and the number of transplants increased, the management of organ allocation among centers became more difficult and more important.

The allocation rules of one OPO now affected other OPOs. Some
transplant programs insisted on good HLA (human leukocyte antigens)
matching, and others felt this less important. There were differences regarding acceptable cold ischemic time (the time after which organs are
removed and put on ice when there is no blood circulating), post-removal
treatment of organs, and other practices. Different practices put some hospitals at a permanent disadvantage in accessing transplantable organs. If a
center set high matching standards, it would procure many organs it did
not wish to use locally, so it would export them to other centers. If all
hospitals used the same standards, there would be no net effect; everyone
would export more organs out of their area, a larger percentage of transplants would be done with organs obtained in other regions, but the total
number of transplants in any given region would not be much affected.
But if some hospitals rarely exported organs and continued to import them,
the exporting centers would always be sending away more organs than they
received. Interdependency increased pressure for fair play, or at least consistent rules.

Technology also played a role. Innovation in immunosuppression and surgical techniques made nonrenal transplantation a clinically sound activity. But for nonrenal transplant to grow, it needed both insurance funding and a regular supply of organs. The first seemed to require authoritative approval of the innovations; the second, changes in the procurement system and shared rules for organ allocation.

Calls for reform in the organ transplant system therefore found an echo within the professional communities. Too few interests were prepared to defend the status quo, so the federal government stepped in. In 1984 Congress passed the National Organ Transplant Act, which effectively banned the procurement of human organs by for-profit organizations. It also authorized a widely used mechanism for managing (as well as slowing and limiting) change—the "blue ribbon" task force.[4]

National Organ Transplantation Task Force

In 1985, the federal government formed that Task Force on Organ Transplantation. They did so partly in response to congressional pressure, which, in its turn, reflected important segments of the organ transplant community's desire to address the issues discussed above. In general, the transplant community led and embraced the task force as a way of putting its house in order and insuring that the technological changes in immunosuppression and nonrenal transplantation would be facilitated by public policy—and as a way of insuring that it remained in control of the systems designed to obtain and distribute transplantable organs.

The most concrete outcomes of the task force fulfilled the professional community's goals. The cost of new immunosuppressive drugs would be paid for by public money for renal transplantation. Nonrenal transplants were considered clinical, not experimental, procedures. A national organization to oversee the procurement and allocation was set up (the Organ Procurement and Transplantation Network—OPTN) at government expense, and its direction was placed firmly in the hands of the professional community. There were extensive public investments in data collection and recordkeeping.[5]

Institutionally, the transplant community capitalized on the task force's report primarily by taking control of the OPTN. The tasks of the OPTN were of great importance to the transplantation system. It was charged with setting organ-sharing policy and with gathering data to track both organ procurement and allocation. In addition, it would be given a contract to track transplant outcomes at the hospital level. Finally, it could set standards for transplant service participation in the OPTN. As OPTN participation was a requirement for receiving Medicare payment for transplants, those rules were effectively certification rules for all transplant services. These would all be the responsibility of the Secretary of Health and Human Services, and she would discharge that responsibility via a contract with an outside agency to be known as the OPTN. The transplant community formed a group—the United Network for Organ Sharing (UNOS)—primarily to obtain the OPTN contract.

UNOS itself grew out of a much more limited regional cooperative organization. Southeastern Organ Procurement Foundation (SEOPF) was a regional group that worked to encourage organ sharing among its members. It focused on insuring better placement of organs by sharing tissue typing information among its members. While it was limited in its membership and goals, it did provide both a model of cooperation and an institutional basis for the formulation of UNOS, and allowed the professional transplant community to bid on, and win, the OPTN contract. This ensured that the OPTN would be structured very much along the lines of a professional association, with policymaking dominated by transplant surgeons and programs and with a high degree of deference to local autonomy. Thus, while public involvement in decisionmaking was greatly expanded, it only moderated, rather than superseded, the independence of the professional transplantation system.

In these ways the task force's outcomes were just what the transplantation community hoped. In some ways, however, the results were rather more than was hoped for. The task force was a public body, it held most of its debates in public, was open to input from all segments of the interested public, and had some members not involved in the medical aspects of transplantation. As such, it represented what is sometimes referred to as a "socialization of conflict";[6] that is, a broadening of constituencies involved in an issue and a shift in the terms of debate. Questions of equity that had previously been largely issues of fairness among transplant hospitals become also questions of fair access to transplants among individuals. Racial and class disparities were discussed. Appropriate national rules regarding the export of organs or the transplantation of foreign nationals became an issue. A new basic principle was formulated: that the transplant community acted as a public steward for donated organs and was responsible for their use to the public through public organizations. In the short run, professional dominance was assured, but the foundation was laid for outside intervention in the rules of organ procurement and distribution.[7]

Post–Task Force Developments

This process of "socialization" was continued in the succeeding few years with the increasingly interventionist role of the Secretary of Health and Human Services in organ allocation policies. Two factors have played a role, the first allowing and the second encouraging the Secretary to intervene. Because the OPTN is funded by public money and its rules affect an institution's Medicare eligibility, it acts under color of law. In effect, it acts as an arm of the Medicare system, which is under the jurisdiction of HHS. This has always given HHS the legal right to set many transplant policies, but only recently has it shown any willingness to do so.

Ethical considerations have provided the impetus for these policies (although institutional rivalries among transplant centers have also contributed). Whether the Secretary's intervention is wise or not, it has been based on the principle that organ allocation ought to be decided solely on the basis of patient characteristics—excluding institutional concerns and geographical location. Much of the transplant community has resisted this approach because it appears to endanger the viability of smaller transplant programs, especially nonrenal programs, and because of a presumed negative impact on donations. Nevertheless, HHS's action represents a natural progression in the evolution of organ allocation policy. The stewardship principle of the task force implies that the use of human organs must reflect public principles about equity and justice. Public institutions have a natural claim on the right to identify those principles.

Public debate on the ethical principles of the use of human organs has been the formal rule at least since the task force report of 1986. What has changed is the working definition of "the public." The Task Force on Organ Transplantation included numbers of non-clinicians, primarily academics. Patients groups testified and debates were conducted using public criteria. Nevertheless, transplant professionals predominated and the "outsiders" were people with long associations with transplant issues. In the last several years, however, the circle of involvement has widened to include state legislatures and some members of Congress as well as the HHS.

Often sound issues are raised; generally they are pursued with the proverbial "more heat than light." This reflects the far more diverse perspectives coming into play. Public agencies use the language of individual equity and fair access. Their constituencies (at least HHS's) are national and their concerns are with social impacts. UNOS, representing the transplant system, has a locally oriented and institutional constituency. It often focuses on the impact of allocation policy on transplant programs. The traditional tension within the organ transplantation system generated by the fact that transplant services are directly affected by rules for allocating organs to individual patients has become somewhat externalized. Unfortunately, the need to balance these demands is easily forgotten and seems to have been forgotten in the last round of debate.

The very public nature of these disputes between UNOS and the Secretary in the later half of the Clinton administration partially reflected the failure of the organ transplant community to effectively incorporate the broad social responsibility implied by the stewardship principle. In its concern for legitimate, but parochial, disputes, it had lost touch with the need to address broader ethical issues in organ use. Its resolutions may have been generally acceptable; its explanations and terms of debate were certainly not. At the same time, the level of abstraction of the debate can easily go too far. Organs are allocated to patients through transplant programs, and the impact of the rules on the ability of those programs to "deliver" the transplant cannot be ignored. An adversarial form of debate is an indulgence.

Organ Transplant History as a Model

Organ transplantation has struggled with two basic social challenges throughout its history. The first relates to organ supply. Technological advances have improved the desirability of a transplant as a medical treatment; other technological advances have expanded the kinds of transplants that can be done. As knowledge of these advances has spread through the medical profession and the general public, the growth in the demand for organs has exploded.[8] This follows a well-known pattern in the medical field. But, the supply of transplantable organs did not—could not—grow at the same rate. Shortages became more acute and there was a (slow) acceptance that they would be permanent. Innovation and success has therefore focused public attention on organ use.

When demand exceeds supply, choices must be made among competing demands. In transplantation, that means *who* shall receive priority over whom. Because organs are obtained as gifts in the context of public action, the use of market forces to direct allocation was not permissible. The first impulse has been to seek a professional solution to substitute for the market solution. Medical efficacy seemed both "fair" and professionally comfortable. It left the judgements in medical hands and allowed decentralized decisions within broad guidelines. This allowed individual clinicians to exercise their own judgements so long as they did not offend professional norms. This assured professional peace while protecting professional dominance.[9]

At the same time, organ transplant experience has shown that medical efficacy only narrows the problem; it does not eliminate it. In almost all instances a large number of potential patients are, to the best of anyone's clinical knowledge, equally likely to benefit from a transplant. To select among them, other criteria must be employed. Much of the debate in the organ transplantation field therefore revolves around criteria on which allocation choices should be made, and who shall be allowed to select those criteria.

Who shall decide and by what rules are two sides of the same coin. Underlying the allocation debate in organ transplantation is the tension between institutional and professional interests and the "public interest" as understood by outside actors. The ultimate beneficiary of a transplant is a patient, but the immediate recipient of the gift is a hospital and a surgeon. Without organs, hospitals cannot operate a transplant service. While transplantation is a large-scale activity in very few hospitals, transplantation services serve other important functions. They attach prestigious doctors to the hospital, they allow training programs, and they add to the hospital's prestige.

Surgeons depend on the gift to ply their trade. Like hospitals, transplantation is a core activity for only a few surgeons, but it is professionally satisfying and prestigious. Moreover, physicians' responsibilities are to their patients, and they therefore favor policies that allow them to serve their patients: the broader social implications of the policies are secondary.

But in the history of organ transplantation these institutional and professional concerns often generated disagreement. Competing allocation rules had differential effects on different kinds of transplant programs—large programs versus small, urban versus suburban versus rural, public hospitals versus private, predominately white hospitals versus those serving minorities. These differences opened the way for other voices to be heard.

"Public interests" not embedded in the transplant community came to play an increasingly large role in allocation debates as the transplant community failed to resolve its differences or did so in ways unacceptable to important outside constituents. As a result, organ allocation rules become more subject to outside scrutiny and finally to rulemaking by government. Whatever the substantive validity of alternative rules, there was a significant loss of control by the organ transplantation community.

Differences

Mao said, "History is a comb nature gives us when we are bald." An un-compromising statement about the limits of learning from the experiences of others, but a warning that ought not be entirely ignored. The organ trans-plantation system differs from the tissue banking system in important ways, both technical and organizational.

Technically the central difference is processing. Human organs are transplanted essentially unaltered from donor to recipient. There are only a few different kinds of organs that can be transplanted, and once procured, the only issue that the organ allocation system must deal with is selecting among a fixed, preexisting pool of recipients. The criteria for choice may be complex and have impacts on institutions and professionals in the sys-tem, but the choice itself is a single event that occurs but once and always at the same point in the process.

The situation in tissue banking is very different. As has been described in earlier chapters, to be of use, tissue must be transformed. This is particu-larly true of bone, which represents about 85% of all tissue transplanted. Most bone is wholly transformed prior to use: it can be processed into paste, powder, or chips in myriad configurations and targeted to a great many different uses. Decisions regarding the differentiation of the "product" can begin as early as the decision about which bone to take, and continue with decisions about which processor to use and what processing to employ.

A large part of tissue banking costs is for tissue processing; for a 1995 report we prepared for the Food and Drug Administration, we found it to be almost 20% of total costs, and as processing has become more complex that number may have increased.[10] Nor is tissue processing a simple, static issue. Technical innovation has been very rapid in this area. Not only are there competing ways of processing the same products, but there is con-stant innovation in the development of new final products, new uses for processed tissue, and so on.

In tissue banking, therefore, the allocation choice is not only among patients receiving the tissue but must be made regarding what tissue will actually be "manufactured," by whom, aimed at what patent population or need, and under what terms. As tissue can be used for everything from saving the lives of burn victims, to saving limbs to making lips pouty, the choices faced are far more complex than those facing the organ transplanta-tion system.

Organizationally the tissue banking world is also quite different. Con-flict within the organ transplantation community over allocation rules was partially responsible for the effective involvement of outside decisionmakers. This internal conflict reflected a number of considerations, including professional differences on clinical matters. But the institutional interests of key players played a major, perhaps *the* major, role. Allocation rules immediately affected every hospital and surgeon in the field. Moreover, the procurement and allocation system is largely under the control of the same transplant doctors and centers. Transplant hospitals and surgeons run the organ allocation system and dominate the boards of most organ procurement organizations. Therefore, allocation practices are of essential and immediate importance to them and largely within their control. This is not the case in tissue banking.

The users of tissue are far more dispersed than the users of organs. Tens of thousands of dentists and surgeons use tissue; thousands of hospitals—virtually all of the acute care hospitals in the country—use tissue each year. There is no general shortage of tissue—some tissue is in short supply, but many kinds can be obtained as a routine component of surgery. Clinicians using tissue do not dominate tissue bank boards, especially when those banks are part of OPOs. There, the pressing institutional need to control allocation does not exist. Indeed, in many instances tissue procuring agencies allocate little or no tissue themselves but depend on tissue processors to do so.

In tissue banking, therefore, the nature and behavior of tissue processors becomes an issue of importance with regard to tissue use. There is no equivalent in organ transplantation. Tissue processing is a highly specialized, technical activity. It requires substantial capital investment and therefore a large amount of tissue to operate economically. Many of the processors are for-profit firms. There is no prohibition against for-profit firms' processing tissue or distributing and selling the final product. Effective tissue processing requires facilities and processes akin to those of pharmaceutical manufacturing. Capital costs are substantial and volume important. The costs of processing are a large part of the costs of tissue and are unregulated. The value of some tissue is high and the profit in "manufacturing" it for some uses is great.

The present result is a situation without precedent in organ transplantation. The complex mix of generally nonprofit tissue procuring banks, for-profit processors, unregulated pricing, and multiple and conflicting final tissue "products" is a major cause of the concerns about ethics in tissue banking and a major impediment to resolving concerns. Consistency is the hobgoblin of little minds, but complexity can be a real demon for policy reform.

The relationship between a tissue bank and the several processors it works with is, in a legal sense, strictly contractual. In another sense the processor acts as the *agent* of the tissue bank. The degree and nature of this "agency" relationship is not universally agreed upon, but the idea of agency in this context brings us back to some of the similarities between the ethical obligations of organ and tissue banking.

Finally there are several macro-organizational differences of importance. The FDA regulates tissue banking to ensure the safety of the transplantable tissue. Most major tissue banks also belong to the American Association of Tissue Banks, a professional association that plays an analogous role. In both cases the focus is on donor screening, quality processing, and record keeping, and the goal is to keep infectious tissue out of circulation.[11] Neither the Association nor the FDA, however, concerns itself with allocation issues or with the ethical conundrums that flow from them. Each local unit in the tissue banking system is free to set its own rules for the sorts of tissue it procures, how it deals with informed consent, and the final use to which its tissue is put. Not only is there no authoritative, system-wide decisionmaking body analogous to the OPTN, there is not even a permanent forum for the community to come together to discuss these matters.

This situation is so extreme that even data about tissue banking are impossible to come by routinely. The number of tissue banks is not exactly known; the number of donors can only be obtained via periodic survey of banks; the same is true of the number of transplants done. No data system exists on an ongoing basis, although the AATB does survey its members annually. No national data exist that allow the tracking of tissue from donor to patients, so no scientific analysis of allocation patterns is possible.

This makes tissue banking vulnerable to anecdotal policymaking. The occasional story of misbehavior cannot be set into a context of a great mass of routinely ethical behavior. Uses of tissue or treatment of donors that seem inappropriate to the public cannot be characterized by the community as aberrant, as no data exist demonstrating the norm. The absence of agreed-upon rules even makes it impossible to demonstrate that the tissue banking community as a whole condemns the reported actions. As tissue transplantation is not nearly so visible to the public or policymakers as organ transplantation, there have been few "scandals" so far. Nevertheless, tissue banking lacks the institutional structures and the data to effectively defend itself when such charges do emerge.

Similarities

There are at least three similarities that connect issues of obligation and allocation in the tissue and organ transplantation world: the overlap in actual donors, the ethical basis for the gift of donation, and the tension between institutional and public interests.[12]

In addition, federal regulations require that all tissue and organ procurement in a given catchment area be coordinated, although the actual pattern of coordination shows variability. This aspect of law reflects, in part, the fact that organ and tissue donors are often the same people. Most organ donors are suitable tissue donors, and many, in fact, become tissue donors. A primary goal of the law is to prevent multiple requests to families or competition among different kinds of organizations seeking the gift. Therefore both the law and the source of tissue and organs bind tissue banks and organ procurement agencies together.[13] Indeed, in a great many places the organ procurement agency and the tissue bank are part of a single institution and the same personnel represent them to hospitals and patient families.

The donor pool for tissue and organs overlaps, but the ethical and legal foundation of donation is identical: altruism. Moreover, this is officially sanctioned altruism. Under law, the "gift of life" must be a gift or it may not occur. This has led to an acceptance in organ procurement of the principle—already discussed—of stewardship. In principle this requires that the use made of the gift is not at the discretion of the receiving agency but must adhere to public expectations of fairness and to the expectations donor families have when they decide to donate. Given the legal, human, and institutional interpenetration of organ and tissue banking, the lessons learned by the former and the expectations applied to it cannot reasonably be ignored.

Finally, there is the similarity that underlies the institutional differences. The transplant system proved vulnerable to outside criticism because it had institutional relationships that suggested interests different from the public interest. Tissue banking shares this vulnerability because human tissue has become so valuable and can be put to such different uses. Some uses for tissue can bring far more income into a tissue bank than others. Even when the bank does not sell tissue to end-users, its relationships with processors can potentially be influenced by differential income across uses and partners. Furthermore, the expectations of the public and donor families hold the procuring tissue banks responsible for final use practices regardless of who distributes their tissue. Just as in organ transplantation, the expectation of equitable use of the gift remains focused on the organization that requested the gift—no matter how many steps there are in the chain between the gift and final use.[14]

What Lessons?

Debates in the tissue banking community are structured to focus on the differences between tissue and organ systems. Tissue allocation debates revolve around the issues of informed consent and the appropriate role of for-profit firms. These are the areas in which tissue allocation is most different from organ allocation.

There is no equivalent of the for-profit/nonprofit debate in organ transplantation. Family consent is, of course, important in both, but the technological differences between tissue and organs make consent issues starkly different. There are very few contingencies or complications regarding the uses an organ can be put to; organs undergo no transformation in function, and allocation rules are explicit, public, and more or less universally applied. Ethics debates in tissue banking therefore focus on just those areas where the differences with organ transplantation are greatest. The similarities between the two worlds therefore seem less salient than the differences.

There is a price to pay for focusing on differences, however. Focusing on informed consent and for-profit versus nonprofit issues minimizes the utility of 25 years of debate regarding organ allocation. Emphasis on similarities may therefore provide a productive viewpoint if not carried too far or applied too rigidly. The starting point of an analysis based on similarities might be found, not at the allocation end of the procurement process, but at the donation end. Organ and tissue are obtained under similar public frameworks and from donor families under similar (sometimes identical) circumstances and conditions. Obligations follow from the donation end of the procurement-use chain and these obligations may bear in similar ways on both OPOs and tissue banks.

Organ procurement agencies have recognized a series of obligations that follow from their functions and public role. OPOs have a privileged position in public policy. As nonprofit organizations they are exempted from taxes in return for public service. Under state and federal law, they are given special rights to ask for and accept human organs as gifts. Many of the activities of these agencies are paid for by public funds, and their importance and legitimacy is attested to by public action in a wide variety of ways—from state income tax check-offs to official organ-donor weeks. OPOs have, as a result, both legal and ethical obligations to the public and to public agencies.

OPOs also have a special obligation to donor families. Asking for a free gift of a part of a deceased relative is universally recognized as forming a responsibility to the giving family. The family has a right to be informed, in general terms, of the disposition of the gift, to receive comfort and recognition from the OPO, to be treated with respect, and to have their gift treated in ways consistent with the high motives that caused it to be given. Finally, OPOs have an essential obligation to recipients. Recipients are, after all, the only reason and justification for their activities, and serving them is the final test of the OPO's success.

Tissue banks share all of these obligations. Those to families and recipients are essentially indistinguishable from the OPO's. Obligations to the public are closely parallel although direct government involvement and funding of tissue banks does not exist. But, in both cases, there are three essential constituencies to which organ and tissue banks are responsible. These responsibilities are not necessarily in conflict, but neither are they perfectly congruent. For example, donor families may want to know how and if their gift has been of use; recipients have a right to privacy. Recipients have an interest in increasing the supply of organs and tissue; the public puts limits on methods of motivating donors and forbids their coercion. Families may wish to limit and direct the use of their gift; the public forbids agencies to act in discriminatory ways.

The obligations owed to these groups contain a variety of elements, both procedural and substantive. The experience of organ transplants over the last decades shows that the central substantive issue concerns the ultimate disposition of the gift. In organ transplantation the allocation debate has taken many forms, but it has slowly resolved itself into a discussion of *who* gets the organ. Intermediate concerns, such as institutional interests, indirect impacts on donation willingness, etc., have increasingly been dealt with in the context of the acceptability of rules for deciding who is next in the queue.

The queue for organs makes allocation debates far simpler than those facing tissue banks. In organ transplantation the ethical quandary is how to order a single queue. The product being queued for is predetermined. (There is only one queue for any patient, as the different queues for different organs contain virtually no overlap of individuals.) For tissue banking, however, the decision must be made about what product will be produced and then how to order access to that product. If skin is procured or processed in one way it is suitable to treat burns and is unavailable for other uses. The same is true of bone and other tissue. The ethical debate therefore also has at least two steps, both to be measured against the acceptable final uses for the tissue.

The first is how to decide what "products" a tissue bank will procure tissue for. Some have suggested that patient need is a starting place and have suggested that tissue could be categorized (1) to save lives, (2) repair or treat non–life threatening conditions, and (3) for cosmetic uses. Definitional problems are daunting, but still, such an approach raises the issue of how to treat the third category. Two alternatives would be to never procure tissue or process tissue for cosmetic use, or to do so only when there is no need for tissue in the other categories. What of tissue that can *only* be used for cosmetic purposes so procuring it does not diminish the availability of other types? Debates on these issues could be conducted with reference to the bank's obligation to its three central constituencies. However resolved, this is only the first step. Once decisions are made about what tissue to produce, there remains the issue that preoccupies organ transplantation—allocating that tissue among potential recipients.

Here the issue is both much harder and easier than that facing organ transplantation. It is easier because there is not a shortage for most kinds of tissue. Therefore, the order of the queue is not of great practical importance in many cases. It is harder because, for the forms of tissue in short supply, no agreed-upon criteria of allocation exist. Indeed, the institutional arrangements in tissue banking almost preclude the development of shared criteria.

For-profits, nonprofits and "agency." If a tissue bank develops criteria for evaluating the final use of the tissue they procure, there remains the problem of implementing those criteria. Most tissue is not processed or distributed directly by the tissue bank procuring it. Much of the debate about the appropriate roles of for-profit firms are about whether tissue banks ought to turn their tissue over to such firms for processing and distribution. Much of this debate has been essentially ideological because there were no outcome criteria to apply as standards for acceptable behavior. The discussions are about who should act as the tissue bank's agent rather than about what is expected of that agent. Once outcome expectations can be defined, operational solutions can be searched out. The issue of the organization of the agent becomes secondary to the behavior of the agent.

The problem then becomes one of information, oversight, and monitoring. As steward for the gift, the tissue bank is, or ought to be, expected to be able to answer final-use questions in any case. It is responsible for the behavior of its agents, and if an agent acts according to its expectations its profit status may matter less. This certainly can extend to issues of cost as well as to those of use. The cost of tissue is effectively an allocation matter, and a tissue bank can legitimately concern itself with it.

Prospects

Two factors changed the way the organ transplant community dealt with allocation issues. On one side the interdependency of the system increased. Transplant centers came to depend directly on others to ensure a flow of organs. Equally important, the system's visibility demonstrated a public or even political interdependency. The behavior of one agency reflected on and affected the reputation of the others. In the early years, however, the community as a whole had no way of controlling individual agencies and little agreement on what behavior was acceptable. The result was the intervention of the federal government: first to impose a system of self-policing, and then, to a degree, a system of outside policing.

Tissue banking may be close to reaching a similar point. Certainly it is in an analogous situation. In fact, its situation may be more perilous. The profit motive and the lack of public consensus about the legitimacy of some uses of tissue expose the entire system to serious attacks. The confusion within the community of how to manage informed consent is as much a symptom of this vulnerability as a cause of it.

The ethical challenges facing tissue banking are also more intellectually difficult than those facing organ transplantation. The multiplicity of uses, the gray areas between cosmetic and therapeutic uses, the general treatment of tissue by clinicians simply as a sort of medical supply, all make the final-use issue complex. Institutionally, of course, the long chain between procurement and use, with its many diverse agencies, adds to the operational problem. Only the relatively good supply of tissue compared to organs provides a bright spot in the picture.

Perhaps the gravest difficulty facing the tissue transplant industry is the absence of any institutional framework in which to resolve these issues. There is no place for the entire community to come together and seek consensus—much less for it to act authoritatively. The experience of organ transplantation indicates that voluntary professional associations find it very hard to play this role. UNOS only came into this role after government intervention, and then only became an authoritative decisionmaker via its

OPTN contract. But the failure of organ transplantation to act on its own might be a lesson tissue banking can learn from. In the long run the public will have to be satisfied that donated tissue is being used in an ethical way everywhere in the nation, every time. If the tissue banking community can act before some scandal mobilizes government action, then it can remain master of its own house. If not, not.

References

1. Titmuss R. *The Gift Relationship*, New York, Vintage Books, 1971.
2. Prottas J. Organ and tissue procurement: medical and organizational aspects. *Encyclopedia of Bioethics*, 1996.
3. Prottas J. The organization of American organ procurement. *The Journal of Health Policy, Politics and Law*, Vol. 14:1, Spring 1989.
4. National Organ Transplant Act, Publication No. 98-507 3 USCC: 301. 1984.
5. Report of the Task on Organ Transplantation, *Organ Transplantation*, U.S. Department of Health and Human Services, April 1986.
6. Schattschneider EE *The Semisovereign People*. New York, Harcourt Brace Jovanovich, 1969.
7. Report of the Task on Organ Transplantation, *Organ Transplantation*, U.S. Department of Health and Human Services, April 1986.
8. See the website of the United Network for Organ Sharing—*www.unos.rog*—for waiting-list information.
9. Prottas, J. "The Politics of Transplantation." In *Organ and Tissue Donation*, Spielman, B. (ed.). Carbondale: Southern Illinois University Press, 1996.
10. Prottas J. "A study of the tissue procurement and distribution systems in the United States." Report to the FDA, October 1995.
11. Office of the Inspector General, Department of Health and Human Services, *Oversight of Tissue Banking*, January 2001. American Association of Tissue Banks, *Standards for Tissue Banking*, Washington, D.C. March 1999.
12. Prottas J. Competition for altruism: bone and organ procurement in the United States. *Milbank Quarterly*. 1992;70(2):229–317.
13. National Organ Transplant Act, Publication No. 98-507 3 USCC: 301. 1984.
14. Office of the Inspector General, Department of Health and Human Services, *Informed Consent in Tissue Donation*, January 2001.

IV

ETHICAL ISSUES

Up to this point, our book has presented an account of the history, structure, economy, technology, clinical applications, and regulation of the tissue industry. It has compared and contrasted the organ and tissue transplantation industries and it has presented the perspective of donor families. The following four chapters deal head-on with the unique ethical problems raised by modern tissue transplantation. In these chapters we see the consequences of a system that tries to embrace altruism and commercialization simultaneously.

Norman Fost tells how one of the nation's most active *organ* transplantation programs created a policy in response to a highly publicized conflict-of-interest problem. Because the problem arose from its tissue banking activities, the University of Wisconsin Hospital Ethics Committee was asked by the university administration to draft a policy on tissue transplantation. This policy, which is discussed by Fost, attempts to deal with two problems: the proper range of tissue use and involvement of for-profit companies. One of the problems the committee confronted was the paucity of data upon which to base their judgements.

Stuart Youngner explores the adequacy of informed consent as the optimum model for managing the ethical problems raised by commercialization. Like Fost, he concludes that informed consent alone is not up to the task. The inevitability of personal and political slants makes discussion of economic issues problematic. Equally problematic are the less-than-ideal conditions under which information must be communicated to grieving families.

In the most philosophical chapter, Courtney Campbell analyzes the nature and the meaning of the gift and the notion of stewardship. Like Fost and Youngner, he concludes that in the "commercialized reality" of tissue transplantation fuller disclosure via informed consent is inadequate to protect the interests of those who donate.

The book concludes with a chapter by the editors that draws together the preceding chapters and offers some recommendations for the future.

10

The Gift and the Market: Cultural Symbolic Perspectives

COURTNEY S. CAMPBELL

Tissue banking in the United States is currently in the midst of an ethical identity crisis. The stage for this crisis was set in the late 1980s, when the tissue banking community underwent a significant change in both philosophy and practice. The immediate catalyst for this ethics crisis was the entrance of for-profit companies in the distribution and marketing of tissue. As Helen Leslie and Scott Bottenfield presciently observed, "many believe that the 'crossing over' of this humanitarian effort into the commercial arena will have a lasting and adverse effect on the efforts of all transplant organizations by establishing a negative image of the transplant community in the public's eye."[1]

This crisis of ethical identity is not only a matter of public image; it unavoidably presents challenges as well to the moral commitments and integrity of the tissue banks and foundations themselves. Despite the fact that some members of the tissue banking community find the concept of and attitude toward human tissue as a "commodity" to be distressing and morally foreign, the language and practices of the community in fact display ingrained patterns of objectification. I will discuss this further later in the chapter.

Public representation of the tissue banking community also seems to presume a (lamentable) intrinsic connection between tissue banking and market systems. Senator Ron Wyden (Democrat, Oregon) has complained that "people are literally being turned into profits" through the process of procuring and distributing tissue.[2] As shown by the metaphors of "industry" and "business" in various media stories, the intimacy of a "community" represented by the discourse of tissue banks themselves has been displaced by depersonalizing language that situates tissue banking squarely within a profitable and ever expanding marketplace of biotechnology and bioengineering. The industrial representation of tissue banking implies a perception that it is a business that runs according to the moral logic of markets; *caveat emptor*, or "buyer beware." In this public understanding, the donations that initiate the tissue recovery process have been displaced by a goal of, as Senator Wyden put it, turning profits.

The crisis of ethical identity for tissue banks can be attributed in part to the different roles or functions they assume in overseeing the retrieval of tissue, its processing, and its distribution. A focus on tissue retrieval tends to highlight the act of donation or the gift of tissue by a donor or tissue source. Thus, a responsible tissue bank should act in accordance with a model of "stewardship of the gift," a perspective that reflects a central assumption of donor families and many tissue bank directors.[3] As I will show in this chapter, a stewardship role for the tissue bank would respect the intent of the original donation, ensure that the technological transformation undergone by the gift does not erode the donative intent, and facilitate a distribution process that embodies both equity and efficiency.

As Julia D. Mahoney argues, however, "requiring the initial link in the distribution chain [*of human tissue*] to be a gift simply postpones commercial activity."[4] Hence, focusing on secondary links such as post-retrieval processing and bioengineering to develop a product for use in treatment procedures, can support an understanding of the tissue as a "commodity." Finally, a focus on tissue distribution can underlie the self-description of tissue banks as a kind of "middleman" between donor and recipient, a metaphor that locates the tissue bank squarely within a market model of matching supply with consumer demand. Thus, the different roles assumed by the tissue bank evoke different and at times conflicting or even compatible ethics. An important moral question is whether elements of donation, gift, and stewardship are retained in the subsequent links of the distributional chain; that is, as the tissue is retrieved, processed, bioengineered, and distributed. I will pursue this question through an analysis of the ethics of the gift, the ethics of stewardship, and the ethics of property.

Gift

As James F. Childress observes, several ethical controversies over the use of human body parts reflect the complexity of emotions, beliefs, sentiments, and practices surrounding the human body.[5] A perspective on the body as a machine or as personal property will engender a different set of communal attitudes and medical practices than will a perception of the body as a temple or an image of the divine. In addition, the plurality of attitudes about the dead body[6-8] can heighten rather than diminish the potential for ethical and professional conflict. But, it is evident from many sources that one prominent way of thinking about organs and tissues retrieved from the dead body is that they represent "gifts" or "donations" from either the decedent who authorized such use in advance or proxy decisionmakers. This altruistic characterization has become formalized through such legal mechanisms as the Uniform Anatomical Gift Act.

Paul Camenisch has developed an insightful interpretation of the ethic of gift in everyday discourse and practice. Gifts create, or in some cases affirm, moral relationships.[9] From the standpoint of the donor or giver, a gift has an instrumental function of providing benefits to the recipient, but also an expressive or symbolic function: in an act of genuine giving, one not only gives a gift but symbolically gives a part of oneself to the recipient. Because the gift involves more than a transfer of a good, but also conveys a self that is, for example, caring, thoughtful, generous, and so forth, the gift communicates an invitation by the donor to the recipient to enter into a moral relationship (or affirms and renews an existing relationship).

The intended recipient can, of course, decline the gift; the recipient is under no moral obligation to accept the proffered benefits or the relationship, even though the giver may interpret this refusal as a rejection of his or her self. Acceptance of the gift, however changes the moral status of both gift and relationship. As Camenisch observes: "the recipient's consent to enter into the gift relation with the donor . . . is rightly presumed to be expressed in the knowing acceptance of the gift."[9] The acceptance of the gift involves a "concurrence of wills" between donor and recipient about the meaning of the gift, the intention for its use, and the relationship of giver and recipient.

While the initiation of a gift relationship is nonobligatory for both parties—that is, the giver is under no moral requirement to give, and the recipient is under no duty of acceptance—once a gift has been accepted, the concurrence of wills has occurred and the relationship has been enacted, and certain kinds of expectations or responsibilities are assumed by both donor and recipient. Here I will focus on the specific responsibilities of the recipient.

Camenisch distinguishes three elements of a recipient's "grateful response." A first element is the *grateful conduct* of the recipient; that is, various actions (expressing thanks, honoring the giver, imitation, a return gift) by which the recipient expresses gratitude to the giver. Grateful conduct seeks to perpetuate and cultivate the gift relationship with the donor.

A second element of grateful response is that of *grateful use* of the gift itself. In contrast to the responsive action embedded in grateful conduct, grateful use is more directly focused on the gift. The concurrence of wills that initiates the gift relationship implies that the recipient's will is to use the gift in a manner consistent with the intent of the donor. This may mean that certain possible uses of the gift are foregone or prohibited, while others are obligatory or mandatory as guided by "the nature of the gift itself and what we can discover of the donor's intention for its use."[9]

Embedded in the two action-oriented elements of conduct and use is a third, attitudinal element, *gratitude*. A feeling or sentiment of gratitude may underlie a world view, such as a religious understanding that sees life as a "gift," or a specific practice irrespective of one's world view, such as that expressed in the language of "gift" and "donation" that permeates organ and tissue transplantation.

Camenisch's analysis of "the paradigmatic case" of gift and response illuminates some moral dimensions of tissue banking, while others require modification and refinement. The features of both grateful conduct and grateful use are implied by the Statement of Ethical Principles of the American Association of Tissue Banks (AATB),[10] which commits the AATB to: value humanity and personal respect in the acceptance of cell and tissue donations; and honor and treat with respect the gifts that have been donated.

These policies are consistent with a report by the Office of the Inspector General, which states that "the foundation of tissue banking" comprises the expectations and altruistic motivations of donor families. These expectations include (*1*) enhancing the lives of others, (*2*) respect for the donor and the family, and (*3*) trust in the tissue banking community.[3] In this framework, the tissue bank is not merely a middleman in a commercial transaction, but having "accepted" a donation, becomes a steward, entrusted to act with integrity in realizing the aims of the donor. Acting as a proxy for the ultimate recipient, the tissue bank assumes one set of responsibilities directed to the donor, such as honor, value, and respect for the donor. A second set of responsibilities involves respect for the gift itself, which in a gift relationship should be guided by considerations of the donor's intent.

There can be far-reaching implications of not respecting the intent of the donor for use of tissue, or not providing the donor full information about possible uses. Leslie and Bottenfield observe that "it is only through the humanitarian actions of donors and donor families—people helping people, the noblest of principles—that tissue transplantation is made possible."[1] The corollary to this reliance on moral nobility is that if the public perception, as articulated previously, is primarily one of people helping businesses make profits, the humanitarian and altruistic impulse tissue transplantation relies on could well be undermined.

In general, tissue banks that neglect the actual and symbolic significance of the human cadaver risk failure in their efforts to generate the supply of tissues for needy patients.[5] In addition, a longstanding concern in organ transplantation is relevant here: public perception of unfairness or inequities in distribution can diminish their interest in and motivation for donation. Thus, the role of tissue bank as responsible steward, and not simply as facilitator of a commercial transaction, can be critical to retaining the ethic of the gift throughout the retrieval, processing, and distribution of tissue for transplantation.

Mediating the Gift

There are at least two problems with direct application of the gift ethic to the context of tissue transplantation. First, the gift relation paradigm presumes a personal relationship between benefactor and beneficiary. Second, as Erika Blacksher observes, "when we sell a gift, it is no longer that. The act of selling erases the act of giving."[11] Given these substantial differences between the paradigm of *gift* and the practice of tissue banking, including commercialization and commodification of donated tissue as well as use of such tissue for cosmetic purposes,[3] one can ask whether it is moral sentiment or public relations that motivates the language of "gift" in the tissue bank community.

Responsible stewardship is especially salient in considering tissue banking, since, unlike the paradigm case of the gift ethic, there is no immediate or direct gift relationship between the tissue source and the ultimate recipient. The tissue bank or foundation is an intermediary institution through which the exchange of the gift from the donor to the recipient occurs. Indeed, society has gone to some length (e.g., anonymity and nondisclosure of donor identity, or imposing constraints on direct donations) to ensure that no direct gift relationship is established between persons. This institutional blocking of a direct gift relationship preempts the "potential tyranny of the human gift" that scholars have voiced concerns about in transplantation settings.[12, 13] Thus, tissue banks become the mediators of a gift relationship that most commonly is enacted between strangers.

To rephrase an observation of Michael Ignatieff, the moral relations that exist between me and my body tissue and the needs of numerous strangers at my door pass through the arteries of blood and tissue banks and organ procurement organizations. Thomas Murray has described impersonal gifts, over which institutions such as tissue banks have stewardly responsibility, as "mystifying" and the "most peculiar" of gifts.[14] The peculiarity resides in the fact that in the standard instances of gift-giving, the moral point of the gift is to invite another into a moral relationship. But in the case of impersonal giving, such as the donation of blood, tissue, or organs, the possibility of a moral relationship is blocked by circumstances and procedures (particularly so when the person is deceased in the case of the latter two instances of bodily gifts). Thus, it can well be asked what the moral point of such a gift would be.

Murray encourages us to think more broadly about moral relations; instead of focusing on dyadic relationships that are presumed in the paradigm of personalized giving and receiving, we also need to consider the kinds of relationships we have with the larger community of human beings. This larger community is sometimes portrayed in post-modernist bioethics[15] as not a community at all, but rather a collection of atomistic individuals whose main moral concern is to avoid harming each other. Moreover, atomistic individualism is reinforced by massive and impersonal bureaucratic systems, typified by the marketplace. In this social context, when we make gifts and donations, such as contributions to a social or political "cause"—for example, reducing world hunger or protecting the environment—we may wonder whether the contribution really does much more than pay administrative overhead and provide us with a tax deduction. In this system, a gift of the body would seem to be a kind of social and economic anomaly.

Rather than being concerned with the effectiveness of a gift in achieving a practical end, Murray focuses on the expressive and symbolic purpose of the impersonal gift. We can make moral sense of the donations of human tissue if we understand them as a way of "promoting solidarity" and "serving essential social values" that otherwise may be ill-served or neglected by commercial and contractual endeavors.[14] The impersonal gift is an invitation into a moral relationship with the community as a whole, a contribution to the common good, which thereby reminds us that our moral relations have a broader circumference than those of kinship or the minimalism of contractual, legal obligations. There are fundamental human goods and needs, such as the relief of suffering, that we should support and serve, even though the coordination or actual servicing of these needs and goods occurs through an intermediary institution like a tissue bank. The gift displays moral purpose as an expression of solidarity and interdependence with a broader community.

The giver entrusts efficient (and grateful use) of the gift to an organization that assumes an intermediary role of responsible steward in administering and distributing the gift.

Impersonal gifts that affirm interdependency are not as alien to social practice as may initially appear. One form of impersonal donation that is increasingly widespread at the start of the twenty-first century is that of recycling household materials, such as plastic or cardboard food containers.[16] Donating these materials for recycling is a gift in that the original possessor could just as easily toss the materials into the garbage bin, as did the preceding generations. Instead, however, the responsible citizen donates the materials to recycling organizations with the knowledge and expertise to use and transform the plastics, paper, or cardboard into beneficial products for the community.

When one participates in recycling programs, one expects no direct benefit to a specific individual, initiates no personalized gift relationship. The impersonal gift instead contributes to a cause that is best served by a larger organization committed to communal benefit. The recycling participant affirms a shared commitment with unknown others, and by "acting locally" on this commitment enters into a gift-based moral relationship with the community. The organization that retrieves and transforms the recyclables into something of value for the community is best able to enact a vision of "thinking globally." In short, something of value is contributed by a person to an organization through whose work the society realizes a greater benefit than if the contributor had retained or discarded the material.

I have developed the recycling analogy[17] here in part because it offers some instructive parallels with impersonal gifts of body tissue. As with all analogies, some caution is appropriate here. While both unneeded body tissue and materials used for recycling may, in one perspective, be viewed as "surplus" or even "waste," and thereby undergo technological transformation to develop a communally beneficial product, subjective meaning may be attributed by the donor to body tissue that is unlikely to occur with conventional recyclables. Body tissue, such as blood, is intimately linked with the donor whose body the tissue is retrieved from, whereas a newspaper or a milk or cardboard container is an object distinct from oneself. What Murray describes as the "impersonal" nature of a donation of body tissue does not, then, stem from the tissue's lack of personal significance to the donor. Rather, the description is a consequence of the absence of a personally identifiable donor–recipient relationship. The donation of body tissue, like the donation of materials for recycling, is given to an abstraction, "the greater good of the community."

Nonetheless (provided consent has been obtained), the retrieval of such tissue should be treated as the retrieval of a gift, because either the decedent or a proxy could just as readily retain the tissue or abandon it. It is the general cause, a cause affirmed by the community as a whole—relieving suffering, enabling needy others to live—that gives motivation and moral point to the gift. The tissue bank or foundation is thus entrusted with stewardship of the gift.

Stewardship

An ethic of stewardship in medicine or medical research is not yet adequately developed, which may reflect a mistaken assumption within medical practice that contemporary practitioners or researchers have not received gifts from past generations, let alone the patients upon whom they carry out their "practice." As May[18] has observed, however, stewardship is closely aligned with a concept of medicine as a covenantal practice, an outlook that is morally distinguishable from medicine as a contract with a commercial and entrepreneurial orientation.

The steward mediates the gift relationship. This can be an all-encompassing responsibility, as suggested in the theologically based conception of stewardship voiced by the Protestant reformer John Calvin: "We are stewards of everything God has conferred on us by which we are able to help our neighbor and are required to render account of our stewardship."[19] Or the stewardship may be much more limited, such as a focus on financial gifts by an eleemosynary institution or bodily gifts by a tissue foundation. But the basic themes expressed by Calvin are relevant to any conception of stewardship: gifts received are to be used to benefit others, and the steward is accountable for the actions undertaken to fulfill the stewardship.

The discourse of stewardship directs attention to the feature of the gift relationship described above as *grateful use*. It provides a moral connection between the gift that has been given and use of the gift in a responsible manner. In so doing, the steward must express respect for both donor and donation.

With respect to the donor, the steward is authorized to use the gift in such a way that it brings benefits to the intended recipient(s). This authorization presumes that mutual trust or a fiduciary relationship between donor and steward is embedded in the larger gift relationship: the donor's expression of trust in the steward is consonant with the steward's virtue of trustworthiness. The donor then relinquishes possession of the gift to the steward, expecting that the steward will act according to moral standards, including fidelity to the donor's intent, in using the gift. This means that the steward is held accountable for faithful and responsible stewardship. If the steward is unable to conform to relevant moral standards—that is, if the steward lacks trustworthiness—the gift should not be given, and the donor should seek another steward. If the steward is unable to comply with the donor's intent (e.g., designated donation), the gift should be refused.

As an intermediary, the steward receives and accepts the gift on behalf of, or as proxy for, the intended recipient. Should there be procedural barriers that prevent the recipient from fulfilling the responsibilities of grateful conduct, grateful use, and gratitude to the donor, as there are with tissue donation, fulfillment of these responsibilities falls to the steward. The steward is thereby entrusted to act to benefit intended recipients rather than promote his or her own personal gain or preferences. Since the steward is a repository of trust for both donor and recipient, it follows that the steward should embody the highest standards of moral character; a perceived failure will bring on accusations of betrayal from donors and recipients.

We can summarize the foregoing in a framework of the elements of responsible stewardship derived from relevant theological and philosophical sources, as well as social practices:

1. Giving: A donor or giver offers a gift that intends to confer benefits for its recipients.
2. Authorization: The donor authorizes the steward to oversee the responsible use of the gift.
3. Trust: The donor entrusts the steward to respect both the gift and the donor's intent.
4. Agency: The donor expects and trusts that the steward will use moral agency and practical wisdom to best fulfill the donative intent.
5. Maximization: The donor invites the steward to use creativity to enhance or improve the value of the gift so that it can confer maximal benefits.
6. Community: The steward directs the disposition of the gift, as well as any improvements or enhancements in its value, to the common good, rather than advancing personal preferences of the steward.
7. Mutual aid: The steward's priority in the disposition of the gift is meeting the fundamental human needs of the community. As articulated in the philosophy of stewardship of John Locke, the responsible steward "tends to the preservation of the life, liberty, health, limb or goods of another."[20]

8. Accountability: The steward is responsible to the donor to give an account of their actions in honoring the donor, respecting the gift, and conferring benefits on the intended recipient(s). The requirement of accountability, or answering for one's actions, encompasses the obligations of gratitude, grateful conduct, and grateful usage.

It follows from this framework that a stewardship may be irresponsible to the extent that the donor is dishonored, the gift disrespected, or parties other than the intended recipients receive benefits from the gift. The context of tissue transplantation raises the prospects of each of these forms of irresponsible stewardship.

Dishonoring the donor. How might the donor be dishonored? One form of dishonor is misidentification. The language and identity of the donor are permeated with ambiguities in organ transplants, and this is surely prevalent in tissue transplants as well. It is important to differentiate between the human or cadaveric source of the tissue and the person who actually makes the decision to donate. This difference, however, is routinely confused by the term *donor*. Childress contends that "it is inappropriate to describe as donors individuals who never had the capacity to decide or never decided to donate."[5] It is similarly erroneous to refer to someone who sells body tissue as a donor, as is commonly done by the term *sperm donor*. In this situation, it is not the capacity to decide, but the motivation and compensation that place the choice outside the donation context. To expand the use of the term *donor* in either of these directions simply makes it morally vacuous.

A second form of dishonoring might involve objectification. The discourse at the initial conference that led to this book revealed surprising and distressing patterns of objectifying the donor. From various presentations, we learned that not only is the "donor" a statistic, but that donors are: *"recovered," "processed," "followed," "maintained," "aborted,"* or *"done."*[21] This phraseology is used as linguistic shorthand for the tissue retrieved from the cadaver with the donor's authorization. Members of the tissue banking community contend they seek continual reminders of the connection between the processed tissue and its human source. But the use of such language objectifies (and perhaps misidentifies) the donor, transforming the donor into a passive, inert entity that cannot express the generosity embedded in the language of *donation*. The objectified donor is *acted upon* by others (tissue retrievers, processors, etc.), not acting altruistically *for* others (recipients). In contrast to the affirmations of respect and value for the person by the AATB,[10] such discourse diminishes the humanity and dignity of the person from whom the tissue is retrieved, suggesting that they are merely, and no more than, an amalgam of extricable tissue.

A third form that dishonoring the donor might assume is neglecting to express grateful conduct or gratitude. In ordinary forms of gift-giving, few things are more destructive of relationships than ingratitude. This is because within a gift relationship, the failure to show gratitude implies not only indifference toward the gift, but also rejection of the giver. A gift that is received but not gratefully acknowledged may also diminish the prospects of future gift-giving. Since tissue transplantation currently relies entirely on gifts and donations of tissue, gratitude and grateful conduct are vital to its ongoing success. The practice of formal and informal activities recognizing and supporting donor families is one illustration of how the institutional intermediary of the gift can manifest gratitude and grateful conduct. Indeed, recent recommendations suggest that processors and distributors provide information to recipients of tissue products that "clearly indicates it is derived from *donated* human tissue."[3]

Moral Stresses: Body Tissue as a Commodity

Can the gift as well as the donor be disrespected? The controversy over this question involves issues of commodification of body tissue and reliance on commercial mechanisms for processing and distribution. The commodification of the initial gift might be seen as a necessary moral compromise in order to efficiently generate enough tissue to meet a burgeoning demand and to allocate technological resources to process the tissue. Significantly, sociologists Renee Fox and Judith Swazey suggest that a parallel transformation occurred with organ transplants in "the commodification of body parts for transplant."[13] They contend that "maximizing and optimizing" language reflects a pervasive trend towards efficiency as the primary value in transplantation, around which various business, advertising, and fund-raising strategies are developed and for which sales forces and information technologies are mobilized to increase the supply of tissues and body parts.[5]

Yet the ethical framework of stewardship we delineated does not preclude such a transformation: the criteria of "maximization" and of "community" require the steward to enhance or add value to the gift so that its benefits can be more widely distributed amongst a larger pool of recipients. Indeed, in the biblical "parable of the talents" (Matthew 25), which provides one kind of theological warrant for stewardship, the steward who hid the gift he received and did not improve on it was soundly rebuked and the talent was taken from him. And it is clear in the case of most gifts of body tissue, such as skin and bone, that the intermediary steward, such as the tissue bank or foundation, must improve or add value to the gift in order for the gift to be at all suitable for a recipient.

Thus, the stewardship framework provides a moral (and background theological) warrant for enhancing the value of the gift as long as two principal provisos are met: (1) the intent of the donor is respected, and (2) the benefits of enhancement are directed towards the larger community, and not claimed solely as proprietary interests by the steward. Both of these provisos can typically be met by certain practices already embedded in tissue banking, such as informed consent. The central question is whether enhancing, maximizing, or adding value to the gift transforms it into a different kind of entity—a commodity whose processing and distribution are governed by the realities of the commercial market.

In many respects, the discourse and practices of tissue banks make it difficult to see how enhancing the gift can be carried out without the gift's being transformed into a commodity as an inevitable part of the process. For example, the storerooms of tissue banks contain "inventory," the "finished product" that is ready for shipping to "customers." Distributors seek to ensure distribution of their inventory prior to its "shelf life" expiration.

Moreover, the commodification and commercial dimensions of the practice seem integral to the "banking" language that attends the storage of various forms of body tissue and body parts. In addition to tissue banks, of course, modern biomedicine has also given rise to blood banks, DNA banks, and sperm banks, among others. While the banking metaphor does refer to repositories for storage and safekeeping, one implication of the metaphor is that we see, and treat, such tissues as economic assets with a particular kind of quantifiable value. Thus, commodification and commercialization can be manifested in body tissue retrieval, storage, and use, described in economic terms and driven by maximizing utility, which may supplant the moral language of generosity and community.[13]

It is precisely this commercialized reality that Mahoney believes must be acknowledged if the moral context of tissue banking is to be fully understood and comprehended. Mahoney contends that avoiding the language of markets and property rights in human tissue manifests a "failure to acknowledge openly the obvious: Tissue transfers—whether or not for compensation—from a lower-value user to a higher-value user create value and, therefore, the potential for monetary returns."[4] Mahoney notes that the debate over the question of "commodification" of human tissue is narrowly focused only on the *initial* acquisition of the gift; however, at subsequent processing and distribution stages, "it is virtually impossible to imagine how human biological materials would be distributed if commerce in such materials were prohibited."[4]

Mahoney makes a compelling case that denial, ignorance, or even deception at the initial gift exchange cannot prevent the commercial realities that otherwise permeate the processing and distribution chain of human tissue transplantation. Yet it is precisely the values affirmed and diminished by the commercial model of tissue transplantation that some authors deem inappropriate to, and even incompatible with, the donation of body tissues. While Mahoney maintains that the moral context of tissue processing and transplantation is inevitably commercialized, Murray contends that such an economic paradigm distorts the real nature of organ and tissue gifts. This, in turn, leads to mistakes at the level of normative ethics and public policy. In particular, Murray is concerned that the commodification of the gift treats relationships as mere means to the efficient achievement of social ends ". . . in the market the relationship exists in the service of the transaction; in gifts, the transaction is in the service of the relationship."[22] That is, the commercial market transforms relationships into "providers–consumers." This diminishes the symbolic and expressive nature of the gift itself, including what the gift conveys about the donor or giver.

Fox contends that proposals such as Mahoney's, to situate organ and tissue exchange squarely within an economic and market model, essentially "de-gift" the donation. Transplantation in the twenty-first century has lost its aura as an awe-inspiring event and has become routine; the increasing prevalence of transplantation technology has made ordinary what was historically remarkable: deliverance of another person from the doors of death, or restoring lost functions. What awe remains does not derive from the expression of human moral character through the gift, but is rather the awe inspired by technological sophistication. Thus, in Fox's opinion, strategies that enable commodifying the gifts of body tissue are a small part of the process of "profanation" of transplants.[23]

There are then two different understandings of how a tissue donation may be dis-respected. The first way[23] is to simply "de-gift" the donation—treat the tissue as merely "raw material" for use in a scientific or clinical process in creating a "finished product," and abandon any semblance of connection to a meaningful gifting relationship or exchange. "Gift" or "donation" language is then revealed as simply appealing rhetoric for what is essentially a process of resource extraction from the body. A second understanding of the process is to acknowledge the reality of the gift of transplantable tissue, but then contend that a moral betrayal has occurred when certain ends (commercial) erode the meaning attributed to the gift.[14]

Both of these arguments for how a gift or donation of body tissue may be dis-respected presume that the "gift" understanding is fundamental to research or using body tissue for transplantation. As suggested by the legal and economic analysis of Mahoney, however, which is reinforced by the sociological analysis of Lori Andrews and Dorothy Nelkin, a gift metaphor is not the only way, nor in scientific and commercial biotechnological contexts the dominant way, of understanding a transfer of tissue from person to medical intermediary. Indeed, it may be symptomatic of the "profanation" of the gift that Andrews and Nelkin only use the language of "giving" once to refer to modes of tissue transfer. They put forward instead the idea of the body, and of body tissue, as a "resource" that may be extracted, harvested, and mined.[24]

The "resource" understanding has various appeals to it. While bioethicists' focus on contractual relationships makes "gift" language somewhat of an anomaly, the discipline has historically been nurtured on ethical dilemmas in "resource allocation" or fairness in distributing "scarce resources." Thus, the set of ethical concepts used in other resource contexts might be readily applied to the resource of transplantable body tissue, now largely divested of its nature as a gift.

Moreover, in an era in which human beings are deemed "resources" for larger institutional or corporate ends (e.g., "human resources"), the economic concepts of efficiency and maximization of the resource do seem common linguistic vernacular. Not surprisingly, the language of "stewardship" does not surface in literature based on commercial and resource understandings; resources need "managers" (not stewards) and a managerial ethos focused on accumulative value.

Scientifically, the resource understanding makes the human body of the twenty-first century analogous to the land of the nineteenth century American West. The body becomes a resource whose extractable, exploitable contents are of more interest than the integrity of the whole. Body tissue is a resource because it contains information that may generate knowledge, or provide the raw materials to which value is added in the development of various therapeutic or rehabilitative objectives. The contemporary equivalent of the resource miners of the nineteenth century—the biomedical research scientist, supported by the capital of investors in a biotechnological firm—assumes a dominant role in the processing, distribution, and control of human tissue, advancing "claims" that establish property rights, patents, and royalties from commercial products.

Finally, the resource metaphor transforms the moral question into a policy issue. The major question in using a resource is ownership of that resource, now thought of as "property." "The concept of property is that of a system of rules to govern control of, and access to, some resources, whether material or incorporeal. And property rights are basically 'the rights of ownership.'"[25] Andrews is very clear that a property understanding of the body and body tissue is needed in a biotechnological age because it gives the person control over access to their body tissue and a right of consent to any educational, research, or therapeutic use.[26] Property can of course be "gifted" from one person to another, so a gift relationship is not incompatible with property understandings; still, the variety of modes of commercial property exchange can diminish the prevalence and significance of gifts. In addition to allocating dispositional control, Mahoney believes a property understanding is more conducive to the promotion of scientific knowledge and to medical advancements.[4]

Since donations of body tissue are mediated through banks and foundations, the status of the recipient shifts; the initial recipient of body tissue is a member of the research or processing community who transforms the "raw materials" of the body into something that can be beneficial to the consumer. In Mahoney's account, it distorts the institutional context of tissue banking to propose a model of stewardship to describe the complexities of processing and distribution. A "nonprofit intermediary organization is entrusted to act to carry out the wishes of the donor, rather than to use the contribution to benefit itself. . . . organizations that receive or obtain human tissue, however, are not understood to be serving an analogous intermediary role and, as a result, are often able to capture the economic value of what they obtain."[4] No strong claim of gratitude or reciprocity is established, as the work of the scientist or processor made possible the retrieval of the tissue in the first place, as well as its development into a finished product. Were it not for the initial labors of the resource extractors, such as scientists and physicians, there would be no "gifts" of the body worth receiving. The main responsibility of the researcher-recipient of the tissue resource or property therefore becomes to ensure that informed consent is secured.[16]

Moral Transformations

The resource model of human body parts, and putting the body in a property and economic context may well involve moral compromises on the themes of gift, stewardship, and relationality. It is important to ask what is lost morally when a gift of body tissue undergoes what Mahoney portrays as its inevitable transformation into a commodity. As noted, since the concept of property is broader than and encompasses transfer by gifts, there might seem to be no necessary incompatibility between property and gift-giving, or between enhancing the value of a resource and stewardship of a gift.

The concern about transforming a gift into a commodity is that the personal meaning of gift-giving, and its centrality in initiating and affirming relationships, will be depersonalized. It surely is the case that something of moral worth has been radically impoverished when the ideal of the giver–steward–recipient relationship that organ and tissue transplantation has historically relied upon as its moral model becomes, in Mahoney's language, a relationship between "lower-value users" and "higher-value users." A moral reality of stratification, power, depersonalization, and instrumentalization are presupposed by this terminology for tissue transfers, against which the concept of a gift relationship seems sentimental naïvete. Thus, the "ubiquity of commerce" in human tissue processing and distribution appears to eviscerate the moral emphases of donation, relationships, and stewardship. Through market mechanisms that bring together "users" and "consumers" rather than donors and recipients this depersonalization can be replicated throughout the transplantation system.

Commercial pressures likewise can divert the gift to other uses and recipients than originally intended by the donor. Such diversion is especially problematic when, without the donor's knowledge or consent, a gift of body tissue generates substantial revenues and profits for a processor or distributor. As Murray suggests, this is a kind of moral betrayal of the gift relationship: "It is one thing to have someone offer to buy something. It is quite another to give it to someone with whom we believe there is a more or less personal, noncommercial relationship, and to learn only later that what was given as a gift, especially if it was a 'sacred' gift, has been diverted to commerce."[14]

If Mahoney's description of the ubiquity of commerce in tissue transplantation is valid, then the concerns raised both inside and outside the tissue bank community about commodification can be seen as focused on a very limited circumstance: the nature of the transfer of tissue in the initial stage from a donor to a bank or foundation. But two additional questions concerning fairness may then be raised. First, given the commercialization of every subsequent stage in the distributional chain of tissue transplantation, is it fair to the donor to require altruism in the initial transfer? Does our admiration for altruism in the donation undermine our commitment to justice in transfers of goods for human benefit? Second, given that reliance on market mechanisms has led to wide disparities and stratification in access to health care resources, does the pervasive commercialism of tissue distribution provide for an equitable distribution of transplantable tissues?

An example of the prospect for moral contradictions on both these questions of justice may be found by examining the philosophy and practices of some companies involved in tissue banking. In April 2000, Regeneration Technologies Inc. (RTI), which is reported to process a third of the nation's donated tissue, decided to seek over $86 million through an initial public offering of its stock. The IPO was defended by one RTI board member as "something that is very accepted in our business system in this country—that there is a return on investment." Simultaneously, the corporate culture of RTI instills a "philosophy of honoring the gift of tissue donation and using that gift responsibly to help as many patients as possible."[27]

Few would dispute RTI's claim that achieving a return on investment is a legitimate goal of a business in a capitalist economy. Meanwhile, RTI's "philosophy" explicitly acknowledges and legitimates the gift exchange and responsible stewardship. The problem of fairness arises when the gift and the business models are juxtaposed so explicitly. Standard business practice does not rely on philanthropic donations for its raison d'être, but rather through contracts in which an exchange of goods and services is conducted. It is little wonder that for some persons in the tissue banking community, disclosure requirements to donors about the uses and the profits to be made from transforming the gift into a commodity investment are worrisome; indeed, nondisclosure might be defended as preferable lest prospective donors be deterred and the tissue supply diminished. Nonetheless, even if (in the hands of tissue banks or processors) body tissue is really a business "investment," then rules of fair commerce would seem to require full disclosure and even to permit the tissue source ("donor" may no longer be appropriate) to have some services provided or some share in the revenues. This is part of the general moral logic of the banking industry.

Issues of fairness in distributing of tissue may emerge with respect to the economic priorities of a tissue bank. The priorities may contravene the stewardship responsibility of mutual aid, which, as delineated above, gives priority to the use of gifts to attend to the fundamental needs of members of the human community. Some questions about fair distribution have been raised, however, by journalistic reports that a substantial portion of donated skin is processed and distributed for use in cosmetic procedures rather than in life-saving procedures for burn victims.[28] It is important to note that, at the level of microallocation of skin, unlike organ transplantation where a single organ often meets the patient's medical needs, patient care for a burn victim requires numerous skin grafts. In the United States, more than one million people suffer burn injuries on an annual basis, about 45,000 of them will require hospitalization.[29] Of course, not all burn injuries require a skin graft.

The question of fair distribution arises not only when needy patients require numerous grafts, but also when needy patients may have to go without a graft because of the skin has been distributed for cosmetic purposes. This priority in distributing donated skin is described by one member of the AATB Skin Council as "a big moral dilemma for tissue banks."[10] It is clear why prioritizing skin for cosmetic rather than reconstructive or life-saving surgeries might be an economic dilemma for tissue banks, who are lured by what is a "bigger marketplace, a bigger opportunity, and a better reimbursement." In certain instances, it appears, the banks' economic viability depends on the profits generated by skin processing for cosmetic purposes.

There is also little question that skin banks face an increasingly competitive economic environment, which has contributed to a sharp decline in the number of skin banks. This economic climate fosters the treatment of skin and body tissue as a commodity.

But short of situations that might be described as "economic necessity" ("necessity" being a term to describe situations in which the traditional rules must be violated for survival), it is not clear that giving precedence to donated skin for traditional burn use rather than elective or cosmetic use should pose a moral dilemma. If the skin is donated with informed consent as a "gift," and if the tissue bank is acting as a responsible steward to ensure benefits to intended recipients rather than an individual or affiliated entrepreneur, then the stewardly duty of mutual aid clearly gives priority to using skin for treating burns, since this need for tissue is a fundamental human need in a way that cosmetic enhancement is not. The primary expectation of families regarding donor tissue is that the tissue will meet "important medical needs."[3]

Cosmetic usage of skin donations thus requires two conditions to be justifiable. First, the tissue source and his or her family should be informed of this possibility and give their consent. Second, use of skin for cosmetic procedures should not cause an artificial scarcity in the supply of skin for patients, such as serious burn victims, who have legitimate medical needs for a skin graft. If there is sufficient skin to meet these basic human needs, then surplus skin could be used for cosmetic purposes.

Altruism and Justice

While a tissue donation is initiated by a gift, the ubiquity of commercial interests in subsequent exchanges prior to transplantation in a recipient raises questions about whether any meaningful content is retained of the ethic of the gift and of stewardship in tissue processing and distribution. In order to encourage both donation and the moral sentiments that are associated with donation, as well as to ensure efficiency in using human tissue, it seems that society has opted for an approach that seeks to allow both a gift and a commercial ethic. In this respect, acknowledging the "gift" of tissue seems a matter of moral symbolism. Whether this is an untenable compromise can be examined by briefly considering some alternative social directions.

A first approach would involve arguing that human tissue is already commodified, as illustrated most starkly by the case of reproductive tissue. Thus there seems little point in arguing for retaining the gift ethic in transplantation simply on the basis that we avoid risking commodifying and commercializing human tissue. *That* question has, from this perspective, already been answered, even if knowledge of the answer is not widespread. The general public simply needs to become more aware of the inevitability of commerce in tissue processing and distribution; tissue banks, OPOs, or other designated requesters should ensure through the informed-consent process that donor families understand this. That is, better use of existing informed-consent mechanisms is a necessary technical improvement in a system that is already largely commercialized.

The problem with this largely procedural and technical resolution to the question is that it neglects some significant issues of substantive ethics, especially pertaining to justice and fairness. As delineated above, fairness in tissue acquisition is relevant in a thoroughly commercialized model of tissue banking. As stated in the OIG report, "it should not be surprising that donor families could feel misled as they question why 'everyone is making money off of this altruistic gift except the donor and the donor's family.'"[3] It's not clear how an understanding of tissue as a commodity could answer that question in any way but to acknowledge the unfairness and offer some kind of financial remuneration for the tissue. This is a policy step that, currently at least, seems to have minimal support from participants in the tissue bank community, however much it might be supported by autonomy-based arguments of contemporary bioethicists.

Moreover, there seem to be issues of fairness in distribution that cannot be resolved simply through fuller disclosure in informed consent. There do not appear to be the general shortages in supply with human tissue that plague the solid organ transplantation system. Yet artificial and economically driven shortages could occur insofar as certain tissue is used for cosmetic purposes rather than the more fundamental needs of burn patients for skin grafts. While this prioritization may violate stewardship, it does not violate business principles based on utility that seek to maximize return on an investment. The economic priorities of some tissue banks may not ensure equity in distribution.

Thus, the current approach may reflect more than a mere compromise in the direction of moral symbolism. To be sure, tissue banking relies on some very potent cultural symbols, including notions of gifts, trust, and stewardship, and the pricelessness of the body. But symbolism is not the only reason supporters of a gift ethic can appeal to. In the domain of tissue acquisition, the discourse of "gift and stewardship" encourages a morality of aspiration and ideals, seeking to elicit the best from human beings through altruistic donations. In tissue allocation, such discourse seeks to ensure that distribution does not fall below standards of fairness and equity. In both instances, then, the ethic and the stewardship of the gift seek to morally differentiate and elevate the practices of the tissue banking community from standard business practice and the ethics of commodity exchanges. In this respect, the gift–stewardship–recipient model seeks to ensure the perpetuation of both love and justice in tissue transplantation.

References

1. Leslie HW, Bottenfield S. Donation, banking, and transplantation of allograft tissues. *Nurs Clin North Am*. 1989;24:891–905.
2. Wyden R. "The Business of Body Parts." *The Oregonian*. June 13, 2000:A11.
3. Office of the Inspector General. Informed consent in tissue donation: expectations and realities. January 2001.
4. Mahoney JD. The market for human tissue. *Virginia Law Rev* 2000;86:163–223.
5. Childress JF. Obtaining the gift of life: ethical issues in the procurement of organs for transplantation. *Social Responsibility: Business, Journalism, Law, and Medicine, v. XXI*. 1995;21:66–85.
6. Gaylin W. "Harvesting the Dead." *Harper's Magazine*. September 1974:24–30.
7. May WF. Attitudes toward the newly dead. *Hastings Cent Studies*. 1972;1:3–13.
8. Feinberg J. The mistreatment of dead bodies. *Hastings Cent Rep*. 1985;15:31–37.
9. Camenisch PF. Gift and gratitude in ethics. *J Relig Ethics*. 1981;9:1–34.
10. American Association of Tissue Banks. Statement of ethical principles. Available at: http://www.attb.org.
11. Blacksher E. On ova commerce. *Hastings Cent Rep*. 2000;30:29–30.
12. Parsons T, Fox RC, Lidz VM. "The 'Gift of Life' and Its Reciprocation." In: Mack A (ed.). *Death in American Experience*. New York, Schocken Books, 1973:1–49.

13. Fox RC, Swazey JP. *Spare Parts: Organ Replacement in American Society*. New York, Oxford University Press, 1992.

14. Murray TH. Gifts of the body and the needs of strangers. *Hastings Cent Rep*. 1987; 17:30–38.

15. Engelhardt HT Jr. (ed.). *The Foundations of Bioethics, Second Edition*. New York, Oxford University Press, 1996.

16. Campbell CS. Religion and the body in medical research. *Kennedy Inst Ethics J*. 1998; 8:275–305.

17. Goldsmith R. "Jersey Leads in a Medical Revolution." *The Star-Ledger*. June 18, 2000.

18. May WF (ed.). *The Physician's Covenant: Images of the Healer in Medical Ethics*. Philadelphia, The Westminster Press, 1983.

19. Calvin J. *Institutes of the Christian Religion*. McNeill JT (ed.). Philadelphia, Westminster Press, 1960.

20. Locke J. "The Second Treatise of Civil Government." In: Laslett P (ed.). *Two Treatises of Government*. New York, Cambridge University Press, 1963.

21. *Ethical Issues in Tissue Banking Conference*. Islin, NJ; June 20, 2000.

22. Murray TH. "Organ Vendors, Families and the Gift of Life." In: Youngner SJ, Fox RC, O'Connell LJ (eds.). *Organ Transplantation: Meanings and Realities*. Madison, Wisconsin, The University of Wisconsin Press, 1996:101–126.

23. Fox RC. "Afterthoughts: Continuing Reflections on Organ Transplantation." In: Youngner, Fox, O'Connell. *Organ Transplantation*. 252–272.

24. Andrews L, Nelkin D. Whose body is it anyway? Disputes over body tissue in a biotechnological age. *Lancet*. 1998;351:53–57.

25. Childress JF. "Human Body Parts as Property." In: Childress JF (ed.). *Practical Reasoning in Bioethics*. Bloomington, Indiana, Indiana University Press, 1997:282–300.

26. Andrews LB. My body, my property. *Hastings Cent Rep*. 1986;16:28–38.

27. Campbell R, Heisel W, Katches M. Anatomy of an IPO: making charity pay. Available at: http://www.ocregister.com/news/rti007cci.shtml. Accessed May 7, 2000.

28. Heisel W, Katches M, Kowalcyzk L. Skin merchants: lives on the line. Available at: http://www.ocregister.com/health/body/day2.shtml. Accessed April 17, 2000.

29. American Burn Association. Burn incidence and treatment in the U.S.: 2000 Fact sheet. Chicago, Illinois, 2000. Available at: http://www.ameriburn.org/pub/Burn Incidence Fact Sheet.htm.

11

Developing Hospital Policy: The University of Wisconsin Experience

NORMAN FOST

In the spring of 2000, about the same time that the *Orange County Register* published its articles critical of the rapidly growing field of procurement, processing, and sale of human tissue,[1] the head of the University of Wisconsin Hospital organ procurement program was found to be working for a for-profit tissue procurement company without the knowledge of his employers. The local and national press coverage led the Wisconsin state legislature to schedule hearings on the matter. Consequently, the UW Hospital Ethics Committee was asked by the hospital's administration to review the issues and draft a hospital policy on tissue procurement. This chapter reviews the critical issues in that review. Although the committee was not charged with developing a consent form, our findings were reflected in a revised consent form that is included at the end of this book as Appendix D.

The University of Wisconsin (Madison) Hospital is a large academic medical center with one of the most active organ transplant programs in the country. The program is particularly renowned for its success in organ procurement. As chair of the Hospital Ethics Committee (HEC), I organized a working group from the HEC to identify the issues and draft a proposed policy after receiving the hospital administration's request. This process included interviews with faculty and staff from the transplantation program and hospital administration. A draft policy was discussed at several meetings of the full HEC and approved by the HEC on November 30, 2000.

Identification of the Issues

Tissue is not a precise concept, and a discussion of hospital policies involving tissue procurement could include blood, skin, bones, connective tissue, corneas, gametes, embryos, stem cells, and so on. Such a discussion might also include a wide range of fetal tissues that are sought for purposes of research or transplantation. Discussion of all entities within this range would involve a wide variety of ethical, legal, and policy issues. We elected to limit our review to the tissues at the center of the current debate: skin, bone, and connective tissue.

The news accounts claimed that the most controversial aspects of the tissue industry—the use of tissue for cosmetic purposes and the role of for-profit entities—were probably not well understood by the general public, particularly by those who are asked to consent to post-mortem tissue donation. While the extent of cosmetic uses was unclear, and details about the alleged "profiteering" were unavailable, our committee agreed that many donors probably were unaware of these issues, and we thought it plausible that some of them would find this information relevant in deciding whether or not to agree to donation.

We therefore elected to focus our analysis on two sets of issues: (*1*) the range of uses for tissues, and (*2*) the involvement of commercial, for-profit organizations in the processing and distribution of tissues. For each of these issues there were two central questions: what should be disclosed to potential donors, and what role should these issues play in the hospital's selection of companies with whom they cooperated (Table 11.1)?

Table 11.1. Issues Under Discussion

	Uses of tissue	Role of profit
Disclosure/consent	How much information should be disclosed to potential donors?	How much information should be disclosed to potential donors?
Selection of tissue banks	Should banks be selected based on a commitment to use tissue for important health purposes, and agreement to disclosure of range of uses and role of profit?	Should nonprofit tissue banks be preferred in the hospital's selection of tissue banks?

Uses of Donated Tissue

Post-mortem tissue can be used for a wide variety of purposes, including life-saving applications, such as skin grafts for patients with extensive burns; procedures that restore function and avoid major disability, such as bone replacements for patients who have undergone cancer surgery; and purely cosmetic purposes. Press accounts focused on the last category, particularly the claim that potential donors might be surprised and distressed to learn that tissue from a recently deceased relative was being used for a relatively trivial purpose. We had little reliable information on what proportion of tissue was used for these various purposes, or what donors knew or believed about these applications. Nonetheless, it seemed plausible that some donors might not agree to all of these uses, and that meaningful consent should include some information about the range of uses.

The central problem involved the complexity of the term *cosmetic*. While all cosmetic procedures involve efforts to change appearance rather than function, the term encompasses a wide range of procedures. At one end of this continuum, the most troubling applications would involve use of tissue to enhance the beauty of someone who was already well within the normal range for physical appearance. The worst case might involve a patient who was at the high end of physical beauty and used post-mortem tissue for a marginal gain for reasons of pure vanity. At the other end of the continuum, however, *cosmetic surgery* might involve infants with severely disfiguring malformations, or older trauma victims whose disfigurements could be profoundly handicapping for purely aesthetic reasons. Presumably most donors would be sympathetic to the use of donated tissue for patients with severe deformities, and some might be unwilling to consent to donation if they thought the tissue was being used for beautification of an already attractive person.

These distinctions between "treatment" and "enhancement" have been explored in other debates about the appropriate use of health care resources and the proper ends of medicine.[2, 3] This is beyond the scope of this chapter. Suffice it to say that this alleged distinction has many difficulties and cannot be summarized in a way that would be practical or meaningful to a bereaved family member contemplating donation of post-mortem tissue.

Apart from the nuances of the treatment/enhancement distinction, we were concerned that the word *cosmetic*, without further explanation, might have a pejorative connotation. That is, some potential donors might not appreciate the range of cosmetic uses and, without further explanation, might assume that cosmetic uses of tissues were undesirable and not worthy of donation. For this reason we agreed we could not avoid some discussion of the term. Potential donors needed to know about the worst possibilities, but not be misled in a way that would inhibit consent for uses that they would support.

In addition to the problems of the content of disclosures about cosmetic uses, there were procedural questions about consent. Some initially thought that potential donors should have the opportunity to designate or limit the range of uses. While restrictions are feasible in some cases—for example, some tissue banks honor limitations that skin not be used for purely cosmetic purposes—we concluded this was generally not feasible due to pragmatic considerations in the way tissue is processed and distributed.

This left two main options: (1) positive consent ("opting in"), meaning donors would be asked to agree to specific uses of tissue, including cosmetic uses; and (2) passive consent ("opting out"), meaning donors would be told about cosmetic uses, so that their consent for tissue use would imply cosmetic uses.

While reliable information was not available, the committee had the impression from our limited sources that objectionable uses of tissue constituted a small percentage of its use, and the vast majority of donated tissue was likely to be used for important health purposes. For this reason, we concluded that it would be sufficient to inform potential donors of the possibility of objectionable cosmetic uses, so that those wishing further information would be alerted, and could choose to opt out if they wished.

In addition to consent as a mechanism for protecting donors from unwanted uses of tissue, we thought it would also be appropriate for the hospital to form relationships with tissue banks that have a commitment to using tissue for important health purposes.

Profit, Profiteering, and Undue Profits

The central criticism in the articles in the *Orange County Register* was that some companies involved in tissue processing and distribution were making undue profits, or that executives were drawing inappropriate salaries or other emoluments, and that some donors might be reluctant to consent to donation if they knew this. Thus, the HEC had extensive discussions about the relevance of profits in moral judgements about those working in the field, and whether there was an obligation to inform potential donors of these monetary arrangements.

For-profit has a legal definition for tax purposes, but some committee members thought this was not a critical distinction with regard to the moral issues. For example, federal law prohibits profiteering from organ sales, but many people have become rich by working in the transplantation industry, even though fully employed exclusively by "not-for-profit" organizations. Indeed, millions of people working in not-for-profit health care institutions, including myself, have become moderately wealthy; that is, we have profited from the misery and illness of others.

It was also recognized that many for-profit organizations behave in an exemplary fashion, with high levels of commitment to the underserved, to the community, and to widely shared moral principles. In contrast, some not-for-profit organizations have relatively little concern for community goals, and while they maintain a not-for-profit tax status by investing residual income in the enterprise, the amount of residual income available for such activities may be substantially reduced by paying unnecessarily high salaries to physicians, administrators, and others. Some CEOs of for-profit companies work in small, spartan offices and drive old, cheap cars, while some CEOs of not-for-profit companies work in luxurious offices and drive expensive cars. Not-for-profit health care plans have been known to invest in services that are likely to be remunerative, and to avoid services that may be more effective in promoting health but which are unprofitable. "Cherry-picking" in health care plans is not restricted to for-profit organizations. In summary, the distinction between "for-profit" and "not-for-profit" organizational structures seemed of uncertain moral relevance.

As with the "cosmetic" issue, partial disclosure of the "profiteering" issue could result in misunderstandings, with the consequence that potential donors might be scared away with the false impression that "for-profit" implied "morally wrong," and "not-for-profit" implied "morally unproblematic."

There was another reason why *profit* should not be considered a dirty word. The rapid growth of the tissue banking and transplantation industry has arisen primarily from the private sector, using private capital; in contrast to organ transplantation, which has been heavily subsidized by federal and state governments through Medicare and Medicaid. Even the least controversial uses of tissue, such as a skin grafts for severely burned patients, would not have progressed to its present level without the involvement of private venture capital.

These complexities about the role of profits in health care made it difficult to reduce the issues in a way that was consistent with the realities of consent in the post-mortem setting. Thus, the most contentious discussion was over the concept of *profiteering* or *undue profits*. Some thought it was important to state our opposition to this, and to inform patients that such behavior might occur. Others, ultimately a majority, believed the words were so imprecise, and raised such complicated questions about possibly undue income among our own colleagues, that such terms could not be used without a lengthy essay. We ultimately decided not to use such terms, either in our recommendations to the hospital, or in proposed language for potential donors. We compromised with the conclusion that potential donors should be informed that processing is done by commercial businesses, "some of which earn substantial gain." This recommendation parallels the longstanding "Moore" principle, which requires that research subjects be informed when investigators using residual tissue for research purposes anticipate possible commercial gain.[4]

Selection of Tissue Banks

While there was agreement that donors should be informed about uses of tissue and about the involvement of commercial entities in tissue transplantation, there was also agreement that consent was of limited value in ensuring an ethically acceptable program. This was due in part to the complexity of the issues, combined with the limited time available for education and discussion in the post-mortem setting, as well as the difficulty of asking families to engage in discussion of complex economic and policy issues while trying to deal with the death of a loved one.

For these reasons, the committee thought that it would also be desirable to reduce the possibility of objectionable uses of tissue by selecting companies who agreed with what we considered important principles; namely, disclosure of the range of uses of tissues, and disclosure of the commercial nature of their business. The committee concluded it would even better if the hospital could restrict its relationships as much as possible to nonprofit companies, and to companies that had a commitment to use tissues for important health purposes.

Pre-mortem Consent to Donate Organs

The HEC considered the question of whether the requirements for disclosure reviewed above should apply to individuals who had designated themselves as donors on their driver's licenses. We concluded that there was no practical way to document disclosure of the relevant information in that setting. While consent to donate solid organs cannot be equated with consent to donate tissues, we concluded that evidence of pre-mortem willingness to donate implied a favorable attitude toward donation by the patient, and that next of kin could protect the deceased patient's interests if the guidelines proposed here were followed.

Conclusion

The primary purpose of the guidelines developed by the UW Hospital Ethics Committee was not to develop a comprehensive consent policy for tissue donation, but to advise the hospital on what we perceived as the most contentious issues; namely, the range of uses for such tissues and the role of commercial entities in processing tissue. The basic elements for consent to use post mortem tissue have been developed by other groups.[5, 6] It was our expectation that the guidelines would inform the development of a specific hospital policy and consent document, and that did occur.

We concluded that donors should be informed about the range of possible uses of tissues, including cosmetic uses, and should be informed about the involvement of commercial entities, some of which earn substantial financial gain. We also concluded that the hospital should prefer companies with a commitment to the principles in the guidelines.

The members of the UW Hospital Ethics Committee contributed substantially to the above analysis. In particular, Robert Miller, J.D., made major contributions to the drafting of the guidelines.

References

1. Available at: http://www.ocregister.com/health/body. Accessed May 21, 2000. Additional articles were published throughout the summer; available at: http://www.ocregister.com/archives.
2. Parens E (ed.). *Enhancing Human Traits: Ethical and Social Implications*. Washington, D.C., Georgetown University Press, 1998.
3. Fost N. Is the treatment/enhancement distinction useful? In Allen DB, Fost N, (eds.), Ethical issues in access to growth hormone therapy: where are we now? *The Endocrinologist* 2001;11(#4, Supp.1):72S–77S.
4. Moore v. Regents of University of California (1990) 51 Cal.3d 120, 271 Cal.Rptr. 146; 793 P.2d 479.

5. American Association of Tissue Banks, Association of Organ Procurement Organizations, Eye Bank Association of America. Model elements of informed consent for organ and tissue donation. *Joint Statement*. November 30, 2000.

6. Office of the Inspector General, U.S. Department of Health and Human Services. Informed consent in tissue donation: expectations and realities. January 2001. OEI-01-00-00440. Report Available at: http://oig.hhs.gov/oei.

12

Informed Consent

STUART J. YOUNGNER

Informed consent is perhaps the ethical issue that most concerns critics inside and outside the tissue transplant industry. This is partly because it is often seen as a "solution" to other problems that have caused controversy in the field.

Why has informed consent caused such a fuss in tissue transplantation when it did not cause much of a stir in organ transplantation? What concern there was in organ transplantation came primarily from the transplant community itself—not from outsiders as with tissue—and stemmed from the shortage of organs and the fact that often people were either not asked to donate or declined when asked. In response, the passage of so-called required request laws attempted to ensure that family members of every potential donor were approached about donation.[1] Required request failed.[2] More recently, routine referral laws have attempted to improve the quality of informed consent by having experienced, motivated persons make the request and requiring that every single hospital death be reported to the local organ procurement organization (OPO).[3] While the transplant industry has emphasized informed consent as a way to "offer the donation option" to families, the driving motivation has been the organ shortage.

The concern about informed consent in tissue donation is different. It was spawned, not by a failure to obtain sufficient tissue, but by the failure to provide adequate information when that tissue was obtained.

While the rate of consent for tissue donation (about 35%) is considerably lower than that for organs (about 50%),[2] a donor shortage is not a major problem. This is because, unlike with organs, the number of potential tissue donors is not limited to brain-dead patients maintained on ventilators. It is estimated that the number of potential solid organ donors in the United States is around 11,000–14,000, whereas there are at least a hundred thousand potential tissue donors.[4] The waiting list for organs as of August 2, 2002, was 80,294, and many people on it die waiting.[5] Tissue for transplantation is relatively abundant, and although accurate national data are absent, tissue shortages are regional and limited to certain tissue types. Moreover, tissue from a single donor can go to 50 to 100 recipients. So, for example, in 2000, 6081 cadaver donors provided 17,255 organs,[5] while more than 20,000 donors provided cadaveric tissue for more than 750,000 allografts.[6]

The use of organs has been relatively transparent to the public. A kidney, for example, goes quickly from donor to recipient and is recognizable as a kidney from start to finish. Yes, there are costs, but the necessary hospitalization, surgery, and medical management are well known, publicized, and not dissimilar to other forms of medical care. People are generally aware that surgeons, hospital directors, and executives of pharmaceutical companies that produce antirejection drugs make a good living. For, profit companies and indeed for-profit hospitals are an accepted part of the health care industry. This financial aspect of transplantation has evolved along with the rest of the health care industry in the United States. Therefore, there is little perceived need to tell potential organ donors about commerce and the market—they know already, and, apparently more or less accept it as the status quo. Even if some citizens complain about the cost of or lack of access to health care, no one claims ignorance. It is hard to imagine that *the Orange County Register* would have printed headlines about organ donors' not being told that hospitals, physicians, and the pharmaceutical industry were making a lot of money from organ transplantation.

The situation is different for the tissue industry, which has developed rapidly, with little time for public exposure and scrutiny. When the sensational stories surfaced in the *Orange County Register*, the implication was that someone had been keeping a secret from the public in general, and from donor families in particular. The "secret" is that a lot of money is being made as tissue is commodified and passed down the chain of distribution to the recipient and that occasionally it is used for enhancement purposes. Rather than changing the commercial status quo, some have suggested that a robust informed-consent process could go a long way toward neutralizing these socially contentious (and perhaps unresolvable) issues for donor families, the tissue industry, and our society. That is, if we tell potential recipients how the industry works, our responsibility to them ends. While this notion has some merit, it oversimplifies a very complex problem. It relies too heavily on a rights or consumer model that fails to capture both the vulnerability of potential donor families and the sense of responsibility of many tissue banks.

To better understand this problem, I will first explore the general meaning and social purpose of *informed consent*, and next raise the question about whether informed consent is the best model for the transaction between donor families and requestors from the transplant industry. Concluding that it is, I will explore how a robust notion of informed consent might apply to the request for tissue. Next will be a review of some limited empirical data about what donor families have been told and would want to know, and a review of recommendations from the Inspector General's Report, and two sets of guidelines, one from the National Donor Family Council and the other issued jointly by the American Association of Tissue Banks (AATB), the Eye Bank Association of America (EBAA), and the Association of Organ Procurement Organizations (AOPO). Finally, I will make recommendations of my own, including an emphasis on the tissue industry's responsibility for "good stewardship" as a necessary companion to even the best of informed consent processes.

What Is Informed Consent, and How Does It Apply to Tissue Banking?

> Informed consent is not an ancient concept. . . . The term first appeared in 1957 and serious discussion began in 1972. . . .
> —Beauchamp and Faden[7]

The first organ and tissue transplants preceded the use of the term *informed consent*. Today, informed consent is the primary moral and legal principle that guides medical decisionmaking and participation of human subjects in scientific research. Informed consent serves many purposes. Most important, perhaps, it promotes respect for persons in treatment and research contexts by nurturing their autonomy and protecting them from undue harm. Informed consent also reinforces public trust in medical treatment and research, thereby promoting both.

The term *informed consent* is widely employed to describe the decisionmaking process of tissue donation, but is it really the best one to understand that process? *Informed consent* is normally used to describe the exchange of information between physician or researcher and patient or surrogate in the context of medical treatment or medical research. But the decision to donate tissue for transplantation (unless it was made by the patient prior to death) involves the subject of neither medical treatment nor research. The subject is dead, and the decision usually is made by a family member. The decision is about the donation of a loved one's bone, skin, corneas, or heart valves to treat unknown other persons. Any research is performed on the tissue of a dead person, not on the family members who give consent. In these ways, the transaction in which family members are offered the donation option (or even the one where individuals sign donor cards in anticipation of their future deaths), is unlike other situations in which the notion of informed consent comes into play.

Since we characterize donated tissue as a gift, should we think of it then more like a *charitable contribution*? We are all frequently bombarded by requests to give to charity with minimal attention to an informed consent process or our state of mind. We also receive a financial incentive for charitable gifts—an income tax deduction. Charities generally have an obligation to deliver their largess to the persons or causes that the donor had in mind when proffering their gift. If they do not deliver as promised and word gets out, donations might dry up.

Or should we describe donation as a *business transaction*, a deal over property, applying contract law and consumer protections like truth-in-labeling to protect the donor partners in the business deal? Or should we simply say "donor beware?" While some people argue that the business model should characterize the transaction, Alta Charo, in Chapter 8 of this book, convincingly describes how the legal notion of property and attendant rights does not map one-to-one on human body parts. Moreover, NOTA explicitly rejects the notion that this is a business transaction.[8] So, while there may be a lot of "business" in the tissue industry, and a business model might someday hold sway, it certainly does not today.

While the models of a charitable gift and a business contract have some relevant features, they fail to capture important aspects of the transaction as it has evolved and now exists. First, while their interactions with potential donor families is not strictly speaking a medical one, OPOs and tissue banks (and the people who work for them) feel a tremendous moral and emotional responsibility for donor families. And, while interactions with family members over tissue donation are not strictly speaking a provision of health care, they certainly take place in the context of health care. In this sense, the relationship between tissue banks and OPOs and potential donor families is most often perceived by both parties as a fiduciary one, where one party is needy and vulnerable and the other is entrusted to promote the one's interests above its own. Moreover, the money people donate to charity does not have the profound symbolism of donated body parts of loved ones or oneself. Despite its imperfections, given the current situation and alternatives, informed consent is the best model for optimum decisionmaking.

The Elements of Informed Consent

There are five basic elements to informed consent. First, the decision by the patient must be voluntary, without undue influence or coercion. Second, the person giving the informed consent must be mentally competent— that is, they must have adequate mental capacity to understand and process information. Third, adequate information must be provided to the person, and, fourth, they must understand it. Finally, an actual decision must be registered. Each of these elements is subject to interpretation in any medical context.[7, 9, 10]

In exploring the elements of informed consent for tissue donation, I will focus on two—what constitutes "adequate" information and what is the capacity and desire of distraught families to understand the complex nature of tissue procurement, processing, and distribution.

Provision of Adequate Information

The courts have considered different standards for judging whether enough information has been provided for a truly informed consent. The *least stringent* is the standard in the community or what physicians in the community (in this case, tissue banks and OPOs) normally tell people. This standard has obvious problems, and the courts have generally rejected it. First, if the community standard is below acceptable moral standards, why should it provide the minimum requirement? Second, and probably most important, physicians and researchers, tissue banks, and OPOs may have different values and conflicting interests from those of potential donor families.

If OPOs and tissue banks have a fiduciary relationship with prospective donor families, they have an obligation to put the interests of those families before their own. While physicians are entrusted with the important social role of healing patients and relieving their suffering, tissue banks and OPOs are entrusted by society not only to provide safe tissue to needy recipients, but also to approach families with the donation option. Just like physicians, however, tissue banks are compensated for their activities, have expenses to meet, want to be recognized for their success, and so on. In addition, those asking for tissue also have the interests of unnamed potential recipients in mind—just as researchers have in mind the interests of future beneficiaries of that research. A little later I will examine the significance of conflict of interest for tissue banks and OPOs.

Harms and benefits. What are the potential harms and benefits of donation to the donor family? About which harms and benefits should they be informed? In answering these questions, a second, *more stringent* standard for assessing the adequacy of information should be used: information should be provided at the level wanted by a reasonable or "typical" donor family.

Persons who have donated organs and tissues report feeling better that something good (help for the recipient) came out of a tragedy (the death of their loved one).[11] Other potential benefits include the sense that in some way the dead loved one "lives on" or would have wanted this to happen. Potential harms include disfigurement of the body, or dishonoring the gift and its givers by using it in an unworthy manner—both of which, in addition to their symbolic harm, could cause considerable upset to surviving family members who agreed to donate.

What counts as an unworthy use of tissue? For some, it might be charging unreasonable costs for processing or making actual "profits" from their gifts. For others, it might mean commodification—turning a loved one's bone into screws or powder kept in a jar on a shelf as part of a computerized inventory until it was distributed to faceless strangers. For still others, *unworthy* might mean using a donated part of a loved one to plump up an actress's lips, or smooth the wrinkles of a wealthy but unhappily aging recipient. And all this without any recognition of the source or the spirit in which the gift entered the chain of distribution.

Of course, it is these very things that have facilitated some of the success of the tissue industry, allowing new and better "products" to improve the lives of more and more recipients. The *Orange County Register* thought these uses count as harms to donor families, but let us examine more-authoritative sources.

In Chapter 7, Ellen Kulik, a lawyer and donor mother, eloquently described her outrage at the commodification of tissue banking and demanded that adequate information be given to donor families. "Contrary to many professionals' opinions," she wrote, "families need more information . . . so that after the death and the donation, they are not confused about their loved one's gifts or surprised to learn new information about how the process works." She went on to insist that families should get written information. Without this kind of informed consent process, she warned, there are risks. "The risk to donor families is the unacceptable complication of their grief. The risk to the tissue industry is the backlash of angry families who have been misled and the possible decline in donation rates." On the other hand, in Chapter 6, John Moyer, a pediatrician and donor father, poignantly described how the pain of his son's death crowded out concerns about informed consent. "Was I given full disclosure as to what was going to happen to Andy's tissue?" he asked. "Did it matter? I hurt so badly leaving him there on life support." He went on, "There is profit and loss involved, but is this something a grieving family needs to hear? Maybe, or maybe not."

Two unpublished surveys provide more comprehensive data about the attitudes of families who have been given the option of donating tissue. In August of 2000, the University of Florida Tissue Bank, Inc., in conjunction with Oppenheim Research and the University of Florida Department of Clinical and Health Psychology released the results of two telephone surveys of 507 respondents each.[12] Respondents were selected at random from persons who had been offered the option of tissue donation between one to eighteen months prior to the survey. Of those who donated, 86% said they had enough time to make a decision, whereas 73% of nondonors said they did not. Very few donors (1.6%) and nondonors (6.3%) felt they had been pressured into making a positive decision. Sizeable minorities of:

- donors (28%) and nondonors (36%) said they did not receive enough information about how the tissue was going to be used;
- donors (35%) and nondonors (43%) said it would have been helpful to know that recovered tissue is "sent to companies." Of these, 10% of donors said that knowing would have made a difference;
- donors (41%) and nondonors (49%) said they would have wanted to know that there are costs associated with recovery, preparation, distribution, research, and surgery of the tissue including salaries, materials, shipping, and administration. Costs are recovered by charges to hospitals and patients. Nineteen percent of donors said it would have made a difference in their decision.
- donors (37%) and nondonors (50%) said that profits should not exceed recovery costs. Forty-eight percent of donors and 24% of nondonors said that profits should be permitted.

In the fall of 2000, Siminoff and Youngner, in conjunction with the Donor Family Council of the National Kidney Foundation and the Musculoskeletal Transplant Foundation, mailed surveys to approximately 6000 members of the Council.[13] There were 2033 responses. Of the respondents, 35% had donated heart valves, 64% corneas, 39% bone, 39% skin, 23% tendons/ligaments, and 19% veins. About 50% said they had either forgotten many details of the informed-consent process or did not remember it at all. Only 19% were given a written pamphlet, 23% given a phone number to call for information, 34% provided with a copy of the consent form, and 30% "not provided with anything."

While approximately 90% of respondents said it was acceptable to use donated tissues to treat burns; prevent the loss of an arm or leg; or for back, hip, or arm surgery; and 67% said it was acceptable to use it for urinary incontinence; only 6% said it was acceptable to use it to smooth out wrinkles or for lip augmentation. Ninety percent said they did *not* know that tissue was sometimes processed and distributed by for-profit companies; 79% said they would have wanted to know; and 58% said knowing it might go to a for-profit company would have changed their decision to donate. Sixty-three percent did *not* know that tissue can be processed and stored, 70% said they would have wanted to know, and 11% said they would not have donated if they knew.

Seventy percent disagreed or strongly disagreed with the statement that families should *not* have a say in how tissues are distributed. Minorities of respondents said that donated tissue should *not* be made into special shapes or significantly transformed—for example, surgical screws made from bone (21%) or stored in packaging for long periods of time prior to use (25%). Sixty-three percent found the word "product" to describe donated tissue as somewhat or very offensive.

The two surveys and the deeper reflections of Ellen Kulik and John Moyer indicate that not all donors or potential donors think alike about the issue of consent. Nonetheless, some important trends emerge. First, significant minorities or actual majorities in the surveys rejected the notion that families should not be informed about the issues of commercialization, commodification, and the use of tissue for cosmetic purposes. Many persons rejected these practices, and a worrisome minority of these said that full knowledge would have affected their decision to donate.

Despite the limitations of the studies—including inadequacies of the sampling methods—the voices of many donors and nondonors alike make it difficult to argue that the typical or reasonable potential donor simply does not want information that might be controversial or upsetting. The data also warn that full disclosure (directly to patients or by investigative reporters) might lower donation rates.

Capacity to Consent

In the throes of grief from the death of a loved one, potential donors are hardly in an ideal position to receive and process complex information. But does their despair make them incapable of, or unsuited to, full disclosure? Emotional upset by itself is not cause to declare incompetence. Mental capacity to give consent or refusal must be *severely* compromised before patients or research subjects lose their right and responsibility to make decisions.[14] Such a judgement almost always requires the presence of an identifiable mental illness that is causing the incapacity. While some potential donor families might be suffering from mental illness, the vast majority clearly are not. Furthermore, it is not a *patient's* decisionmaking capacity we are concerned with here, but that of a family member, and our interest and authority to investigate surrogates' mental capacities are limited.

Nor is it acceptable to sidestep informed consent by invoking therapeutic privilege, a vestige of the days of unbridled paternalism when physicians could unilaterally withhold important information or outright lie to cancer patients to "protect" them from being upset. Subsequent study and analysis demonstrated that the cancer patients wanted the information and that physicians were motivated as much by their own fear of death and sense of failure as they were by concern about their patients. The practice of withholding information about cosmetic use and commercial aspects of the industry may be a holdover from the earlier, less complicated era of tissue banking when these issues did not exist. It may also genuinely demonstrate a concern for the welfare of potential donor families. In addition, it may reflect both guilt about approaching families at a time of vulnerability and discomfort about the increasing commercialization of their industry.

Additional complexities. Even if we are willing to tell families about potentially upsetting aspects of tissue processing and use, what exactly should we tell them? Certainly, most family members are in a state of anguish. Furthermore, a majority of tissue requests are made over the phone by persons who have never met the people they are speaking with. Is it feasible to give a robust description of the structure and function of the tissue transplant industry in this context? Even if one attempted it, what words and tone should be used? Should we explain the similarities and differences between profit and not-for-profit organizations? Should the realities of our market economy be presented? Extolled? Criticized? In what balance? Words like "for profit" or "making money" used out of context can be unfairly provocative and manipulative. Yet avoiding their use altogether would allow many people to naïvely imagine that their gifts of tissue make their way to grateful recipients without money ever changing hands or acting as an incentive.

Some may argue that the way out is to simply get more people to fill out tissue donation cards and use those cards to bypass family objections. This strategy would hardly solve the problem of informed consent for tissue donation, however, since it would displace responsibility of informed consent from health professionals or trained requestors to clerks in state license bureaus. These bureaucrats are unlikely to be sufficiently trained or motivated to make first-person consent for tissue donation a meaningful process.

Conflict of Interest

In their socially sanctioned role, physicians and other health professionals have specific moral responsibilities. The physician's role defines his or her duties.[15] For treating physicians, the duty is to provide good care to patients; for researchers, the duties are twofold: both to the integrity of the research *and* to the research subject. Thompson has termed these socially entrusted responsibilities *primary interests*. These responsibilities may overlap and even conflict—especially, for example, if a physician does research on his or her own patients. As mentioned earlier, the tissue banks and OPOs have primary interests both in securing tissue for transplantation and in making sure that donor families are respected. These might be considered conflicts of mission or loyalty. In the case of research, the Declaration of Helsinki and recent revisions[16] make it clear that the goal of doing important research must not outweigh the interests of the research subject. Analogously, in tissue procurement, the interests of potential recipients must not be served at the expense of tissue donors.

In addition to conflicts of loyalty, clinicians and researchers also may have *secondary interests* that conflict with their primary interest or interests. A secondary interest is outside the scope of professional duty and benefits the investigator or physician personally. Secondary interests may include personal financial interests as well as less tangible things such as fame and power. Of course, secondary interests of one sort or another always exist. They become problematic when they are too influential or when they are hidden. One way to deal with interests that are too influential is to eliminate them. For example, physicians have been prohibited from owning radiology companies to which they refer their own patients. Or universities may prohibit a principal investigator from heading a research project funded by a company of which she or he is the president or major stockholder. Lesser conflicts of interest can be dealt with through the informed consent process. Informing a decisionmaker about the conflicts of interest of the other party offers an opportunity for further questions, scrutiny, or refusal to participate.

One noteworthy example of a conflict of interest in tissue banking came to light in April 2000 when a for-profit tissue processor, Regeneration Technologies, Inc. (RTI), filed documents with the Securities and Exchange Commission (SEC) in preparation for issuing an initial public offering for its stock.[17] Included in those documents was a compensation scheme that provided financial bonuses for employees based on their ability to recruit new donor sources or to increase donor activity. Compensation included: $125 to $1250 per incremental donor recovered on behalf of RTI; $50 per donor over a target in a given service area; $100 per donor recovered in a funeral home over the planned five donors per month; $100 per heart valve recovery in a medical examiner's office over the planned two hearts per month; $1,000 for executing a Management Service Agreement, and $100 for all staff of RTI for each month in which productivity targets were exceeded. The failure to disclose such compensation to either donor sources or donor families could certainly be construed as troublesome.

The very act of the tissue bank's "going public" poses a significant conflict of interest, one that is not well addressed by any current legislative or regulatory guidelines. Any company that has shareholders must, by its very nature, serve its shareholders first and its customers second. Business decisions may be in the best interests of the shareholders (including employees and officers), but may not necessarily coincide with public (in this case, patients' or donor families') interests. This is not to say that all publicly traded companies are unethical; nothing could be farther from the truth. It does, however, underscore the complexity of such a situation when multiple and often disparate stakeholders' needs must be juggled.

Another example of a conflict of interest involved employees of a university hospital–based organ procurement organization who, unbeknownst to the university (and against university policy), received compensation (monetary and stock options) from a tissue bank that received donor referrals from the OPO.[18–21] This relationship was revealed neither to the employees' superiors nor to donor families who were approached for consent to donate tissues to the tissue bank. The employees were subsequently removed from their positions at the OPO and one was required to pay back the monies he had received from the tissue bank. This situation is discussed in detail by Dr. Norman Fost in Chapter 11, and clearly shows the slippery slope when financial gains may be made through the referral and procurement of donated tissues.

To summarize, OPOs and tissue banks have two primary missions or interests: to procure safe tissue for transplantation into needy recipients, and to respect the donors. In addition, they have secondary interests—their own job security, salary levels, and recognition and influence within the field. These conflicts of interest, primary and secondary, may adversely affect the informed-consent process by influencing clinicians or investigators to minimize or avoid disclosure of potential harms. Few persons would argue that respect for donors or donor families should be sacrificed even to promote the welfare of potential recipients and certainly not for the personal or institutional welfare of those asking for the tissue. Before turning to some possible solutions to the problems with informed consent, let us examine what has been suggested so far.

Suggested Solution to the Informed-Consent Problems

In response to severe criticism in the press and the attention of federal authorities, donor families and the tissue industry issued guidelines for informed consent. The Executive Committee of the National Donor Family Council of the National Kidney Foundation released two documents. The first, "*A Position Statement on Tissue Donation*," called for more sensitivity "to the needs of organs and tissue donor families."[22] More specifically, while acknowledging that "financial resources are an important factor in maintaining the quality of the services provided," the Donor Family Council urged that the tissue industry operate in a way that would to "minimize costs and maximize benefits to patients." It also stated that donated tissue must be used in a way that promotes healing for people with the greatest need. It encouraged health professionals not to refer to donated tissue as a "product" and urged that all packaging of tissue respectfully acknowledge its source as a gift. It also encouraged the tissue community to pay for additional funeral costs associated with tissue donation.

In its second document, "*Informed Consent Policy for Tissue Donation*," the council called for "full disclosure of the facts."[23] These facts included "how tissue is recovered, processed, stored, and distributed." They called for informing families that if heart valves will be recovered, the heart will be removed and sent to the processing facility. Families should be told that tissue could be used in life-saving and life-enhancing capacities and for medical education and research. Families should have the "right" of restricting use of the tissue they donate, should receive a copy of the consent form, and should be offered "other written material explaining tissue donation." There was no mention of financial issues.

The other set of guidelines was the joint effort of three organizations: the American Association of Tissue Banks (AATB), the Eye Bank Association of America (EBAA), and the Association of Organ Procurement Organizations (AOPO).[24] Their document, like the one prepared by the Donor Family Council, makes it clear that there were other initiatives in progress and that revision is a possibility in the future "as developments warrant."

The document then goes on to recognize the importance of donors and donor families to the success of tissue transplantation. It advocates an informed-consent process "sensitive to the consenting person's situation." Information should be presented "in language and in terms that are easily understood" and under circumstances "that provide an opportunity to ask questions and receive informative responses." Persons seeking consent "should be trained to appropriately answer any questions that the consenting person may have."

In setting out its "basic elements of informed consent" the guidelines encourage requesters to discuss the *benefits* of donation and mention the impact on burial arrangements as well. Interestingly, more-controversial issues—profits, commodification, and use for cosmetic purposes—are left to a section called "additional elements of informed consent." In specifying this "additional information," the guidelines include: possible involvement by a medical examiner; that transplantation might include "reconstructive and esthetic surgery;" and that profit and nonprofit organizations may be involved. At a minimum, the guidelines say, explanations about these "additional" matters should be provided to families who bring them up themselves, or, they may be "appropriate for communication . . . depending upon the circumstances." There is no explanation of just what sort of circumstances warrant actively including this controversial information as part of the informed consent process.

Both the Donor Family Council and AATB/EBAA/AOPO guidelines were issued before the survey of donor families by Siminoff, Youngner, and the Donor Family Council was completed. Its finding of a widespread wish to know and passion about the issues might well have influenced both guidelines to urge greater and more specific disclosure. It is difficult to defend the position that one should wait for families to bring up a controversial issue when most of the respondents said they knew nothing about it.

The Inspector General of HHS, after interviewing 30 organizations involved with tissue recovery, receiving responses from more than 50 donor families to questions posted on an Internet web site, conducting interviews with official of AATB, and reviewing laws, regulations, and association standards, issued a report entitled "*Informed Consent in Tissue Donation: Expectations and Realities.*"[25] It started with the powerful statement that "The expectations and altruistic motives of donor families are the foundation of tissue banking," and concluded that "tissue banking and processing practices have gradually diverged from donor families' expectations in recent years." It explicitly acknowledges the issues causing tension:

- Commercialization of tissue banking. Large-scale financial operations may overshadow the underlying altruistic nature of tissue donation.
- Tissue viewed as a commodity. After processing, tissue and products containing tissue are often marketed and sold as a medical supply, rather than as a donation.
- Cosmetic uses of tissue. Some tissue, particularly skin, may be processed into products that are used for cosmetic purposes that may not be "medically indicated."

Recognizing the fiduciary nature of the relationship and appropriateness of the informed-consent model, it pointedly said that "The special nature of this product, and the circumstances under which it is made available, call for steps to be taken above and beyond those that would apply to most other businesses or philanthropic enterprises."

The Inspector General's recommendations, while recognizing both the complexity and the sensitivity of the issues, are more forceful than those of the professional organizations. Moreover, they are similar to the Donor Family Council's demand that the tissue industry take responsibility for some of the problems rather than simply finessing them through an inherently problematic informed consent process. As far as informed-consent goes, the Inspector General calls on HRSA's Division of Transplantation to:

- Identify principles and guidelines that should underpin consent requests, "such as those outlined recently by the National Donor Family Council and by industry groups."
- Make suggestion about the type, format, and content of written information that should be shared with families.

- Make recommendations about training of tissue bank staff and external requestors.
- Make recommendations on how to evaluate the effectiveness of requestors.

The Inspector General specifically calls on the industry to:

- Give written materials to families at the time of the request or in the days immediately after. This material should include a copy of the consent form, written material on how to follow up if desired, a full description of the uses donated tissue may be put to, and a list of other companies and entities with which the bank has relationships.
- Indicate clearly on all tissue packaging and marketing that contents derive from donated human tissue.
- Fully prepare, train, and evaluate requestors.

Finally, the report calls for the tissue banking industry to work with groups representing the interests of donor families to (1) explore a process for periodic *public disclosure* about tissue banks' financing, (2) examine "what types and how much financial information would be useful" for families and individuals in making decisions about donation, and, (3) consider the potential impact of such disclosures on donation.

Analysis and Recommendations

A great deal is at stake in the debate about informed consent for tissue donation: the welfare of donor families, the availability of tissue for potential recipients, and the vitality of the tissue industry. Called to public attention by the most reductionistic of methods—headlines in the press—the issue is terribly complex and begs for a thoughtful, incremental approach.

First, while *informed consent* is the reigning paradigm, it does not neatly fit with the transaction between requestors and donor families who are, themselves, neither patients nor the subjects of research. Second, what counts as the *truth* is open to interpretation. There are no reliable national data about the distribution and use of tissue. We cannot, for example, say with certainty what percentage of tissue goes to whom for which uses.

Furthermore, judgements about some of the issues are difficult to disentangle from one's own *political views*. Are the market, financial incentives, the commodification of tissue, and involvement of for-profit companies "good" things or "bad" things? How do we distinguish responsible for-profit companies from irresponsible nonprofit institutions? Where do we draw the line between "trivial" cosmetic surgery and "medically necessary" reconstructive surgery? How can we present these issues in a fair, non-manipulative way to potential tissue donors?

To make matters worse, the informed-consent process occurs in the midst of a family tragedy, and the request is most often made over the phone by strangers. There is little time for reflection or revisiting issues. Donor families and others have called for written information to be given or sent to families after they have given verbal consent on the phone. But if written material contains information not absorbed, forgotten, or simply not given in the initial consent, what will happen if families change their minds days later? Bodies will have already been dismantled. This is likely to prove more upsetting to families than if they had said no originally. It could also cause logistical nightmares for tissue banks.

While we should try our best to improve the informed-consent process, the above factors will inevitably render it very flawed. Alone, it will not solve the problems of protecting the interests of both potential donor families and recipients. Part of the answer must come from the tissue industry itself, something strongly suggested by both the Inspector General's report and the Executive Committee of the Donor Family Council—but barely mentioned in the industry's guidelines. Informed consent is one way to deal with potentially upsetting realities and harmful conflicts of interest. Another way is to simply eliminate or reduce the likelihood of some of the realities and conflicts.

The tissue industry cannot have it both ways. It cannot withhold information about cosmetic and other uses of tissue that might maximize profits (or payments for "services") at the expense of the real interests of donor families. It cannot continue to passively abrogate its responsibility to the greater community by failing to centralize data collection and analysis and to enforce standards. Why doesn't the tissue industry take a bit of the sting out of commodification by insisting that all packaged tissue prominently reveal its origins as an altruistic gift? Why doesn't it work with the American Academy of Orthopedic Surgery to make sure that patients who receive tissue also know that it came as a precious gift?

Revealing the disturbing realities to potential donors and giving them a chance to refuse donation or veto certain uses *could* upset them or even discourage them from donating. Why, then, not set an industry standard that says no tissue will be used for puffing up lips or will be so used only when worthier needs are taken care of? Or, as Norman Fost suggests in Chapter 11, inform donors that tissue use will be responsibly prioritized and that efforts will be made to affiliate with responsible partners. Short of these measures, potential donors should be given a veto over certain uses.

Some distribution problems are straightforward. Few would argue that cosmetic uses of skin should have priority over treatment of severe burns. Other problems are more subtle. For example, creation of spacers for spinal surgery from long bones reduces the availability of these bones. It would not make sense to inform donor families about this problem and ask them how they would want bone processed and distributed. The tissue transplant industry, just like the organ transplant industry, will always have complicated choices about distribution. Yet as Prottas notes in Chapter 9, organ transplantation, with UNOS and its centralized, publicly available data and real regulatory teeth, promotes trust that the problem is recognized and solutions are being pursued. Donor families help guide UNOS policy. They could do the same for tissue. Public education about the organization and financing of the tissue industry, a suggestion made by the Inspector General, could also lessen the need for informing individuals at the time of death and relegate judgements about the pros and cons of the market to the political, rather than the informed-consent, process.[25]

The tissue industry (including the surgeons who do the transplants) should attempt to improve the informed-consent process. But more important, it must demonstrate that it is a good steward of the precious gifts it has been entrusted with. Otherwise, it will be seen as self-serving, trust will erode, and outsiders will step in to fix a problem that in reality the tissue industry can best fix itself.

References

1. Health Care Finance Administration (HCFA). *Hospital Protocols for Organ Procurements and Standards for Organ Procurement Agencies.* 1986:42 (USC 1320b-8).
2. Siminoff LA, Arnold RM, Caplan AL, Vernig BA, Seltzer DL. Public policy governing organ and tissue procurement in the United States. *Ann Intern Med.* 1995; 123:10–17.
3. Department of Health and Human Services (HCFA). Medicare and Medicaid Programs; Hospital Conditions of Participation: Identification of potential organ, tissue, and eye donors and transplant hospital's provisions of transplant-related data. Final rule. *Federal Register.* 1998;119 (Codified at 42 CFR S482.45).
4. Association of Organ Procurement Organizations. *2000 Tissue Banking Survey of AOPO Members.* One Cambridge Court, 8110 Gatehouse Road, Falls Church, Virginia 22042.
5. United Network for Organ Sharing. Available at: http://www.unos.org. Accessed August 9, 2002.

6. Office of the Inspector General, Department of Health and Human Services. *Oversight of Tissue Banking.* January 2001. OEI-01-00-00441.

7. Faden RR, Beauchamp TL (eds.). *A History and Theory of Informed Consent.* New York, Oxford University Press, 1986.

8. National Organ Transplant Act (NOTA), Publication No.98–507, 3 USC §301, 1984.

9. Buchanan AE, Brock DW (eds.). *Deciding for Others: The Ethics of Surrogate Decision Making.* Cambridge, U.K.: Cambridge University Press, 1989.

10. Meisel A, Roth LH, Lidz CW. Toward a model of the legal doctrine of informed consent. *Am J Psychiatry.* 1977;134:285–289.

11. Siminoff LA, Chillag K. The fallacy of the "gift of life." *Hastings Cent Rep.* 1999; 29:34–41.

12. Scott M, Oppenheim A, Rodrigue J (eds.). *Adequacy of Informed Consent for Tissue Donation: A Survey of Donor Families.* Gainesville, Florida, University of Florida Tissue Bank, Inc., 2000.

13. Siminoff LA, Youngner SJ. Survey of donor families about informed consent for tissue donation. Prepared for the Donor Family Council of the National Kidney Foundation; 2000.

14. Youngner SJ. Competence to refuse life-sustaining treatment. In: Steinberg MD, Youngner SJ (eds.). *End of Life Decisions: a Psychosocial Perspective.* Washington, DC: American Psychiatric Press, Inc., 1998:19–54.

15. Thompson DF. Understanding financial conflicts of interest. *N Engl J Med.* 1993; 329:573–6.

16. World Medical Association: Declaration of Helsinki. Recommendations guiding physicians in biomedical research involving human subjects, Sections II and III. *JAMA.* 1997;277:925–926.

17. Regeneration Technologies, Inc., S-1 Registration Statement. Date filed: 4/27/2000, pp. 280, 286–287. Copyright ©2000 EDGAR Online, Inc. (ver 1.01/2.003)

18. Marchionne M. "UW Organ Donation Director Resigns." *Milwaukee Journal Sentinel.* May 12, 2000.

19. Marchionne M. "Problems Found at Tissue Bank." *Milwaukee Journal Sentinel.* April 30, 2000.

20. Hoftieezer Simms P. "Hospital Employees Suspended in Probe." *Madison Newspapers, Inc.* April 21, 2000.

21. Ross JR. "UW Hospital Suspends 3 in Tissue Case." *Madison Newspapers, Inc.* (Associated Press), April 22, 2000.

22. National Donor Family Council (NDFC) Executive Committee. *Position Statement on Tissue Donation.* New York, National Kidney Foundation, 2000.

23. National Donor Family Council (NDFC) Executive Committee. *Informed Consent Policy for Tissue Donation.* New York, National Kidney Foundation, 2000.

24. American Association of Tissue Banks (AATB), Eye Bank Association of America (EBAA), Association of Organ Procurement Organizations (AOPO). *Model elements of informed consent for organ and tissue donation: joint statement.* 2000.

25. Office of the Inspector General, Department of Health and Human Services. *Informed Consent in Tissue Donation: Expectations and Realities.* January 2001. OEI-01-00-0044.

13

Concluding Thoughts
and Recommendations

STUART J. YOUNGNER, RENIE SCHAPIRO,
AND MARTHA W. ANDERSON

The preceding chapters present the first comprehensive examination of the tissue transplantation industry. From them emerges the picture of a rapidly developing health care enterprise at the cutting edge of biotechnological and commercial development. Equally apparent is the human dimension—the hundreds of thousands of people who are helped through tissue transplantation and the tens of thousands of families who make the generous gift of tissue from their newly deceased loved ones. The values of the market, the value of altruism in organ and tissue donation, and the Hippocratic values of healing are all very important in our society—and all are at play in the complex functioning of the tissue transplant industry.

In putting this volume together, we have attempted to provide the context in which these values sometimes clash as human tissue passes down the chain of distribution from donor to recipient. To conclude the book, we will now highlight some of the major issues facing the industry and suggest strategies for dealing with each.

First, the public remains poorly informed about the tissue industry, its strengths, and its problems. This situation puts an unreasonable burden on the informed-consent process—for example, by putting those who request tissue in the position of confronting grieving families with new and complicated information about the alteration, distribution, and commercialization of tissues. In addition, from the tissue banking industry's perspective, a better-informed public will be less apt to react negatively to information about the business practices in the field. Relying on the press to inform the public risks oversimplification or worse. Our society has done a much better job educating the public about organ transplantation. Of course, the organ transplant industry has had more time to educate the public, but it is also, with government assistance, more prepared to do so. Tissue transplantation must mount a similar campaign.

Second, despite the relatively good record, safety remains a worry—especially because one donor's tissue can go to so many recipients. Lack of obligatory safety standards, for example, invites problems. Lack of knowledge about some infectious agents, such as prions, and the unexpected introduction of others, such as West Nile virus, make absolute safety impossible. The FDA is taking an increasingly active oversight role, something generally (if somewhat ambivalently) welcomed by the industry. Yet the FDA may not have the resources to do what is necessary, and over-regulation can cause problems of its own. It will be important for the industry to work in partnership with the FDA. The FDA's three-pronged approach to safety is a good start.

Third, there is a tremendous lack of data with which to make evidence-based determinations about scarcity, distribution, and safety. The paucity of data makes both criticism and defense of tissue industry practices lack credibility. We believe that the industry should, by itself or with federal assistance, create, maintain, and make accessible a national database. Like OPOs, tissue banks should be required to submit data to a national organization such as the AATB. This may not be easy to achieve in a highly competitive market. We have heard some members of the industry claim that they would consider relevant data to be proprietary information that they would not want to share with their rivals. Others have expressed the concern that a national database would provide "free advertising" for competitors. Such concerns, while understandable, should not be allowed to prevent the establishment of an important service to the greater community.

Fourth, despite its limitations, the informed-consent process must be improved. While it is true that the information is complex and grieving families are not ideal decisionmakers, improvements can be made. Research about what families are told, what they hear, and what they want to be told would be extremely useful in crafting better policies. In response to criticism by the press, by the Inspector General, and by donor families, the industry has begun to beef up the process of informed consent. Many tissue banks now offer educational and informational brochures to donor families that more clearly outline the specifics of tissue donation, including the fact that tax-paying companies may process the tissue, that tissues may be processed into varying sizes and shapes that resemble medical devices, and that tissues may be stored for extended periods of time.

The frequency of discussions between the person obtaining consent and the potential donor family about the tissue bank's relationship to for-profit companies is unknown, although some tissue recovery agencies do disclose this information to all potential donor families. On the other hand, some OPOs are distributing the tissue they recover to the highest bidder—something they are unlikely to reveal to families. Tissue banks now routinely offer donor families followup information including copies of the consent form, and it appears that more tissue donor families are provided opportunities to participate in donor family recognition events. Such efforts to improve the consent process should be systematically evaluated to determine their effectiveness before one uniform informed-consent intervention is imposed for all situations.

Fifth, the model of good stewardship that already characterizes the behavior of much of the tissue transplant industry needs to be strengthened. Donor families are not patients, but they are inexorably tied to the dead patients whom the tissue comes from, and families are so palpably wounded that organ procurement agencies and tissue banks feel a tremendous responsibility to protect and honor them. This caring instinct needs to be recognized, preserved, and nurtured. This is one reason that many in the industry believe strongly that all tissue recovery should be done by 501c3's. It would be ill advised to require that all aspects of the tissue transplant system be nonprofit. Requiring that tissue recovery be performed by such organizations, however, would mean that the finances of the organizations involved with tissue donation and recovery are publicly available and that motivations of such agencies are less likely to be complicated by profit motives.

The tissue industry must take seriously its role of stewardship. To do so it must act collectively; no easy task for an industry whose members are often in fierce economic competition. Stewardship includes not only safety issues but just and efficient distribution of tissues as well. For example, the tissue industry should adopt nationwide rules for the allocation and distribution of tissues, and provide for that system to be discussed and debated in public. Where voluntary action cannot rise to the occasion, government should step in—first to nudge, but if that fails, to enforce compliance.

The advocacy of the Donor Family Council has been an essential ingredient in keeping the industry focused on good stewardship, and the industry should continue to support and empower this group—even when their demands are, in one way or another, "inconvenient."

Sixth, NOTA should be clarified regarding its prohibition of organ purchases and "reasonable" payments. NOTA has served the organ and tissue donation system well for the past 18 years. But the prohibition of purchases of tissues and the definition of "reasonable payments" remain vague and subject to broad interpretation. Furthermore, the requisite chain of custody of donated human tissue is unclear, allowing many different systems, both profit and nonprofit, to be used by tissue banks. Given the public outcry over the financial dealings of tissue banks following the *Orange County Register* articles in April 2000, steps must be taken to insure that appropriate costs are charged but that excessive payments do not occur.

Seventh, orthopedic surgeons should be better educated about the differences among tissue banks and more involved in policy issues. It is vital for a surgeon to be informed about the types of tissues available, and the differences among tissue banks and the options for his or her patients. In a recent study, fewer than 15% of hospitals surveyed reported any surgeon involvement when ordering allograft tissue, and 60% of surgeons did not know which tissue bank their hospital used or what kind of processing techniques were used.[1] Similarly, it is critical that orthopedic surgeons become more involved with promoting awareness of tissue donation, rather than viewing allograft as simply another medical device.

Finally, while it is clear that the model of the gift of donation remains the dominant one, our society's infatuation with market values has led to increasing calls to use market forces, such as financial incentives and outright payment for organs and tissue, to increase the supply of organs and tissues. If altruism is displaced and market values dominate, human tissue may some day be regarded as a commercial commodity from start to finish. Gone would be the fiduciary relationship and attendant sense of responsibility for donors and recipients that characterizes most of those who work in health care, whether they be physicians, nurses, organ procurement personnel, or tissue bankers. Whether such a turn of events would enhance or diminish the tissue transplant enterprise (and our society) is debatable. Until it happens, however, the notion of stewardship, so ably described by Campbell and endorsed by the Inspector General of the Department of Health and Human Services, should remain the central tenet of all those involved in the tissue transplantation industry.

This book is the first scholarly and comprehensive examination of the tissue industry, but will not and should not be the last. It is a snapshot in time but the picture we present is not static—far from it. As data about the exact shape of the industry and how it operates become more complete, solutions to some of the problems addressed here may become more apparent. The industry seems to recognize that it has reached a stage of development where better organization, governance, and regulation are essential, and it has taken some steps to address its problems. Exactly how tissue transplantation will play out in the face of advances in biotechnology, unpredictable market forces, and government's evolving regulatory policy remains unclear. It is clear that tissue transplantation will continue to help patients as it provides an opportunity for grieving families to give others a gift of life or health. It will also continue to challenge our notions about the proper treatment of dead bodies.

Reference

1. Rapp SM. Few orthopedists are involved in ordering allograft. *Orthopedics Today* 21–4:17, April 2001.

Glossary

ACELLULAR   Devoid of cells, a lack of cells.

ACHILLES TENDON   The tendon originating from the gastrocnemius and soleus muscles of the calf and inserting on the calcaneus bone of the foot.

ALLOGRAFT   Tissue or cells recovered from one individual and intended for transplantation into another individual of the same species.

ASEPTIC   This refers to the condition of being free from all forms of life, including bacteria, fungi, and viruses. *Aseptic technique* refers to efforts to maintain a sterile field during a procedure to prevent infection. These efforts include utilizing sterilized instruments and supplies and requiring staff to wear sterile gloves and other clothing such as caps, gowns, and masks to reduce potential contamination.

AUTOGRAFT   Tissue or cells recovered from an individual and transplanted back into that same individual.

CADAVERIC   Pertaining to a deceased individual, a dead body.

CANCELLOUS   An adjective used to describe something as being spongy or lattice-like in character. When referring to bone it describes the type of bone found in the marrow cavities of the long bones.

CARTILAGE   A form of dense connective tissue composed of cells in a dense matrix. Cartilage comes in several specific types but commonly is associated with the type that is found lining the surfaces of bones forming a joint. It reduces wear and tear on the bones and allows for smooth movement in the joint.

CERVICAL   This term refers to the vertebrae of the neck and consists of the first seven vertebrae of the spine.

CHONDROCYTE   The cell found in cartilage responsible for its production and maintenance.

COLD ISCHEMIC TIME   The time period from when an explanted organ is perfused with cold preservation solution until it is placed into another individual and blood flow is restored.

CORTICAL   This refers to the cortex, which is the outer layer of a structure. When used to describe bone, this is the very hard and dense outer layer of bone found on most elements of the skeleton. It has a very specific structure and is responsible for most of the strength associated with bone.

CRYOPRESERVATION   The use of low temperatures to preserve cells or tissue. Often a chemical substance is added to protect the cells from damage during the freezing and thawing of the material.

DEMINERALIZED BONE   Allograft bone that has been treated to remove most of the mineral component of the bone and consists mainly of the connective tissue matrix and proteins. Demineralized bone has osteo-inductive properties.

DURA MATER   The outer dense connective tissue layer that covers and encloses the brain and spinal cord.

ETHYLENE OXIDE   A gas utilized to sterilize materials that cannot be sterilized with heat or steam. Ethylene oxide has been used to sterilize tissue prior to transplant, but there are concerns that the toxicity that sterilizes the tissue also affects the quality of the graft in the recipient.

FASCIA LATA   A superficial fibrous connective tissue covering and supporting the muscles of the anterior and lateral thigh.

FEMUR   The large bone of the upper leg, often referred to as the *thighbone*. The femur proximally forms the hip joint with the pelvis and distally articulates with the tibia to form the knee.

GAMMA IRRADIATION   A form of electromagnetic waves formed by the decomposition of specific radioactive substances. Gamma irradiation has been used for many years to sterilize food, equipment, materials, etc. In tissue banking it is used to sterilize tissue prior to use.

HLA MATCHING   The degree of match between two individuals with respect to common genes within the Human Leukocyte Antigen loci found on chromosome 6. Three genes are inherited from the father and three from the mother. These genes are responsible for the identification of self. When the body is presented with an organ from another individual with different antigens, the process of rejection occurs. A perfect match is referred to as a six-antigen match where all six loci are identical. In general, the closer to a perfect match the lower the degree of rejection expected.

HEMATOPOETIC STEM CELLS   Undifferentiated cells primarily found in the bone marrow that under direction of various factors can develop into many different forms of mature blood or lymphatic cells.

HOMOLOGOUS USE   When used with bone transplantation, this means that while the graft may have come from the leg of the donor and have been placed in the spine of the recipient, the function of the graft is fundamentally the same, to provide support. Its use is to provide the same function in its new location.

HUMERUS   This is the large bone of the upper arm that proximally articulates with the scapula forming the shoulder joint and distally with the radius and ulna to form the elbow.

ILIAC CREST   This refers to the upper edge of the ilium. The ilium is commonly referred to as the hip bone.

INTERCALARY   This refers to something that is interposed or located between something else. Intercalary allografts are placed between the ends of long bones.

LUMBAR   This term refers to the area of the back between the thorax and the pelvis, often referred to as the small of the back. It is composed of five large vertebrae.

LYOPHILIZATION   The process of quickly freezing something and then placing it under a vacuum to remove the water contained within the substance. The process is also commonly known as *freeze-drying* and is one method of preserving tissue.

MENISCUS   The dense connective tissue bands arising on the outer aspect of the tibial plateau that reduce friction and wear within the knee joint.

MESENCHYMAL STEM CELLS   Undifferentiated cells derived from the embryonic mesoderm that under certain conditions can be directed to become mature forms of connective tissue, lymphatic and blood cells, blood vessels, and several other types of tissue.

MINIMALLY MANIPULATED   The process of not significantly changing the structure and function of something. When used to describe allografts it means that while the shape and look of the graft may not resemble the original tissue, its function and structure are minimally changed.

OSTEOARTICULAR GRAFT   An allograft that is composed of the bone, articular cartilage, and tendons of a joint that is used to replace a diseased or damaged joint in the recipient. In many cases the use of an osteoarticular allograft can prevent the amputation of a limb.

OSTEOCHONDRITIS DISSECANS   This condition results when a piece of cartilage and a portion of underlying bone break away within a joint and cause irritation and inflammation.

OSTEOCONDUCTIVE   The ability or a material of substance to cause bone-producing and remodeling cells to migrate into an area.

OSTEOINDUCTIVE   The ability of a material or substance to induce undifferentiated cells within the marrow or connective tissue to differentiate into cells capable of producing bone.

OSTEONECROSIS   The process of bone dying, "dead bone."

OSTEOTOMY   The procedure of cutting into or through a bone.

PATELLAR TENDON   The extension of the tendon of the quadriceps muscle connecting the patella to the tibia.

PERICARDIUM   The connective tissue sheet surrounding and forming a sac around the heart and great vessels.

PRION   Prions are abnormal protein-like substances that have been linked to Creutzfeldt-Jakob disease and other "slow virus" diseases. They are extremely resistant to most forms of sterilization.

PULMONIC VALVE   The valve located between the right ventricle of the heart and the pulmonary artery that prevents the backflow of blood into the ventricle after systole (contraction).

SAPHENOUS VEIN   A large superficial vein beginning on the surface of the foot and extending to the groin that drains blood from the extremity and directs it to the heart.

SPINAL FUSION   A surgical procedure designed to stabilize and immobilize adjacent vertebrae. This procedure is performed for a variety of reasons including herniated disks, degenerative diseases, and traumatic injury. The use of allograft/autograft bone is very common. It may be used alone or in conjunction with various manmade prosthetic devices.

TIBIA   The larger bone of the lower leg, often referred to as the shinbone. It articulates proximally with the femur (knee joint) and distally with the talus (ankle joint).

XENOGRAFT   Tissue or cells recovered from an individual of one species intended for transplantation into an individual of another species. (also *xenotransplant, xenogenic*).

Appendix A: Model Elements of Informed Consent for Organ and Tissue Donation

AMERICAN ASSOCIATION OF TISSUE BANKS

ASSOCIATION OF ORGAN PROCUREMENT
ORGANIZATIONS

EYE BANK ASSOCIATION OF AMERICA

Adopted November 30, 2000

Human organ and tissue transplantation has become an important and growing part of modern medical practice. Advances in medical science have made it possible for millions of Americans to receive these life-saving and life-enhancing gifts. None of this would be possible, however, were it not for the tens of thousands of donors and donor families who give their organs and tissues to help their fellow men and women.

The decision to donate must, therefore, be an informed consent, and it must be conducted under circumstances that are sensitive to the consenting person's situation. Information concerning the donation should be presented in language and in terms that are easily understood by the consenting person. The consent should be obtained under circumstances that provide an opportunity to ask questions and receive informative responses. An offer should be made regarding the availability of a copy of the signed consent form, and information should be provided regarding ways to reach the recovery organization following donation. Consent should be obtained in accordance with federal, state and/or local laws and/or regulations. The person seeking the consent should be trained to appropriately answer any questions that the consenting person may have. In addition, coercion should not be exerted in any manner, nor monetary inducement offered to obtain consent for donation. The identification of who may be the appropriate person to consent to donation, and whether the consent of any person in addition to the donor needs be obtained, should be evaluated in accordance with the applicable laws and organizational policy and is not addressed in this statement.

The following list of "Basic Elements of Informed Consent" is intended to highlight the information that may be considered critical to informed decision making by a family member or other legally authorized person, who is being approached for consent to organ and/or tissue donation. This listing, whether communicated verbally or included on consent forms, is not intended to preempt any applicable federal, state, or local laws or regulations that may require more or less information to be disclosed for informed consent to be legally effective.

Basic Elements of Informed Consent

In seeking informed consent, the following information should be provided to the person(s) being approached for consent:

1. A confirmation/validation of the donor's identity and his or her clinical terminal condition.
2. A general description of the purposes (benefits) of donation.
3. Identification of specific organs and/or tissues (including cells) that are being requested for donation (with subsequent information provided on specific gifts recovered).
4. An explanation that the retrieved organs/tissues may be used for transplantation, therapy, medical research, or educational purposes.
5. A general description of the recovery process (including timing, relocation of donor if applicable, contact information, etc.).
6. An explanation that laboratory tests and a medical/social history will be completed to determine the medical suitability of the donor, including an explanation that blood samples from the donor will be tested for certain transmissible diseases.
7. An explanation that the spleen, lymph nodes, and blood may be removed, and cultures may be performed, for the purpose of determining donor suitability and/or used to determine compatibility of donor and recipient.
8. A statement granting access to the donor's medical records, and that the medical records may be released to other appropriate parties.
9. An explanation that costs directly related to the evaluation, recovery, preservation, and placement of the organs and tissues will not be charged to the family.

10. An explanation regarding the impact the donation process may have on burial arrangements and on appearance of the body.

11. Any additional information required by federal, state and/or local laws and/or regulations.

Additional Elements of Informed Consent

1. In some situations, there may be additional information that should be known by the consenting person(s), or that might be helpful for family decision making. At a minimum, if the donor family inquires about any of these or additional matters, explanations should be provided.

2. The guiding principle for the use of these "Additional Elements of Informed Consent" is to advance simplicity and reasonableness in seeking informed consent, i.e., include these elements or additional comments if they are appropriate and might clarify any exigencies. For example, if there is the likelihood that the patient will become a Medical Examiner's case, then it should be appropriate to so inform the family. If it is unlikely that donated tissue is going to be used for esthetic surgery, then it would not be reasonable to address this issue in the family approach.

3. One or more of the following elements of information may also be appropriate for communication to the person(s) being approached for consent, depending upon the circumstances surrounding the donation and the potential gift(s):

4. A description of any involvement by the Medical Examiner and/or Coroner, including an explanation that an autopsy may be performed.

5. An explanation that transplantation may include reconstructive and aesthetic surgery.

6. A reference to the possibility that the final gift may take a different form than originally recovered.

7. An explanation that multiple organizations (nonprofit and/or for profit) may be involved in facilitating the gift(s).

8. Reference to the possibility that tissue and/or organs may be transplanted abroad.

Appendix B: Bill of Rights for Donor Families

As of December 3, 2002. Subject to change.

- This document is intended to represent the rights and legitimate expectations of families of loved ones who die and who are (or may be considered) potential organ and/or tissue donors. This document is also intended to serve as a guide for services that are (or should be) offered to such families.
- The term "family" identifies legal next of kin but is also intended to embrace other individuals who may have a significant relationship with a potential or actual organ and/or tissue donor, whether through biological, matrimonial, legal or affectional ties.
- The term "donor family" identifies family members who may be or have already been approached to give consent for organ and/or tissue donation from the body of a loved one after death has occurred.
- This document does not address the situation of living persons who are contemplating or have consented to organ and/or tissue donation during their lifetime.

Families have the right:

1. To a full and careful explanation about what has happened to their loved one, his or her current status, and his or her prognosis.
2. To be full partners with the health care team in the decisionmaking process about the care and support given to their loved one and to themselves.
3. To a full and careful explanation about how the (impending) death of their loved one was or will be determined, with appropriate reference to the concepts of cardiac and/or brain death.
4. To be given opportunities to be alone with their loved one during his or her care and after his or her death occurs. This should include

offering the family an opportunity to see, touch, hold, or participate in the care of their loved one, as appropriate.

5. To be cared for in a manner that is sensitive to the family's needs and capacities by specially trained individuals.

6. To be informed if their loved one had previously made a decision about organ and/or tissue donation (including the decision not to donate) and if there are legal implications of that decision.

7. To be given the opportunity to make organ and tissue donation decisions on behalf of their loved one, where appropriate and in accordance with applicable laws. This opportunity should be included in the normal continuum of care by the health care provider after death has been determined and the family has had sufficient time to acknowledge that death has occurred.

8. To receive information in a manner that is suited to the family's needs and capacities about the need for organ and tissue donation, the conditions and processes of organ and tissue donation, and the implications of organ and tissue donation for later events, such as funeral arrangements, viewing of the body, and related practices.

9. To be provided with time, privacy, freedom from coercion, confidentiality, and (if desired) the services of an appropriate support person (e.g., clergyperson) and other resources (e.g., a second medical opinion, advice from significant others, or the services of an interpreter for those who speak another language) which are essential to optimal care for the family.

10. To have opportunities to spend time alone with their loved one before and/or after the process of removing donated organs and/or tissues, and to say their "goodbyes" in a manner that is appropriate to the present and future needs of the family, and consistent with their cultural and religious identity (e.g., asking the family if they want handprints, footprints, a lock of hair, etc.).

11. To be assured that their loved one will be treated with respect throughout the process of removing donated organs and/or tissues.

12. To receive timely information that is suited to the family's needs and capacities about which organs and/or tissues were or were not removed, and why.

13. To receive timely information regarding how any donated organs and/or tissues were used, upon request and whenever possible. If desired, families should be given an opportunity to exchange communications with individual recipients and/or recipient family mem-

bers. Upon request, donor families should also be given accurate updates on the condition of the recipients.

14. To be assured that the donor family will not be burdened with any expenses arising from organ and/or tissue donation, and to be given assistance in resolving any charges that might be erroneously addressed to the family.

15. To receive ongoing bereavement followup support for a reasonable period of time. Such support might take the form of: the name, address, and telephone number of a knowledgeable and sensitive person with whom they can discuss the entire experience; an opportunity to evaluate their experience through a quality assurance survey; free copies of literature about organ and tissue donation; free copies of literature about bereavement, grief, and mourning; opportunities for contact with another donor family; opportunities to take part in a donor or bereavement support group; and/or the services of a skilled and sensitive support person.

All explanations mentioned in this document should be provided by a knowledgeable and sensitive person in a private, face-to-face conversation whenever possible, in a manner suited to the family's needs. Also, these explanations may need to be repeated or supplemented more than one time.

This *Bill of Rights for Donor Families* has been officially endorsed by the following organizations:

- North American Transplant Coordinators Organization
- Division of Transplantation, Health Resources & Services Administration, U.S. Department of Health & Human Services
- American Association of Critical-Care Nurses
- National Donor Family Council
- National Kidney Foundation

This document was prepared by Charles A. Corr, Ph.D.; Lucy G. Nile, M.A.; and the members of the 1994 Executive Committee of the National Donor Family Council (NDFC) of the National Kidney Foundation. Revised by the 2002 Executive Committee of the NDFC.

The mission of the National Donor Family Council is to enhance the sensitivity and effectiveness of the organ and tissue recovery process, to provide opportunities for families to grieve and grow, and to utilize the unique perspective of these families to increase organ and tissue donation.

National Donor Family Council
National Kidney Foundation
30 East 33rd Street
New York, N.Y. 10016
(800) 622–9010
www.donorfamily.org
E-mail: donorfamily@kidney.org
©1994, National Kidney Foundation
2002 Edition

Appendix C: Informed Consent Policy for Tissue Donation

NATIONAL DONOR FAMILY COUNCIL
EXECUTIVE COMMITTEE

INFORMED CONSENT POLICY FOR TISSUE DONATION

As with organ donation, the National Donor Family Council (NDFC) of the National Kidney Foundation believes that a crucial element of the tissue donation process is the informed consent of the donor family. With respect to tissue donation, the informed consent of the donor family must, at an absolute minimum, include a voluntary decision based on full disclosure of the facts.

Full disclosure includes the following elements:

1. Donor families should be given a general explanation of the tissue donation process, including:
   - medical and social history
   - communicable disease testing
   - laboratory testing
   - medical suitability
   - how tissue is recovered, processed, stored and distributed

2. Donor families must be told what tissue can be recovered from their loved ones based on medical suitability. If heart valves will be recovered, families must be informed that the heart will be removed from the donor's chest and sent to a facility where the valves will be removed. If the entire eye will be removed for corneal donation, families should be informed.

3. Donor families must be informed that tissue can be used or modified in various ways for transplantation in a life-saving capacity, transplantation in a life-enhancing capacity, and medical research or education.

4. Donor families must be told that they have the right to limit or restrict the use of the tissue.

5. Donor families must be told about the likelihood that the donated tissue will be stored, how it will be stored, the duration of storage, and the possibility that the tissue may not be utilized.

6. The completed consent form must be reviewed with the donor family before final consent, and a copy should be offered to the family. Other written material explaining tissue donation should be offered to the family.

7. Donor families must be given the option of receiving acknowledgement of their gifts. This acknowledgement should include disposition and any recipient information available at that time, while protecting the anonymity of both donor and recipient. To obtain additional information about the gift, the donor family should be provided with contact information (including phone number and address) for the recovery agency.

As approved by the NKF National Donor Family Council Executive Committee and the NKF Board of Directors, September 25, 2000

NOTE: This Policy Statement is subject to further revision based on a survey of donor families currently in progress.

Appendix D: Anatomical Gift Form

University of Wisconsin Hospital and Clinics
600 Highland Avenue · Madison, Wisconsin 53792
ANATOMICAL GIFT FORM

BEFORE RULING OUT A POTENTIAL DONOR - PLEASE CONTACT THE UNIVERSITY OF WISCONSIN ORGAN PROCUREMENT PROGRAM AT 1-866-UWHC OPO (1-866-894-2676)
Please see reverse side of this document for Organ and Tissue Agency Contact Information.

1. PLEASE COMPLETE THIS SECTION FOR <u>ALL</u> DEATHS
Did you seek appropriate consent from the next-of-kin?   Circle **YES   NO**
Did the next-of-kin consent to donation?   Circle **YES   NO** (If yes, plese complete Section 2)

Signature of medical professional responsible for completing this form:_____

Printed Name of medical professional responsible for completing this form:_____
2. THIS SECTION MUST BE COMPLETED TO OBTAIN CONSENT FOR ORGAN AND/OR TISSUE DONATION

I,_____ , _____ hereby give to:
    (Printed Name of Next-of-Kin or Guardian)   (Relationship to Patient)

The University of Wisconsin Hospital and Clinics, The University of Wisconsin Organ Procurement Program, MTF / TranSource, and the Lions Eye Bank of Wisconsin, the organs and tissues marked "YES" below from the body of:

_____ (All others should be marked **"NO"**)
    Printed name of decedent/donor

Organs for transplantation (yes/no)	Tissues for donation (yes/no)	Research and/or education, if unsuitable for transplant (yes/no)
___Heart	___Heart for Valves	___All organs listed
___Liver	___Eyes	___Other, please specify:_____
___Lungs	___Skin	
___Kidney	___Bone	___Only the following Organs,
___Pancreas	___Connective Tissue	please specify:_____
___Intestine	___Saphenous Vein	
	___Other, please specify:_____	

I further consent to the release of medical information and to the removal of blood, lymph nodes, and spleen as needed for infectious disease testing (such as HIV, Hepatitis, CMV, RPR/VDRL) and determination of compatibility between donor and recipient.

I understand that skin, bone and other such tissues may be used for a wide range of uses including reconstructive and cosmetic purposes and that multiple organizations (nonprofit and/or for-profit) may be involved in facilitating the gifts.

I understand that testing and hospital expenses related to donation are the responsibility of the organ procurement organization, eye bank, or the tissue bank, not those of the next of kin. I also understand the funeral and burial expenses after donation are the responsibility of the next-of-kin.

_____   _____
Signature of Next-of-Kin or Responsible Party   Signature of Witness

_____   _____
Address of Next-of-Kin or Responsible Party   Signature of 2nd Witness if Telephone Consent

_____   _____
                                    Date

Telephone Number where Next-of-Kin or Responsible Party can be reached in the next two hours.

_____
Date
See policy Number 4.31

UWH# 9013 (REV. 4/01)   **File in Progress Notes**   **ANATOMICAL GIFT FORM**

Index

Note: Page numbers followed by *f* or *t* indicate figures or tables, respectively.